HOW WALL STREET DOUBLES MY MONEY EVERY THREE YEARS

HOW WALL STREET DOUBLES MY MONEY EVERY THREE YEARS

The No-Nonsense Guide to Steady Stock Market Profits

By Lewis Owen

Published by

BERNARD GEIS ASSOCIATES

First printing, October 1969
Second printing, December 1969
Third printing, February 1970

To my wife, Esther,
whose patience
in all things
sustains me.

With special thanks to Gene Loughlin, Jr.—a good broker who became a good friend.

TABLE OF CONTENTS:

Preface

In 1968, the Securities and Exchange Commission slapped the biggest brokerage house of all for allegedly passing along inside information to favored customers. In an unrelated case, the Federal Court of Appeals had earlier ruled that executives of Texas Gulf Sulphur made an illegal bundle from private knowledge of a big discovery.

What makes these moves of particular pertinence to this book is the way *The New York Times* led into its coverage of them. Here are the article's opening words:

"One of Wall Street's hoariest adages holds that the little guy—the small investor—is always wrong. He sells when he should be buying and he buys when he should be selling—while the big investors are making all the profits."

If you sit and wait for the SEC to make that adage false, you'll only die broke. But what an entire Government agency can't do, *you* can. And that's the purpose of this book: to show you how to swim against the tide and make some of those profits for yourself. And maybe end up a "big investor" too.

Go get 'em, tiger!

A PROFITABLE SHOCK TREATMENT

An Introduction
by Ira U. Cobleigh

Economist and Author of the Best-selling
HAPPINESS IS A STOCK THAT DOUBLES IN A YEAR

This book will shock you—if you are as conventional in your thinking about stocks as most of the "little guys" who dabble in the market. But unless you've done as well as Lewis Owen—that is, unless you've consistently doubled your money every three years—it will provide the most profitable shock you've ever had.

Owen urges you to buy stocks on margin! He tells you to buy only a stock that's rising and to sell ruthlessly any stock that's falling. Also to forget about blue chips, dividends, and mutual funds.

As a man who has been studying the market for many years, not without my own share of success, I have only one piece of advice to give you about this book: Read it and then follow Owen's lead.

For he has written one of the most refreshing and rewarding books ever published on trading to win in the stock market. No owlish, slide-ruling analyst, chartist, or investment adviser he, but an animated and perceptive professional in the advertising business. Owen writes in a brisk style, and intersperses his thoughts on gainful trading with relevant humor and incisive anecdotes. So it makes not only profitable but pleasant reading.

The author's basic approach is refreshingly honest. His is a sort of Pilgrim's Progress in Wall Street. He discusses his early blunders with just as much relish as his subsequent coups. He regards himself, and all other relative market newcomers, as "Little Guys," striving to overcome the four historic roadblocks to Wall Street success: cupidity, stupidity, overtrading, and bad timing.

After years of in and out trading, tape watching, seeing good profits fade into losses by not selling in time, and indulging in such follies as short-selling and day-trading, Owen found out he'd gotten precisely nowhere. In fact, quite the contrary!

He had, however, been paying attention. From those observations, he hit upon tactics that soon put him many thousands of dollars ahead. He now shares these refined and proven methods with his readers, summarizing them in his "Twenty Rules to Help You Make It in the Market."

This is not a book of theories. Owen names stocks, lists his own current portfolio, and cites actual price performances to document the profitability of his techniques for choosing and managing stocks. And he's devastating in his puncturing of many pet Wall Street dogmas.

He proves that you don't need a fortune to play this "Money Game"—$2,000, the amount you need to open a margin account, will do for openers. And he asserts with confidence that you can consistently rack up gains of 30 percent or more annually, doubling your money in three years, if you will follow his guidelines.

This is no book for conservative, long-term investors, or for seekers of dividend income, but it's not for wild-eyed speculators, either. It's for the calmly courageous who are willing to latch their dollars onto active performing stocks and to work at building equity. Are you willing to burn a little midnight oil in order to strike a gusher on Wall Street? Then buckle down to this book, study Lewis Owen's precepts—and go thou and do likewise!

HOW WALL STREET
DOUBLES MY MONEY
EVERY THREE YEARS

Chapter 1

WHERE HAVE ALL THE DOLLARS GONE?

I looked at the brief column of figures—and felt just plain lousy. As the fellow says, somewhere along the line I must have been wheeling when I should have been dealing. Because, after seven years of increasingly frenzied trading, the first of January, 1963, found me a discouraging 20 percent in the hole. Like one nickel out of every quarter—or two dimes out of every dollar. In fact, if you wanted to be really nasty about it—two hundred out of every hard-earned thousand dollars had gone down the drain. And I'd been doing so beautifully.

It all began in 1955, when I was writing TV commercials for Chrysler Corporation. For three years I'd been lyrical about the "chair-high seats" and "top-hat headroom" in the dumpy, conservative old Chryslers, Dodges, and Plymouths of the day. Every week I commuted to Los Angeles to watch over the crazy choreography of the live, one-time-only commercials that were the fare of those benighted days. And every year I hush-hushed out to Detroit to view the new models that were to set the motoring world on its ear.

Invariably, I found the same sawed-off, superbly engineered horseless carriages that were the legacy of Walter

P. Chrysler and of the sawed-off, superb engineers who still ran the company and its styling.

And then, in the early summer of 1954, the miracle happened and the Chrysler products came alive. How bad they look now—the tailfins that started for the sky and soared higher, year after year. But then they were ultra—and we coined "the Forward Look," and knew they'd sell like crazy.

So I bought 15 shares of Chrysler Corporation. And my first halting step into investing had been made.

Even in this timid move, I did one thing that is now high on my list of "do's" for the small investor. I bought an odd lot of stock that was so expensive (59) that I couldn't afford a hundred shares. And today I know that this is a sound move, despite Wall Street's contempt for the odd-lotter. We'll dig deeper into that one later.

But listen to what I did wrong with just that one, inspired purchase. I bought it on a hunch—on the feeling that the cars would sell and the company would prosper. You and I have no right risking our money on unsupported hunches. We have to check them out against the facts of earnings and distribution and other no-fun items. A hunch, like a tip, should only move us to *look* into a situation, never to *buy* into it automatically.

Then, too, I bought the stock before it started to move. Think this is the smart way? Well, you're in for a shock. Because only suckers and the coziest of insiders buy at the low. The wise investor waits for the rise to begin—*because that's the only proof it really is going to move.* And we sure will go into that one in later pages. Never buy at the low. How's that for a switch?

Finally, I held that stock from 59 right up to 100—because my hunch was right as rain. And then I held it right back down to 65 before I sold it, in 1959. I tied up $900 for five years to net $61.53. And I thought I'd made a pretty shrewd move. Later we'll talk about buying on the rise and selling on the drop. Timing, friend, timing—is the essence of investing.

4

But at least I made money on that one. Made money on General Telephone, on Brunswick. Let's see—E. F. MacDonald, Decca, B. T. Babbitt. There was that pile on American Motors in 1959, and IT&T in 1960. How come 1963, all those years later, found me in the hole? Because when I was dumb or wrong it cost me more than I made when I was bright and right—that's how come. And it dawned on me that we all tend to forget our failures and cherish our victories. And it warps our judgment.

That B. T. Babbitt deal was actually my next venture after Chrysler. You remember Bab-O Cleanser—well, your mother does.

I had changed jobs in 1957, after eighteen years with one advertising agency. One of the fellows who worked for me came in and closed the door the way people do when they want to be conspicuously secretive, and asked, "Would anything persuade you to change jobs?" And I was just fed up enough to reply, "Anything." So a couple of months later I was VP at another agency, with a $12,000 increase.

Now, when you get that kind of boost, you have a definite choice to make. You can poof it away or you can do something with what Uncle Sam leaves of it. I decided I'd better hang on to as much as possible because this new place wasn't known for the stability of its jobs. The answer seemed obvious. Invest.

One of my accounts was Bab-O, and the stock was in the cellar. So far down that the B. T. Babbitt Company was, supposedly, going to face a stockholder's suit for running things into the ground. What's more, everybody around the place said the company was going to push the stock up to foil the dissidents, because the higher the stock the lower the squawk. Don't know how somebody was supposed to do it—and, if there are any lawyers listening, I'm sure nobody did. But at the time it sounded very in, so I bought 250 shares at 4½ and sold it seven months later at 6. Which was not all the money in the world, but was better than a poke in the eye with a sharp stick.

But, by golly, I'd stumbled on the principle I had neglected to apply with Chrysler but that I'll drill through your head if you get nothing else out of this book. *Don't ride a stock down.* Babbitt hit 8 and started to slide and I got out at 6 with a 33 percent profit. This has been attached to the other rule I just mentioned. Altogether it reads: "Buy on the rise—sell on the drop." Don't argue with me till you read the reasons in a later chapter.

As if it weren't enough to hit on one good rule (which I didn't really recognize till I started soul-searching years later), I bought in again at 4⅛ and rode that trade to 9½ in a year and a half, which developed long after into another firm one: "Don't hesitate to go back into a stock you've sold." Of course you've got to add another dimension to that one, too—because anyone will buy a stock at a *lower* price than he sold it at. But only the wisest investor will go back into a stock at a *higher* price than he sold it at. How many of us have stubbornly watched a stock soar again without us, after we prudently dumped it during a sell-off? Put a marker on all these pearls for discussion after a while.

The trade winds blew too hard

This thing sort of gets into your blood, and as I put in more money I began to do more trading. Rather than lose you in detail, let's just say that I bought two issues in 1957, ten in 1958, eighteen in 1959, and by 1960 I was going great guns. *Sixty* purchases in that one year. My broker wasn't churning me, but I was sure churning me. No wonder when I toted up the score after the rude awakening in 1962 I found I'd paid out $3,800 in commissions during 1960 alone, which helped me net a loss of $3,300 on the trades.

I couldn't blame my broker. Who cares if the broker gets fat as long as you grow a little, too? But in the winter of my 1962 discontent I saw the *real* price I'd paid.

Seventy-five hundred dollars had gone in commissions through the years, so my broker was the richer and only I was the "broker." Interest charges on my margin, plus taxes, added another $1,000. On such a little account. The question was—can you pay such costs and still make money? Or is the only course the one the columnists urge? Buy good stocks and stick with them through thick and thin.

I had to find out. It was easy to blame the 1962 bear market, which knocked 200 points off the Dow Jones Average. But I had always kept good records—as I shall insist you do—and they showed me an interesting fact. Early in 1962, when the Dow Jones took a dive, I had already taken my own, personal half-gainer. In fact, as the D-J went down, I went back up. And then, when it took the glory road again I hit the skids in one sensational nine-month slide. So, somewhere, this particular Wolf of Wall Street was outfoxing himself.

You couldn't blame penny-stockitis, that deadly disease symptomized by a weakness for expensive bargains. Not with Pfizer, Jones & Laughlin, Raytheon, General Dynamics, Collins Radio, National Airlines, Monsanto, MMM, IBM.

IBM? H'mmm. That's four shares at 406, in 1958—and, after a three for two split, two more bought at 408 in 1959. Let's see (head for Standard & Poor's *Stock Guide,* supplied free by friendly neighborhood broker)—a 25 percent stock dividend in 1964, another three for two in 1966, and two for one in 1968. That's thirty shares today at about $350, or $10,000 equity on a $2,500 investment ten years ago. Very good.

Only I sold my eight shares in 1959 and 1960 for $4,000. Chalk one up for the buy-'em-and-keep-'em school. And the never-sell-IBM school, which isn't necessarily the same group of nontraders.

But you don't get to lose by turning a 60 percent profit in a year or so. Time now to drag out this one: "Bulls make money and bears make money, but pigs always lose"

—a hardy Wall Street perennial that is used alternately to comfort people who sell IBM, and to chide those who still hold Thiokol because they were waiting for it to go to 100 instead of just 72.

And, by golly, I held that, too—but only for two months, in '60 while it slid from 60 to 50. I had tried to guess the bottom, with all the siren songs of "It can't drop farther" and "It's in a buying range" ringing in my ears. And a riff through the records showed that I did that again and again, just like all the other Little Guys. In a deep, Cassandra voice I say unto you, "Let it turn around, booby; let it establish a nice solid base, let it consolidate, let it build a support area, let it prove to you that it doesn't want to keep dropping—and then let it start that golden rise again, before you buy a stock that's been in a slump." You're no genius, nor am I. We're just a couple of nice fellows trying to keep from losing our small sockful while we build it into a small fortune. And I darned near lost mine.

Bad luck comes in bunches—and hunches

For one thing, like all new investors I thought I was my own best research department. I would read things or hear things, and a voice would say, "Buy it!" And I'd buy it. Just like that story about the fellow who was leaving Las Vegas with his last ten dollars when a Deep Voice from nowhere said, "Go back—go back."

He went back and the Voice said, "Go to the Casino— to the roulette table." He went to the table and the Voice thundered, "Put ten dollars on red." So he put his last ten dollars on red—and it came up black—and the Voice said, "Damn." And don't think I haven't cleaned *that* one up.

For example, in 1959 I read an article about Fairchild Engine & Airplane buying plans and U.S. manufacturing rights to a wonderful new turboprop Fokker. A feeder line transport. The Voice said it had to be a winner—and it was. Only the company got so bogged down in Dutch metric systems and Dutch tooling and Dutch engineering practices that it took years of red ink to launch the wonderful wide-windowed beauty that the little airlines swoop about in today. So I bought it at 9 and had enough sense to get out at 8½, six months later, before it really fell. A great hunch.

A company named American MARC announced a diesel outboard in 1959—under development, of course. Showed it at the New York Boat Show and the finish seemed a little rough, but for "rough" read "rugged." I knew it had to go. It went. The motor hasn't been heard from since.

Oh, there were successful hunches. National Air Lines (1958) had no jets on its Miami run and neither did its rivil, Eastern, but—*psst*—National had swung a deal to lease one of Pan Am's big, brand-new Boeings during Pan Am's slack winter season. So, scoop-te-do, National went from 18 in October to 24 in April and you can't knock that.

But for every National there was a Lionel—in at 32, out at 25, and as high as that since. So I had to learn not to trust my hunches, and so must you.

I had to learn so very many things. Not the stuff you usually find in books—the language and the technicalities and all that. I didn't have to know that the New York Stock Exchange was founded under a buttonwood tree in 1792, or how to understand sentences like, "These earnings are capitalized at a multiplier rate which will vary with the quality of the issue." But I had to learn the things even your best friends won't tell you, because they don't know.

This book tells you what I learned and how I learned it.

Come to think of it, we'd better get the ground rules established on that. I've waited till you got these pages all dog-eared and thumb-smeared before telling you this, so you couldn't get your money back—but this book probably isn't written for you.

Can you qualify to read this book?

There's only one kind of person I can help, and his name not only isn't "legion," it's scarcely even "platoon." In these pages I'm going to teach you just two things—how to *protect* your capital and how to *make it grow.* Growth —the only sensible goal. On the way I'm going to tell you to join the "I hate dividends" club. I'm going to tell you— horrors!—*to buy on margin.* I'm going to fly in the face of the conservative, so-right advisers who talk price-earnings, and yield, and averaging down, and mutual funds, and bonds, and a lot of stuff that might be just great for a lot of people. But not for any Little Guy who wants the most out of the market.

All in all, I'm going to tell you a lot of things most investors, and most investment counselors, don't believe and won't follow. But if you're one of the skeptics, your doubts are a reflection on you, not on me. Because you're not thinking like a Little Guy—and you sure had better! Otherwise you're dead.

So this book is written for the Little Guy. But not just any Little Guy. The guy with guts. With intelligence. With patience enough to spend time making his money grow. With thick enough skin to go his own way, but enough built-in sensitivity to feel the strange pulses of the market.

Think that describes you? Then read on. But decide right now to put the time and thought into it that the stock market requires. Not just money—Wall Street eats money. Time and thought. Including the time and thought to absorb this book.

Statistics say only 15 percent of those who buy stocks make money. If that seems a shockingly low figure, consider why people buy stocks, and what it gets them. Millions buy for income and, after taxes and inflation take their toll, end up contented losers. Millions buy stock in the companies they work for, and go up or down with its fortunes without ever coming near making theirs. Millions buy on hot-shot tips, grab unknown Canadian mining stocks, pounce on new issues of nothing companies. Millions go short. Millions act blindly. Millions put mortgage money behind their hunches, throw sweat-stained dollars down the drain as though they were baseball trading cards. No, by golly, nobody ever traded a Willie Mays for two Larry Dobys with anything like the abandon shown by most market devotees.

Okay—there's no bigger bore than a reformed drunk, or a fellow who's given up smoking. Well, add me to that list. I'm a reformed damn-fool investor. I learned the hard way how not to invest. And then I learned how to make money at it. And, in order to help you take a shortcut to success, I'm going to lead you through the whole sorry story of my folly and my awakening. So pay attention— we may ask questions.

Cry for the Little Guy

First of all, recognize that the stock market is a tough way to make a buck. Especially for the Little Guy. He doesn't have a big enough account to merit the kind of attention the big boys get. He doesn't have the time to give the market. He doesn't have the quick information system. He doesn't have the knowledge required to interpret what's happening so that he can make his decisions wisely. Today, in a frantic attempt to clean up their own bookkeeping mess, many brokerage firms are shunning the $500 account, forbidding purchase of stocks under $5, stupidly urging the small investor to buy mutual funds instead of bothering them, because they "can't make money on those small transactions."

Oh, cry for the Little Guy, with every man's hand against him. Only the bitter part is, he's his own worst enemy. Your broker, if you can find one bright enough to welcome small accounts, would sooner you made money than lost it. The big investors do look down their noses at this odd lot of odd-lotters, as witness *The Money Game,* the best seller written by "Adam Smith," a money man, funny man, which refers to the investing public as "John Jerk." But it's only the small investor's own actions that make him an object of their scorn.

Wall Street as a whole wishes he'd mend his ways. They spend millions to educate the small investor because they want him to trust them with his money—a trust that only comes from winning. So how come he's a loser? Let me give you one beautiful case history in losing. Mine.

"So he mounted his horse and rode off in all directions"

That famous quote from Lincoln Steffens is a perfect description of the average investor. And, boy, was I average!

Every small investor makes two basic mistakes. First of all, he fails to act with consistency—with aim or direction. He's all over the lot, running after the high-risers, clutching at tips. Like a kid on a dark lawn chasing fireflies.

Secondly, the Little Guy tries to act like a big man. And that's the biggest mistake of all. He's not a Wall Street trader in miniature. Or an Investment Fund, Junior Grade. He's a Little Guy, and unless he acts accordingly, he'll be like a midget in a basketball game—with about as much chance of scoring.

You'll probably be able to recognize yourself in the goofs I made on the way to a net loss. Give a good, hard look at your own mistakes as I touch on mine. Take comfort that I don't make those kinds of mistakes any more—and that you, too, can turn over a clean new gold leaf. I still make mistakes, and always will, but I know today how to keep them minor. Here is the kind I used to make, when I was riding hard for a fall. In all directions.

My records from those early years look like an exercise in how to support a broker. Into a stock one month, out the next. Into AMF, for example, on August 18, 1960, at 68—out on August 31 at 66. What sent me into them and what scared me out of them, neither records nor memory tell me. But I do see a pattern that follows down through the years. Its name is "impatience." Jump in, shuffle your feet for a month or so, jump out and try something else. The only thing worse is *too* much patience.

Buy Vendo in October at 36⅝; sell it in November at 37½. I cleared $7.89; my broker made $75.06. Buy Ennis Business Forms at 21 in April; sell it at 21 in June. Big deal.

Watch that tape-watching

And suddenly as I write this it all comes back to me. Tape-watching did it. I'd had a two-year contract in my new job, and it called for "discussion" after eighteen months, to see about renewal. Well, by the eighteenth month I'd had it, so to everyone's surprise I "discussed" the fact that I wouldn't be renewing. The old curmudgeon who owned the agency checked his lawyer, as I had checked mine, and found he'd been hooked. So he bade me a very cordial good-bye and mailed me my check for the next six months. Actually, it delighted his flinty heart, because nobody'd ever taken him before. This strangely likeable old coot is worth a paragraph or two. He was actually called by his initials, like "A.K."—which they weren't. He ruled with an iron fist, complete with heart to match. Instead of a Christmas bonus, one year, he sent out a memo suggesting we economize a little, like turning out the lights at night— and maybe there'd be some profits to split up next time. On the bulletin board there immediately (if briefly) ap- peared the lines ". . . and I heard him declare e'er he drove out of sight, 'Merry Christmas to all and turn out the light.' "

He wasn't exactly the most ept man in the advertising business. He advised an aging client to okay this big, full-color campaign for his cement company, saying that the man wasn't going to last much longer and his successor might not have such great vision. The poor client had a seizure right then and there, and his successor not only didn't okay the campaign, he didn't even okay the agency. Which illustrates two things: A.K.'s keen foresight and the lack of gratitude in the advertising business.

At any rate, the point is that while I hunted another job and lived off A.K.'s tear-stained checks, I made my headquarters at my broker's. Even got a key to their wash-room. I'd spend all day, between interviews, watching the tape and the tape-watchers. And talking to the fellows. Well, that's no good.

There are two reasons why it's no good to watch the tape. For one thing, you get to think you know what's going on, and you lose the sense of strangeness that is the Little Guy's suit of armor. But worst of all, you lose all sense of time. You watch a stock sit still for a week and you believe it's never going to move. You feel you've got to do something, because you see all those forces interacting right before your eyes—with XYZ leaping half a point a trade, and PDQ painting the tape on the upside. While your own stocks just lie there.

And my records show the result.

Adams Millis bought June 7, 1960, at 30⅛. More on June 14 at 35⅛. Out on June 17 at 44⅞, for what had to be my coup of the year. Then buy it back at 45½ on June 20. Add more the next day when it slipped to 42½. And sell in three chunks in July at 38, 34, and 33. Net loss $189.89, instead of the $1,261.00 profit I held for a moment.

Mind you, buying more as a stock goes up is aces in my book—the only way to go. But such frenzied trading, plus the sin of riding that stock all that way down—and buying more as it went down—marks the little wise guy, rather than the wise Little Guy.

But let me tell you about Tang Industries. Bet you think I'm making up these names. I bought it at 9½ on July 1 and sold it at 10½ on July 7—just enough to make the broker $34.00 and me $62.60. But I bought it again *that afternoon* at 14½ and it went to 18. It started to slip and I told my broker to sell at 16, instead of "at the market" (see Chapter 22). By the time I learned I'd missed the trade, I could only get 10½ again. Which was worth $39 to my broker, but lost me $442. There *must* be an easier way to make a living.

You show me a guy who can buy National Video at 21 and sell it at 24 a week later and I'll show you a guy who was dumb enough not to wait five years to sell it at 125— and smart enough not to wait seven years to sell it at 15. You can't lose them all.

Incidentally, some wiseacre is going to discover that I've bought all the good ones through the years, and that if I'd only held them I'd be worth skeen million dollars today. And he's not going to get any argument from me. But I had a lot of losers, too. Anybody can pick a portfolio of winners in retrospect. The trick is to do it in advance, or to milk the good ones and ditch the bad ones, the way I'm going to show you how to do.

I didn't milk them very long in those days. Like Lockheed. In and out at 21½ in four days, because that tape was zipping by and I couldn't wait for the 70 it eventually reached. Or Comptometer, with an $800 loss inside a week.

But you surely get the message about the Russian roulette that's inspired by tape-watching. Not in everybody, granted—but, unless it's the only warm place in town, don't hang around the board room. Go in, take a look, then git.

Or else you may even go to selling short, like I did.

Selling short or "going short" is a very simple and legitimate operation that always seems complicated and crooked to the uninitiate. That's part of its appeal, I suppose—it's rather racy to be betting that something's going down when you know 99 out of 100 are hoping it will go up.

You go short by telling the broker to sell a stock short. He actually borrows the stock and sells it, the money going into your account. But you can't touch that money—in fact you have to put up additional money just as though you were buying it at that price. To close out the transaction ("cover"), hopefully after the stock has obediently dropped, you have your broker buy shares at the new price. He pays for them out of your account, leaving the price you originally paid plus the difference between the first price and the second. In other words, your profit is the amount it went down (minus commissions) where in a regular transaction it's the amount a stock goes up. I'll make that clear enough, and explain why it's a shirt-loser in Chapter 25, but for now just let me give you a couple of horrible examples.

In 1960 my first such venture cost me $320—to short Ideal Cement at 24¾ and cover ten days later at 27¼, because the nasty thing went up instead of down. But then it went down again and it was obvious the only thing wrong was that I'd been too hasty. That is, I thought it was obvious.

So when I saw a real black-and-white situation, I bit again. Got into it because my Telautograph had gone from 12⅞ to 24 in five days. I bought some more and watched it drop to 21 next day. Sold some and finally got out completely at 15 a week later. Net loss $135.

But since I'd taken such a shellacking, I could see that it was a real good short sale. So I sold short at 14⅛ and covered two days later at 17⅜—for another $374 loss. That was behaving like a true odd-lotter—buying when I should have sold, selling when I should have bought. But did I have to compound it by going short? You ain't heard nothing yet!

I shorted Chrysler and five sweating weeks later had a profit of $88.40, when I covered. Oh boy, how long had this been going on? Not long. I shorted Lockheed and lost $213 in a couple of weeks. Beckman Instruments made me $112. Hot dog, this is the life!

Chrysler then went from 38 to 49 while I held my breath and another short on it. To the tune of a $738 loss.

You're listening to the man who shorted IBM at 555 and covered at 613 six weeks later. That's calling them.

But I was really with it and it sure was fun and this wasn't money, anyway. And I hadn't learned to check my equity every month by writing down what each stock was worth and putting that total against what I owed on margin, and subtracting my whole original investment to see where I really was (Chapter 32)—or I'd have been scared out of my half-wits. Because it *was* money. And it was *my* money. And I was merrily pouring it into the gutter while I thought I was strolling the Street.

It wasn't enough to be selling more shorts than Jockey Knit; I had to discover day-trading.

Day-trading—the fool's pair o' dice

The SEC has changed the rules since then and put a limit on this kind of nonsense, though you can still make an ass of yourself day-trading. An impoverished ass—and that's the worst kind. But at the time, in 1960, you could day-trade till the bulls came home, and I went for it big.

The gimmick in day-trading is that at that time you could buy about 3⅓ times 70 percent of your equity. Don't worry if it sounds complicated, there's always someone to figure it out for you. It means that, if you had $10,000 worth of stocks and cash in the account, you could buy over $23,000 worth of stock in a day-trade. Even though it's less now, it's still a big temptation. The only thing is, you have to sell again before the trading session is over. If you sell short, you have to cover by the close, too. Fair enough? Like hell it is!

When you trade, you give away a point in commissions and stuff before you make a penny. Okay, it's less on a low-price stock, but the percentage is even higher. That means you lose when your stock breaks even and you break even if it moves a point in the right direction. A point in the wrong direction loses you $2 a share right off the bat. It's brutal, it's dangerous, it's senseless. It's shooting craps, that's what it is. Today, even the SEC and the brokers recognize that, and they only let an investor do it occasionally—which is too often.

I started with a day-trade in IBM. Nothing small about me. When I found what a tremendous stake I could raise, I went whole hog and bought 50 shares. At 448, yet. To save you the trouble, with commissions that comes to $22,471.91—and how's that for high rolling! Especially when the afternoon found IBM ahead and I sold at 450¾. Now that was a trade. Except that the broker took $118.95 and, with taxes, left me 40 cents in the hole. *In the hole, mind you,* after being right.

But it must have felt good. A month later another 50 IBM day-trade had me buying at 490¼ (up 40 points from my previous trade, you'll note)—and chewing my nails down to 486¾ for a $305 loss. And you know there were days when I didn't earn that much at my job.

How would you like to hear about a day-trade in Transitron? One with 500 shares that started at 27½ and ended at the same level—costing a neat $353.26 in commissions. Not while you're eating, eh? Well, just let me add that it was a short sale, too. So I was doubly dumb.

But that IBM bit was my cup of tea, so I tried another 50 shares at 600¼, and sold it just before the close at 599¾, for a loss of $155. And the point is that IBM had gone from 448 to 600 in less than six months, while I screwed around like a big shot. I risked everything, time and again,

18

to lose more than $500, while just three shares bought at that original 448 would have made me that much. And at that I was lucky. It could have been disaster, in a stock that can fall 10 to 15 points in a day.

I pulled other boners as I battled the tape. And even after I was working again and had given back their key, I still had the fever and acted the fool. Of course I had some winners, too, although the trend was down throughout all of 1960.

You actually wouldn't believe 1961. I went up handsomely for six months, then lost my shirt for six months. The value of my stocks was identical, within a couple of hundred dollars, at both ends of the year. On stocks sold, I lost exactly $4.19. Not that I was in the market to break even, but if I had known what was coming in 1962, I'd have figured I had done very well.

To show you the way things went, let me give you one page in my notebook of those days:

BOUGHT	NO. SHS.	ISSUE	PRICE	AMOUNT	SOLD	PRICE	AMOUNT	PROFIT (LOSS)
11/ 2/61	100	Lithium Corp.	12⅞	1,307.38	1/18/62	12⅛	1,189.86	(117.52)
11/ 3/61	100	Raymond Inter.	13⅝	1,383.13	1/17/62	12½	1,226.99	(156.14)
11/ 3/61	100	Gamble Skogmo	34⅞	3,523.94	1/17/62	35	3,458.03	(65.91)
11/ 8/61	50	IBM	600¼	30,079.51	11/ 8/61	599¾	29,913.91	(155.60)
12/18/61	100	Allied Artists	6⅛	625.63	5/10/62	3⅞	387.50	(238.13)
1/17/62	50	E. F. MacDonald	63	3,182.75	3/14/62	100	4,954.00	1,771.25
1/ 5/62	300	Brunswick	47⅛	14,265.18	1/ 5/62	44⅝	13,245.94	(1,019.24)
3/21/62	50	Great A&P	56½	2,856.13	6/21/62	42¾	2,108.23	(747.90)
6/ 6/62	100	Amer. Viscose	52⅞	5,287.50	6/ 6/62	51¾	5,124.63	(162.87)

How did that one winner get in there?

The roller coaster's steepest on the downside

The big bear market of 1962 didn't mean a thing to me. It started late in 1961 and ran right into June, with the Dow Jones Average dropping 27 percent in that 7 months. I had started my own private bear market—in June of 1961—

and interrupted it for a recovery (just to show my independence) when the Dow was doing its worst. Then threw my money away like a fool in a nine-months' spree, while the market tacked back into the channel again.

It is far easier to lose on Wall Street than to win. We'll talk later about the "house odds" that are stacked against you, but they're not the main problem. We'll discuss the yo-yo pattern so many rising stocks follow—going too high, then settling back most disconcertingly. But that's not what does the damage. Nor can the periodic bear markets shoulder the blame. The simple truth is that it's tough for the inexpert investor to hold a stock on the way up, because it's fun to take profits. But it's easy to ride it down, because who needs losses? So the smart money hangs on during the slow, clicking ride to the top of the roller coaster and then gets off. To continue the metaphor, the skilled investors give the car a shove when they sell and—whoosh—down she goes, with you still aboard. Me, too, in those days.

But the actions of the individual stock still don't constitute the big problem. It's the actions of the investor that cause the trouble. Because you literally get so you can't win for losing. You get panicky, and do foolish things, and get in deeper and deeper so that the whole thing compounds and you really take a dive.

And didn't I just?

But I had learned my basic lessons. And although I have made plenty of mistakes in the years since, they were not the fatal kind that put a man under. More important, I never again had a bad year, and I never again expect to have one.

There's a line in a book first published in 1935 and revised down through the years. It's one of the few down-to-earth, plain-language books you'll find on investing; I recommend it for further reading once you've absorbed these pages. The book is *The Battle for Investment Survival* by Gerald M. Loeb,* and the line is, "Knowledge born from

* New York: Simon & Schuster, rev. ed. 1965.

actual experience is the answer to why one profits; lack of it is the reason one loses."

So you'll probably have to make your own mistakes before you develop real skill. But learn from me how to keep their consequences small. Those years of stupid trading taught me some valuable lessons in what not to do—which you don't have to prove for yourself. They also taught me some "do's" to go with the "don'ts." Those you should absorb as well, and put into practice.

After all, I couldn't have done *everything* wrong, or I would have been out of business.

> *What are Little Guys made of?*
> *What are Little Guys made of?*
> *A taste for dice and bad advice—*
> *That's what Little Guys are made of!*

Chapter 2

WHAT I DID RIGHT

There's a familiar illustration of the laws of probability that states that if a million monkeys were set down at a million typewriters, sooner or later they would write *Hamlet.*

Another story, hopefully less familiar, concerns the promoter who never quite made the big time. He brought out a soft drink call "6-up," produced a cowboy movie called "11:59 A.M.," and spent years trying to sell a morning TV show called "Yesterday" and a night show called "This Afternoon."

Up to my 1963 awakening, you can position my investing efforts somewhere between those two propositions. I tried so many things I had to hit it right once in a while. But I never did hit that combination we all hear and dream about—the one that vaults us directly from Wall Street to Easy Street. However, I learned much, and so can you, from the maneuvers that turned out right. So let's touch on them a moment, too.

Back in 1959, when I bought 25 shares of American Motors at 39 (that was before it split in 1960), it didn't seem exactly peanuts to me. The company was making its big comeback then, and George Romney was putting it on its feet. Five months later, at 52¾, I bought 25 more; then 15 at 74⅜.

Just like I knew what I was doing, I sold the original, for a long-term capital gain, at 92½, late in 1959. Then sold the later purchase in January, 1960, at 80⅜. For a beginner, that was just about a perfect ride—and you know where American Motors has been and has stayed ever since. A lot of that 80 and 90 stock is still tucked away in people's accounts, waiting for break-even day. And break-even day isn't about to come.

Remember, that was an odd lot of a fairly high-priced stock. So when your instincts tell you to buy round lots (100 shares) of low-priced stocks, because you can't make anything on just a few shares of the high-priced issues—you think of American Motors on the rise. Or Polaroid, or Xerox, or Syntex, or any one of the issues that have made that wonderful move. It doesn't take a hundred shares to participate in a big way. Unless you don't call a $2,000 profit on a $3,500 investment participating in a big way. (P.S. Pyramid your holdings, average up as it rises, and you'll really squeeze the juice out of it.)

I caught on to that odd lot/average up routine early. We'll cover all the logic of it later.

High price needn't mean expensive

I always say a man can't be all bad if he buys IBM once in a while. Only a Little Guy knows how tough it is to lay out three or five or six hundred for a single share of stock. Despite the day-trading aberrations confessed to in the previous chapter, I held IBM most of my early investing years—and it served me very well.

It's still serving its stockholders well, though I persist in the quaint notion that I can do better today with issues somewhat lower in price. But for the man who really doesn't want to trade, IBM has been the world-beater.

Most people have to be persuaded of that—the instinct

23

is so strong against high-priced stocks with a long growth record.

A while back, a friend wanted to put some inherited money into the market as a first-time investor. I finally made him pin down exactly what he wanted in the market. He wanted growth—not crazy, new stocks but only those which had proved themselves over the years. He didn't want to have to watch the papers every night and worry about them, either.

I referred him to my broker, with the advice that he spell those things out very clearly. A week later I asked how he'd made out. "Oh," he says, "you know all that guy came up with? IBM, Polaroid, and Xerox!"

"Well?" says I.

"Any jerk could have picked those," says he.

"Would you have felt better if he'd given you a hot tip on Consolidated Framus at three dollars and-there's-some-inside-buying-going on?" says I, meanly.

And he would have, because nobody really wants not to have to watch the papers every night. To prove it, he bought all three and watches the papers every night, anyway. What's more, his wife watches the papers, too, so when the stocks go down he leaves the paper on the train by mistake—and I've just spoiled that one for him, haven't I?

At any rate, I somehow brought myself to buy high-priced items like IBM and Minnesota Mining and Jones and Laughlin (which cost me a $7.05 loss in six months of 1961, because the steels have been nowhere longer than you'd think possible). All in all, the higher-priced stocks have been good to me, and they can be to you. I'll be playing that tune throughout these pages.

Getting out is very "in"

Among the things a man does right, you have to list the times he crumpled a fender but escaped a serious crash by fast reaction and clever driving. So, in running a portfolio, getting out in time when you buy wrong is as important as buying right in the first place. We'll dig deeply into the sins of riding a stock down, and being "locked in" (silly phrase), but let me just mention that it was bad enough to stay with Brunswick from 58 to 36 in 1962. But I could still be in today at 17, pretending I don't really have a loss because it's only a "paper loss." American Machine and Foundry, sold at 66, lost me less than a hundred dollars, but it hasn't been out of the twenties since 1962. So, as in any battle, getting out with a whole skin when things go against you is mighty important, too.

Could be it was impatience that drove me out of falling stock in my early days. But it has become a solid principle, now, not to go down the drain with them. Preservation of capital doesn't simply mean avoiding risks—it means cutting losses, too. A whole chapter will spell that one out.

In the missing-fortune-by-an-eyelash category, I could list all the winners I held that didn't really take off till after I'd sold them. I've mentioned National Video—sold at 24, instead of the 125 it hit five years later, adjusted for a split. (Of course it does add interest to realize that this erstwhile glamour stock went off the boards at 12½ early in 1969, when the firm closed down its plants.) Control Data made me small amounts a couple of times, but to sell it at 28 in 1962, then see it split three for two and go to the 160's by 1967, doesn't exactly make a man feel smart. Except that I did make money on it and you can't hate yourself for that. Today, if I get out of a dropping stock that I really like, I go in again when it starts to rise once more.

Actually, while too much in-and-out stuff only enriches your broker, the Little Guy should develop the practice of "tasting" stocks. Only if you own a stock do you really watch it and think about it. Nobody ever got much—either in learning or sustenance—from picking a paper portfolio, because watching somebody else's stocks is like watching somebody else's dinner. So take pride if you buy the right stocks, even if you get off them before they hit their peaks. The man who never even bought them will be the first to taunt you for what you missed. But what does he know?

There are two ways of reading the fact that this chapter is so much shorter than the previous one. You could assume I didn't do as much right as I did wrong—and you'd be quite correct. Or you could figure that reading about another man's smart selections would be Dullsville. And you'd be even more correct on that. Which should carry a message for you, when next you get into a discussion on your investing prowess. Instead of dragging out—and even exaggerating a bit—your marvelous string of victories, try telling about your bad moves. You'll get a rapt audience, and it will help you become the kind of realist who has the best chance of making money in the market.

Chapter 3

SCHOOL'S IN SESSION

So now I've got my feet under me, ready to leap headlong into the job of shaping you up. Call the previous pages my credentials. I qualify by having done all the wrong things and survived it. And by having learned the right things. Somehow I feel like Robinson Crusoe, having to re-invent everything that's taken for granted in other parts of the world. But I never could find proper guidelines, so I've had to put it all together for myself. And it all works.

We've touched on a few of the key points—like buying on margin, buying odd lots, buying on the rise, buying more of a stock that's going up. We've talked pretty much at random, about selling when a stock drops—and about buying it again if it recovers. We've clucked over the folly of short-selling and day-trading. We'll cover all those in detail and add all the other vital bits like the technique of obtaining and using advice, including this book.

You'll learn why you should usually avoid blue chips, dividends, and mutual funds (a position that earns me instant outrage from 20,000,000 of the 24,000,000 investors, 4,300 out of the 4,300 broker-dealer firms—and 101 percent of the funds).

You'll discover some esoteric factors you never before

considered, like the small float and the "self-fulfilling prophecy."

If you have been investing for some time, you may think you can safely skip the next chapter, because it contains the real basics as to what the market is and why. But do so at your peril. At worst it's a worthwhile review, and you're almost sure to find your preconceptions challenged.

Besides, how will you know what to disagree with, unless you read every word?

Before we start the nitty-gritty, though, it would be a good idea to define the goal I've set myself in the market, and which I commend to you. Stated flatly, it may not seem very exciting. *It's a mere 30 percent growth every year.*

That surely doesn't seem very ambitious, does it? Dozens of stocks double every year; some triple or do even better.* But you can't consistently pick only the big winners. So there's a great deal more to investing than that. The market itself—that great, amorphous blob that dominates your investing life—goes up and down. Wars and the threats of war knock some stocks down and boost others up. The actions of other people—odd-lotters, short-sellers, and, with dangerously growing intensity, fund managers—affect the stocks you select and help make you right or wrong, brilliant or stupid.

The first $50,000 is the hardest

Aim for that 30 percent. It will double your money in three years, and then you'll double all that in three more years. And mathematics being what it is, the second $50,000 will take only a fraction of the time the first $50,000 does.

Who knows, you might even make the million dollars in the title of so many best sellers on the subject. If you live

---

* Read *Happiness Is a Stock that Doubles in a Year* (1969 Edition) by Ira U. Cobleigh (New York: Bernard Geis Associates).

long enough. But, even more important, you'll *keep* whatever you make.

A friend who bought an apartment house instead, and weeps a little now and then, told a neighbor that a fellow he knows had sold a book on how to double your money in three years in the market. The neighbor, with the stung pride of the normal investor said, "Hell, I've done better than that. He's not so smart."

"Oh," said my friend. "Well, did you write a book about it?"

"He's smart," said the neighbor.

But my smartness index doesn't depend on writing a book—or on doubling your money, or even tripling it. It depends on having learned or developed simple rules that, intelligently applied, can smooth the market's inconsistencies into a steady upward path.

Your smartness index depends on your ability to grasp and apply those rules. If you do, you have the pleasant prospect of witnessing a growth of your investment that runs $2,000—$2,600—$3,380—$4,394—$5,712—$7,426—$9,654—$12,750—$16,574—$21,746—$28,268.

With that ten-year growth held before you as a carrot, let's plunge into the intricate simplicities that make up this fascinating business of "specuvesting."

Chapter 4

THE WHYS AND WHEREFORES OF THE MARKET

Like the Hollywood star said, "Let's not talk about me, let's talk about *you*—what did *you* think of my last picture?" From here in, having established my credentials as an odd-lot loser who became a round-lot winner, let's concentrate on turning you into a winner, too. Naturally, we'll have to do it in terms of my own experience.

It'll take some doing. I'm going to assume that you know nothing about the market. It will pay you to make the same assumption, because a going-in attitude of ignorance will help you to unlearn a lot of junk that's been standing in your way, and to square away for a successful operation. Paying attention will help keep you from paying something far more valuable—your hard-earned, sweat-stained, ever-lovin' money.

It will ease your mind to know that you don't have to be able to quote statistics and endless facts to be successful in the market. Just be attentive—make sure you understand —then remember the principle or the conclusion. You can forget the rest. That goes for picking stocks or for reading this book. Your aim isn't to sound knowledgeable, it's to make money. Like they say, money talks. You'd do better to tag along and listen.

So listen.

First of all, understand from the very outset that investing is gambling. So, if you don't like the idea of gambling, you probably won't make a good investor. In the stock market you're simply betting your money that you'll get back more than you put in. True, it's a very sophisticated form of gambling—but, whether you're in it for dividend income or for growth, you are gambling.

Furthermore, there are house odds against you, just as there are in any game. These take the form of brokers' commissions, state taxes, and the grasping hand of your Uncle and mine. Win, lose, or draw, your broker and the state get theirs. And the Internal Revenue Department stands by to skim its off the top if you dare to do better than break even.

The only safe, nongambling investment you can make is to deposit up to $15,000 in any federally insured bank and collect the interest. *Anything* more than that can lose you all your money or part of it. And the bigger the profit you go for, the bigger the risk you take. There is, of course, a perfectly safe way of doubling your money. You take it out of your wallet, fold it once, and put it back in. That's an old burlesque gag, I'm told.

Investing is one of the better risks. You don't lose everything when you're wrong as you do in dice or cards, and the odds are fabulously better than in horse racing. It's a lot better than opening your own small business—over half of which fail with a total loss. But investing is an out-and-out gamble that will require all the skill you can muster as well as a generous helping of well-seized good luck if you're to come out a winner.

If you figure to play it ultrasafe—by concentrating, for example, on the "widows and orphans" stocks such as GM and American Telephone—then you not only don't need me, you won't even like what I have to say. Because these can be very poor investments. As this is being written,

AT&T is appealing to the government to relent on the 7 percent profit ceiling it slapped on her. And, meantime, the stock stays in the 50's. The safe-players who bought at or near the "Big T" high of 75 in 1964 should get cold comfort from the dividends they're receiving today—since they've lost one-third of their investment.

This vicious attack on Ma Bell can only be excused by the fact that it proves a very important point, which is this: Don't go into the market for anything but growth. And if you do go for growth, be mentally and financially prepared for the risk this unfailingly involves.

"Prepared" means prepared to lose!

Don't kid yourself—you can lose. So to invest successfully you've got to have some money *that you can afford to lose.* That's not pessimistic, it's realistic. To be specific, if you're to have the best chance for sizable capital gains (and that is the *only* thing you should be interested in), you must have a disposable sum of at least $2,000. This is the minimum required by most brokerage houses for opening a margin account—and we're going the margin route in this book.

And, further, you must not only be able to afford to lose some or all of your investment, you must be able to keep it in the market for an indefinite length of time. It can't be money you're going to need on a certain date—for college, or for a down payment, or a loan coming due. Or to get married, you mad, impetuous fool, you. It's okay if your goal is many, many years away, but don't plan on any short hauls. Your particular stock, or the market as a whole, or the whole darned economy are sure to be down at the very time you *have* to cash in. The man who's forced to make a selling or buying decision based on anything except market factors has just that much better chance of losing his shirt.

Incidentally, for convenience's sake, I'll be using the

masculine gender in this book. But I know that the gals invest—and that some of them are very good at it. Of the 24,000,000 shareholders in the country today, one-third of them are housewives and nonemployed women. The working girls who invest bring the total up to, you should pardon the expression, a fat 51 percent of all shareholders. The fact that one out of every six women holds stock today is only partly due to their clever trick of surviving the husbands, or the widespread practice of putting stocks in the wife's name. The rest of them are in the market because they put themselves there. So, ladies, don't hesitate to do likewise. And take courage from the fact that not only do women invest, but over 1,800 of them are actually registered representatives of New York Stock Exchange member firms. But please don't mask your ignorance with stubbornness, as so many brokers report you do.

However, before joining the dance, anyone must decide how much to invest. I've already mentioned that $2,000 is the minimum needed to follow the precepts of this book —because you need that much to open a margin account. The "why" is in Chapter 18. So you'll need $2,000 at least —and you'll need as much more as you can comfortably spare, because the bigger your account the more room you have to maneuver. And the more service you can demand from your broker, which is strictly a secondary consideration but a very real one.

In short, you should put as much money as you can spare into your account. It may surprise you, but any idle money just sitting there actually draws interest. The one percent or so your broker pays is less than you can get in a bank, but it pays off in other less tangible ways. Of course if you have a balance of about $50,000 sitting idle, your broker will pay as high as 4 percent. But then you ain't no Little Guy, so go read some other book.

The main thing is to figure out in advance how much you'll put in at the start, and how much you'll add every month or every year. The amount should not hinge on how hot you think the latest tip is. Investing is a business—and all businesses have to start with calculating how much you can put into them.

Since we can't put a ceiling on what you should invest and we have already set a $2,000 floor, we'd better work backward from a list of things you shouldn't touch—things that must come first, before you decide on an amount to put into your account.

First, if you have a family, get adequate insurance. Mind you, insurance is just about the worst possible *investment* because it pays off in yesterday's dollars. But we're not talking about investing now—we're talking about the security of your family. And that comes first.

Next, you should have enough in the bank to support your family, on the lean side if you wish, for at least three months. That includes mortgage payment, insurance, food, clothing, everything. If your employment or a good portion of your wages are secure, come hell or high water, then you can shave that requirement. But you need a comfortable bank account and nobody can tell you any more precisely than that.

Finally, if you're building a college fund, or a house-in-the-country fund, or a travel fund—don't touch it. Don't fall for the temptation to build it "the easy way," because as I've said, you'll get caught off base as sure as shootin', and that can really hurt. Especially if your spouse isn't entirely in tune with your wolf-of-Wall-Street efforts.

It may well turn out that when you honestly review your finances, you'll find you can't go into the market at all. So don't. If you *need* the money you invest, then you can't handle your investments wisely. Of all the flat statements you'll read in this book, that is the most unequivocal. The panic induced by unbearable losses will only breed foolishness and more losses.

If you find you don't have the money to spare, and you still want to invest, use the New York Stock Exchange's Monthly Investment Plan (MIP), described on page 106. It's a pale shadow, but it will get you started toward the day when you do have cash to spare.

Four good reasons for investing

If you do have spare cash, invest it. Everyone who can afford it, and who has the stomach for it, should be in the stock market. The reasons that make the most sense are:

1. To beat inflation
2. To put idle money to work
3. To get regular income
4. To get some of those big profits

1. Inflation is a very real problem. The cost of living increased in nineteen of the years between 1945 and 1968. The tempo has picked up, with 2 percent in 1965, 2.9 percent in 1966, 2.8 percent in 1967, and 4.7 percent in 1968. And if you really want to worry, consider the Korean War increases of 5.8 percent in 1950 and 5.9 percent in 1951. This rise has been continuous since Washington whupped the Redcoats—and it actually became a part of governmental policy with Roosevelt's inauguration in 1933. You may feel that's a political opinion, but don't let your feelings cloud the fact that it is so. And that it will continue.

Can the market beat inflation? Consider the Dow-Jones average of thirty leading industrial stocks. It stood at 99.90 in 1933. If that's too much the ancient history bit, then go back only to 1957 and a D-J Average of 435.69, compared to the 820-850 range of early 1968's "bear market," or the 950's reached in early 1969. And it will be back.

Obviously, any investor who was whimsical enough to buy an equal number of shares of each Dow-Jones stock in 1957 and hold them through thick and thin has beat inflation with that part of his money.

From the dividend standpoint, if that's your bag, the same growth has occurred. In 1957, total dividends from the thirty D-J issues came to $21.61. In 1968 these "Dow-Jones dividends" totaled $31.34, so the income growth has been there. Remember, of course, dividends are a snare and a delusion to most investors.

Lately, the government has been taking pokes at inflation

without deflating it much, however. "Cooling down the economy," they call it. The discount rate (the rate Federal Reserve banks charge their member banks) has been moved up and down. There was the helpful 1966 statement by William McChesney Martin, Jr., head of the Federal Reserve Board, that the market situation looked like 1929 all over again. That one supposedly triggered the bear market of 1966. There was the imposing of an income-tax surcharge that triggered nothing much but complaints. Then there was the time the President wouldn't let steel raise prices. And the time, two years later, when he wouldn't again—and they did, anyway. Now we're at it again.

The efforts have been sporadic at best, and none has had much effect on the inflationary spiral—nor will anything except a really big cut in government spending, which neither you nor I are likely to live to see. Inflation is here and it's a very real problem. If you don't think so, try to live on the income your father raised you on. Lewis Carroll had the Red Queen say it: "You have to run as fast as you can to stay in the same place."

So you have to try to hedge against inflation. If you bury your money in a tin can, 1 or 2 percent will leak out every single year. If you put it in the bank, you'll net 2 or 3 percent above the cost-of-living rise—and pay income taxes on the whole 4½ or so. You can buy real estate, but that's tough duty and completely lacks the market's unbeatable negotiability, which lets you sell right now. Or you can start your own business, with that 50 percent chance of failure we mentioned earlier.

On all counts, the stock market is the answer for the average, intelligent person. It's no royal road to riches, but you can keep a country mile ahead of inflation if you use your head. And whether you're thirty or sixty, you owe it to yourself to take a stab at it. It's only fair to state, too, that any comparison of investing with gambling falls apart on this one peculiar fact—inflation can cancel out all the "house odds" in the long run. The market has gone up, is going up, and will go up, because of inflation as much as because of our expanding economy. There is no guarantee that your stocks will go up, too. But the odds are helped by that damnable trend.

2. *Idle money* can disappear. Inflation nibbles away at it, as we've discussed, but there are worse dangers than that. I'm not talking about fat inheritances or big windfalls that can support expensive tastes, but the two or three thousand dollars—or ten or fifteen thousand dollars—that a man may build up through the years or have handed to him once in his lifetime. You have to nurse that pot along. The Bible's point about the wonderful treatment awaiting the prodigal son who wastes his money doesn't apply unless you have a rich father to return to after your foolishness.

It's against nature for most of us to let money sit idle— especially if we've had it handed to us. So the car, the clothes, the cruise all take their toll. And they should. But how about setting aside a little seed corn before it all gets eaten up?

Again, don't invest that money short term between sprees, or to finance the next one. Money in the market should be there for growth—and growth takes time. Figure to plow back your gains and dividends. Pet it, work with it, *build it*. It can retire you some day. And that's better than a new Super-Sport GTX.

3. *Regular dividend income* is like motherhood. You don't dare knock it, but it can arrive too early if you're not careful. If you're already making a good salary *you don't want more income*. Not from the stock market, anyway— because there you *pay* for income, as we'll fully explain in Chapter 26.

The time you do need income is after you're retired, or if you're a nonworking widow, or for any reason find the "right now" more important than the rainy day. If that's your situation, then you can do very handsomely in the stock market, with 5 or 6 percent assured and some possibility of growth.

If you do want income, your broker can help you more

than this book can. But read it anyway, to learn what you should have done ten or twenty years ago.

4. Those big profits are being made every market day, rain or shine, bull or bear. Not by everybody who's trying, and rarely by the same persons, day after day. But the profits are there to be made, and they're being made by little people just like you. Only not very often.

Nevertheless, "getting in on those big profits" is probably the best reason of all for going into the stock market —in fact it's really the only reason. We live in a capitalistic country, in what is mainly a capitalistic world, thank the Lord. All the deep economic theories about how this functions can really be summed up in the homely phrase, "them as has gets." And, while this is usually groaned when your wealthy townsman wins the raffled Chevy, it is actually a fairly accurate statement of the principle of investing in anything. If you have some money, investing can get you more.

The stock market merely gives you a remarkably convenient and flexible way of doing it. Of course, I have to add a home-grown homily to the discussion—when you put your money to work for you, you'd better be prepared to work for *it*.

Four stupid but very popular reasons

So those are the sensible reasons for going into the stock market. There may be others, but I don't know of any. There are, however, a whole host of stupid reasons for taking the plunge. And the stupid reasons are a lot more attractive than the good ones.

That may be why there are a lot more stupid people than bright ones in the market. And why most of them lose money. Their reasons most often include these:

1. To get money quickly for a specific purpose
2. To cash in on a hot tip

3. To show you're as smart as Joe
4. To get some of those big profits

1. Quick money for a purpose is the greatest of all stock market psychedelics. "I can put that into the market for six months and we'll have enough to buy the camper before we need it!" Sure you can—if you don't mind the alternative of spending your vacation at home.

It's been said so often that it bears saying again—if money were that easy to make, your broker would be too rich to bother with your account. He can't make money that fast and that surely, and neither can you.

I've told you about day-trading. Well, six-month trading is just as bad because it sucks in the uninitiates who think it's a perfectly logical approach. They have the vague realization that you pay less tax after holding a stock six months, and they've heard about all sorts of people doubling their money in that time. So why not?

There are plenty of good reasons why not, but the best one is: "Because you'll very likely lose a good part of what you've already got." Why shouldn't you? If only 15 percent of those who enter the market come out ahead, why should you be one of them? And why should it happen on a schedule?

The other popular phrase is: "All I want is five points and I'll get out." That sweet reasonableness, that charming absence of greed, is supposed to indicate that this cool investor knows it isn't easy to make a killing. A man of the world, he simply needs a little stake and has this money just sitting there, so . . .

The trouble is, it isn't a pose. People believe it to be a very sensible expectation. When American Motors was 23, in 1963, a friend of mine had his mother buy 100 shares. "I figure she can make $500 and get out," he said, complacently. And indeed she may, some day—because at least he didn't add the six-months bit. Meanwhile her money sits, with no dividends, and pulsates a good 10 to 15 points lower.

Don't invest for a specific profit, or for a specific period, or for a specific purpose—except to make as much as you can over a long, long time.

2. *Hot tips* are usually worth exactly what you paid for them. Nothing. Virtually the only hot tip that can mean anything to the novice is the carefully given advice of someone intimately connected with the stock market. Nobody else can know with any certainty what the effect of any development will be on the market.

The chemist who discovered the new drug doesn't know. The president of the company which will make it doesn't know. And chances are that even the elevator boy who overheard them all discussing it doesn't know. And anyway, you will be the last to hear about it—and what makes you so much smarter than everybody else?

The old-time humorist Kin Hubbard once said, "Only one fellow in ten thousand understands the currency question, and we meet him every day." Man, is that true of the stock market! You just never run out of experts. And hot tips.

There are three things wrong with a novice going in on a hot tip. First off, it may not be true—or, even if it's true, the rumor may not get enough currency to affect the market. Secondly, it may already be too late—the stock may already have soared—and it takes a great deal of sophistication to be able to tell (or guess) whether a rocketing stock has reached its apex and is about to burn out. As well as a great deal of sophistication to take your loss and get out before you're wiped out, if it does start to plummet. Thirdly, you may get caught in a swindle or in a situation that gets out of hand. When that happens—and it's not infrequent when speculative fever is raging—the SEC or the Exchange itself can suspend trading and *you can't sell your stock at all* until the thing is straightened out—usually many dollars lower.

For a flagrant example of a basically worthless hot tip, which made the sharpies a lot of money and lost the lambs just as much, consider the case of a company named the Dyna Ray Corporation. During the somewhat speculative summer of 1967 it soared in over-the-counter trading from 15 cents a share in March to $10 a share on August 17. Nice move, wot? And then the spoilsport SEC suspended trading in it. They had good reason for the suspension. As they stated: "No current public information is available concerning the company's operations, financial conditions, product lines, plant location or place of business, and recent efforts to communicate with company officials have been unsuccessful."

Dyna Ray was suspended at about $10 on August 17 and reopened at $2 on October 17.

In the stock market, as you can see, wishing *can* make it so—if enough people back their wish with cash. But the bubble will eventually burst, and you may well be the one left with a fistful of soapsuds. So just remember the most unchallengeable bit of pedantry in the market, "investigate before you invest," and forget about the hot tip.

3. Showing you're as smart as Joe may lead to an expensive discovery—that Joe himself isn't as smart as he's led you to believe. Then, being as smart as Joe may result in your being as broke as big-talker Joe. And you will have learned a costly lesson.

The typical small investor has a habit of discussing all his gains and clamming up about his reverses, so the one-way street that Joe pictures to you is smooth and easy, with all the lights green. But if he were to level with you—and with himself—you might see a far different vista. If he's been in the market any length of time, and has ever held more than one or two lucky buys, his progress will have been anything but smooth.

As I said earlier, resolve now that you'll talk about your flops as well as your wins. This is not only more fair to your envious friends, it is excellent therapy for you. If you get the idea that you're Superwolf, you may be led to commit some very expensive follies. Face the fact, going in, that you're going to blow one now and then, and don't be fooled by the big-time operators who never let on that they do. And don't let Joe gloat you into the market.

Besides, there's always the unpleasant possibility that you may *not* be as smart as Joe.

4.   Those big profits, which form the best possible reason for investing, also form the worst. It looks like such easy money. You can see, every day, stocks that go up 2 points, 4 points, 6 points. Man—100 shares—that's $200 —just like that! Well, they go down 2 points, too—just like that!

Unless you follow the market closely, you don't even realize that it's not the same stocks going up all the time. Even people who own stocks can get the mistaken impression that they've got good gains, because they tend to remember the jumps and forget the fractional erosion that eats gains away. But the main trouble with impressions is that they don't count. Only the action of the few stocks you hold counts. You can't buy the market. You can't even buy the Dow-Jones. All you can buy is two—five—ten stocks. And you rise or fall with them no matter what the market seems to be doing.

The market is a matter of timing, anyway. In the period from December, 1950, to December, 1952, the value of all stocks on the Exchange averaged an annual gain of 12.6 percent. From December, 1955, to December, 1957, they averaged an annual loss of 3.3 percent. Same time span, opposite results. Who knows when the next 1957 will take place? Or the next 1962—or 1966—or, sad thought, a summer like 1969? Maybe it's just waiting for you to get in.

Those big profits are there all right, but they have a will-o'-the-wisp quality that can lead you into quicksand if you don't watch your step. So, don't put dime one into the market unless you fully recognize that it has no respect at all for your money or for your eagerness to make more.

There are 24,000,000 stockholders today—and each of them has a reason or reasons for owning stock. The vast majority of all the new investors who enter the arena each year do so for one or more of the seven reasons outlined. *And in too many cases, their going-in attitude foredooms them to failure.*

So what should your attitude be? Actually, if you've read this far you're halfway home. Because you surely shouldn't have any illusions left about the easy money that will come your way.

Chapter 5

THE NUTS AND BOLTS OF THE MARKET

Now you've decided that you want to invest—and you've decided how much to invest. Your next step is a tough one. You have to open an account. And that means picking a broker.

Well, you can walk into any brokerage office and tell the nearest employee you want to open an account. It's that simple. In a well-run office, one callow young "customer's representative" (or "account executive," if they prefer that title) will have been appointed to get the "walk-ins" that day. That's you. And, frankly, you don't want him.

Oh, the howls of anguish from the brokerage houses when I say that. He's been so carefully selected, so lovingly trained. He has endless resources in the company's research department; he can get all kinds of help and advice from his bosses.

But, if you go hunting up in Canada, you want the grizzled old guide who's walked those woods for years—not his book-larnin' son. Same goes in the wilds of the Wall Street woods. You need a seasoned practitioner who has proved himself in every kind of market.

Trouble is, he won't want you. You're just plain too

small. In fact, the brokerage firms have now messed up their business so badly that some of them are actively discouraging the small investor. After years of wooing and weaning he is now being told they can't make money on his small transactions. Various firms are using various restrictions: discouraging odd-lot transactions, refusing orders on which the commission is less than $10, putting a $2,500 minimum on over-the-counter purchases. It's like having the grocer refuse to sell to bachelors.

So ask around. Talk to your friends about their brokers. Then go see one. Talk to him about your aims and the size of your account. Mention your friend; it flatters the broker and makes him more eager. And you'll have twice the hold if you decide to use him.

But don't be diffident about your puny two grand, or whatever. It's important to you and it had better be to him. Remember, you're not asking anybody to do you a favor by taking your account. Those people can't live without business, and that's what you're offering them. So if one makes you feel uncomfortable or unwanted, just thank him politely and tell him you're not quite ready yet, but you'll think it over.

And if all this is too much bother for you, or too distasteful, then pop the money back in the bank. You've already flunked the first elimination test. Because, despite the claims that investing is a game people play for kicks, it calls for hard work, just like anything else that's worthwhile.

In fact, it's actually just like any other work. The market requires the same kind of disciplines and the same attention to detail as does *any* decision-making job. Which brings up an important point. If you're in the business world, and you're not making out—if you can't hold a job, or you never got ahead in the ones you did hold—then you'd better save your money. Take Aunt Minnie's little legacy, or those bonds the Major made you buy, and shop around for a sports car. You'll get a much better ride for your money.

Of course, if you've never worked at all, by all means give it a go. You seem to have a natural instinct for survival —which may be just what's needed.

So let's say you've finally picked a broker. And he can very well be a bright young fellow—because I don't want to be accused of trying to hold back the tide. Just so you pick him and don't just have him thrust upon you.

Actually, the kind of investing you're going to do may be better suited to a fairly youthful broker, because he won't be Depression-scarred. You'd be amazed at what memory of Black Tuesday and breadlines will do to a portfolio. While you are going to be very logical in the conduct of your investing, you don't want such pictures to force a crippling conservatism into your decisions.

One thing more about your new-found broker. You're doing business with him, you're not marrying him. Don't ever broker-hop, but, on the other hand, don't feel it's a crime to change if it turns out he's really not your kind of guy. Just find a new broker and tell him who your old one was—he'll handle the whole shebang.

The ABZ's of buying stock

Buying stock couldn't be simpler. You deposit your money in your account. You'll have to sign some papers, so ask what they are. Ask about anything you don't understand. Your broker will also tell you what buying power it gives you—how much you can invest. Actually, if the current margin requirement is 80 percent, just multiply your money by ten and divide by eight—it's that easy.

Then tell him how many shares of what stocks you want to buy. *Don't* use it all up in one purchase. Even if you get lucky, you won't have learned a thing. Chapter 23 tells why you should diversify, but for now just accept my word and think in terms of several issues.

The whole investment world is your oyster at this point, but you're going to steer clear of bonds, preferreds, convertibles, commodities, warrants, puts and calls, and everything else except common stocks. These are sold on all sorts of exchanges as well as "over the counter."

Mr. and Mrs. Exchange and all the little Exchanges

The "Big Board"—the New York Stock Exchange—is the daddy of them all. The American Stock Exchange, also in New York, is the next biggest and most prestigious. Incidentally, till 1953 it was known as the "New York Curb Exchange." It was held outdoors till 1921. The National Stock Exchange (in New York) is the baby, and is so small that, I swear, the porter answers the phone when someone calls in for a quote. And he sounds sleepy, at that.

On a good day, about 1,500 issues will trade on the New York Exchange, for a total of 12,000,000 to 20,000,000 shares. On the American, also called the "AMEX," it will be 1,000 issues and, say 6,000,000 to 10,000,000 shares. On the National Exchange, a score of issues and 100,000 shares make it a day. This is no reflection on the stocks sold on this teensy exchange—on one of which I recently multiplied an investment by six, thank you.

No stock is listed or traded on more than one exchange in any city because the SEC forbids it. The principal New York and AMEX stocks are, however, also traded on all the regional exchanges. The biggest of these is the Midwest Stock Exchange, a consolidation of exchanges in Cleveland, St. Louis, and Minneapolis–St. Paul. Its volume is 3 or 4 percent of the Big Board's. Other regional exchanges include San Francisco (Pacific Stock Exchange), Boston, Philadelphia-Baltimore, and half a dozen others, all registered with the SEC and subject to the same rules as the New York "parents."

The regional exchanges carry most of the best-known stocks, as well as lots of local stocks that aren't listed in New York. You can probably make out fine with these, though I haven't tried. Which reminds me of an 1831 cookbook passed down in my family. In giving helpful household hints, it states as follows:

A gentleman in Missouri advertises that he had an inveterate sore upon his nose cured by a strong potash made of the lye of ashes of the red oak bark, boiled down to the consistence of molasses. The sore was covered with this, and, about an hour after, covered with a plaster of tar. This must be removed in a few days, and, if any protuberances remain in the wound, apply more potash to them, and the plaster again, until they entirely disappear; after which heal the wound with any common soothing salve. I never knew this to be tried.

Well, I've never traded in local stocks on a regional exchange, though I *have* known it "to be tried." No stock exchange should be avoided, and no stock shunned because of where it's traded. But extra degrees of caution are suggested when you go down from the Big Board, to the AMEX, to the regional exchanges—with an extra warning about stock traded on the Canadian exchanges.

This isn't chauvinism; it's just that requirements for listing get less and less severe in that order and can be practically nonexistent where the famous Canadian penny mining stocks (under $1) are traded. Beware.

Last of all, but no less likely hunting ground than any exchange, is the over-the-counter market. That's where all the unlisted stocks are traded—in other words, *all* stocks except the 4,000 or so that are on the registered stock exchanges. How many? More than 20,000 companies that have "gone public" are traded only over the counter. (This peculiar name has no significant meaning, by the way, and would more accurately be "over the telephone"). Not all these companies are tiny or unknown. Banks by the dozen, insurance companies, mutual funds, and thousands upon thousands of industrial companies are traded in no other way. To be truthful, though, you can run your eye down several columns of the unlisted industrial securities reported in the papers before you find one you recognize. Most of them head for a registered exchange as soon as they can qualify. The popularity of a company's stock is very important for a number of reasons we'll go into later. And being on an exchange makes a big difference.

Surprisingly, most registered issues can be bought over the counter, too. But no space here for explaining that, because you won't be buying them there.

Commissions and other subtle bites

The commissions charged on the exchanges and the over-the-counter market are too complicated to dwell on. You're going to pay it anyway, so why let it bother you? Just remember if the amount of money involved is less than $100 the commission is as "mutually agreed." Nobody will ask you to agree, but it will rarely, if ever, be less than $6. But, mostly, if you figure on about 50 cents a share on every trade—once when you buy and once when you sell (a "round trip")—you won't get too many unpleasant surprises. Actually, it's a sliding scale that hinges on the total amount of the transaction. It's not very much, but it's enough to help support a mighty big fleet of yachts—which I hope doesn't sound too bitter.

When you sell in New York, Massachusetts, or Pennsylvania, you'll pay a state transfer tax. The federal government naturally gets into the act, again on the sale, not when you buy. These are not income taxes; you pay them win, lose, or draw. They're just part of the picture—the "house odds" we mentioned a while back.

Reading the tables and tapes

After you've bought a stock, you'll want to follow its progress. In fact I insist on it. At this point, there are a lot of abbreviations y. shd. kno. so that you can read the published stock reports. Although we won't be buying any preferred stocks, you'll want to know that they're designated "pf," since the company whose common you bought may also have a preferred issue, and it will be listed right under yours. Convertible preferred are "cvpf," which looks like Victor Borge's famous punctuation language. Many issues have several "pf's" with the number after each "pf" designating the amount of interest it pays. Or they may have letters to differentiate between them; like "pfA," "pfB," etc.

An "x" after the name of a stock listed in your newspaper stands for "ex-dividend," and it simply means a dividend is about to be paid to those who already own the stock, but not to anyone buying it on that day. The "x" means "without dividend," and the stock usually starts that day at a price lowered by the amount of the dividend.

If you find "wi" after a stock it means "when issued"; the stock hasn't actually been issued yet because it's split or is brand new, but you can buy it now and get the certificates when it really is issued and—oh, brother. Ask your broker. Don't ever mind seeming dumb.

The letters "fn" mean "foreign issue," and the only reason I mention it is that, like the "wi" symbol, it sometimes results in a stock being listed twice in the tables and this could throw you, since the price will be different.

Warrants have "wt" after them, while "vj" means bankruptcy, so run like a scalded cat.

A section of the stock tables looks like this:

Net Chge.	1969 High.	1969 Low.	Stocks and Div. in Dollars.	Sls. 100s.	First.	High.	Low.	Last.	Net Chge.
¼	16	5¾	Trns Car .10p	76	7⅝	8	7½	7⅞	+ ½
¾	58¾	21¼	TransLux .60	44	24¾	24¾	22¾	23¾	—1
⅛	8⅛	4	Transairco	10	4⅝	4⅞	4⅝	4¾	+ ¼
1¼	27¾	13⅜	Transcon Inv	113	17	17	15⅞	16	— ¾
..	23¾	12¼	Transogrm	7	14¾	14⅞	14¼	14¼	— ¼
¼	34¼	10	TWA wt	214	13⅞	13⅞	12¾	12¾	— ⅜
¼	75¾	64½	Tri Cont wt	1	64¾	64¾	64¾	64¾	.....
1¾	30	11⅝	TriStMot .38f	10	12⅞	12⅞	12⅞	12⅞	.....
½	41½	16⅛	Triang P .15e	53	20⅜	20⅜	19⅜	19⅝	— ¾
⅜	6¼	2½	Tubos Mex	49	3 3-16	3⅜	3⅛	3⅛	+ ⅛
¼	15⅝	8⅛	21 Brand .29f	12	8⅝	8¾	8⅝	8⅝	.....
⅝	58½	20½	Tyco Labs	22	25	25⅛	24⅛	24¼	— ¾
4⅜									
⅛			**U—V—W—X—Y—Z**						
⅛									
⅜	18	9¾	Udico Corp	28	10⅝	11⅞	10⅝	11⅞	+1⅝
⅜	17⅞	8	UIP Corp	17	9	9⅛	9	9	— ⅛
+ ⅛	44¾	14⅛	Unexcelled	25	16¾	16⅞	16	16	— ⅜
⅛	19½	11⅜	Un Finl 1f	5	12⅞	13	12⅞	13	+ ⅜
¼	25½	17¾	Un Invest .70	1	17¾	17¾	17¾	17¾	— ¼
⅝	34¾	[illegible]	[illegible] .80	[illegible]	[illegible]	[illegible]	20	[illegible]	

1969 High.	1969 Low.	Stocks and Div. in Dollars.	Sls. 100s.	First.	High.	Low.	Last.	Net Chge.
13¾	10⅜	Vocl cv pf.66	1	10⅜	10⅜	10⅜	10⅜	—
26⅝	20	Vogt Mfg 1a	5	22	22	22	22	+
26½	10⅛	VolMerch .20	32	12½	12⅞	12⅜	12⅝	+
30¾	12⅝	VTR Inc	58	14¼	15⅝	14¼	15¼	+1
12¾	7¼	Vulc Corp .20	21	7¼	7½	7⅛	7⅛	—
11⅞	6½	Vulc Inc .30	6	7⅜	7⅜	7⅛	7⅛	...
20⅞	10½	Wabash .20	15	12	12¼	12	12	+
30¼	18⅝	Wacknhut .30	x2	25½	25½	25¼	25¼	+
20	12¼	WadelEq .50f	8	13	13	12⅜	12⅜	—
52⅜	14⅛	Waltham Ind	21	17⅞	18	17½	17½	—
70	45⅞	Wang Labs	8	60⅛	60⅛	58⅜	58⅜	—1
17⅞	6	Ward Fds wt	10	7¾	7¾	7½	7¾	+
25½	14	Wards Co .40	2	16	16	15¾	15¾	—
39⅞	19⅛	Weil McL .44	16	29	29½	29	29⅛	+
18¼	10⅝	Weiman Co	18	13	13¼	12¾	13¼	...
15⅝	7	WeldTub Am	27	8⅜	8¾	8⅜	8½	+
23	9¼	WellcoE .10d	5	10⅝	10¾	10⅜	10¾	+
13	5⅛	Wentwth .10g	1	5⅜	5⅜	5⅜	5⅜	—
34¾	22½	West Ch .90	4	23⅜	23⅜	23	23	—
18⅝	9½	We[illegible]	[illegible]	13	13¼	[illegible]	[illegible]	

It's simpler than it looks. The "1969 High Low" is just that—the high and low prices for the year, not including the day for which the report is being given. Most papers don't give those figures, but good big-city papers do, and the blessed *Wall Street Journal* does. Since you're not going to clutter your head with a lot of figures, it's helpful to have them before you.

The next item is "Stock & div in $." The company name may be abbreviated and some of the results are pretty wild. I like "Bklyn UG," which isn't very good public relations for "Brooklyn Union Gas" (for that matter, Coastal States Gas Producing is "CstStGs," which sounds more like Coastal States Gas Escaping). Right after the name is the dividend, if any. Then you may see a small letter, which refers you to the footnotes for some juicy bit like "annual rate plus stock dividends."

"Sales in 100's" is a cinch. Just add two zeros to the number given. That's how many shares were traded that day, or up to the time the tables were printed, if it's an early edition. It doesn't count the thousands that may have been traded in lots of less than a hundred shares, or over the counter, but what do you care?

"First," "High," "Low," and "Last" are surely self-explanatory. They apply to that day's trading. "Net chge" is "net change"—the difference between the previous day's closing price and the closing (or latest) price on the day being reported.

Reading the tape is something else. First of all, you have to know the symbols of the stocks you're watching. They try to make these symbols remind you of the company, but they're not all as easy as IBM or GM.

The biggest and bluest chips were awarded the single letters, way back in time. Therefore, while AT&T would have a perfect three-letter symbol since so many people call it that, it proudly sports its single-letter "T." Standard Oil (N.J.) is "J." U.S. Steel is "X," which shows how prized the single letter is. But usually they're more creative. Like Quaker Oats with "OAT," or Manpower's "MAN."

If John Sexton & Co. (foods) ever gets listed, they won't give it the obvious symbol "SEX." In fact, with Associated Spring Corp. they went completely chicken and found an extra "A" somewhere to make it "AAS." It's just as well that questionable combinations are avoided. After all, if my million monkeys could write *Hamlet,* chance could also put some weird things on the tape. As it is, simply by buying General Interiors Corp., Seligman & Latz, Andrea Radio, Seeman Bros., Terminal Hudson Electronics, National Electric Welding Machine, and Brandywine Racing Association, you could make the AMEX tape read like this:

GIT	SAL	AND	SEE		THE	NEW	BRA
24½	2s26	9⅛	12¾	⅞	8	23⅜	26

So it wouldn't do to permit anything more graphic to creep in. Especially since there are even a few four-letter symbols.

However, for reasons nowhere near as intriguing, tape symbols are affecting the American industrial scene. More and more companies are changing their corporate names to conform with these stock symbols. Insurance Co. of North America took its stock symbol "INA" as their corporate name. Smith-Corona Marchant figured SCM Corporation was easier to remember. Many other such changes testify to the power of the investor today. The popularity of its stock has always been important to a company, and to its management. But, with the whole country going stock happy, it's a number-one consideration in every move they make these days. Even to the name.

THE ABC'S OF INVESTING

There was a time when Wall Street was indeed a numbers game.
But that was in the years before the new criterion came.
Today, there's only one guidepost to aid the sure-thing bettors
And that's to buy the companies whose names consist of letters.

52

Oh, there's GAC and IHC and CCI Marquardt,
Which only qualifies if you ignore the final part.
There's MCA and GCA and INA, as well;
What business they all conduct's impossible to tell.
But MPO will surely go another dozen higher,
Then be replaced or smartly paced by little GTI, or
By MSL or, what the hell, it could be AMP.
While UTD or UMC may pack that TNT.
But don't forget, before you bet your last remaining cash,
Some won't go far although they are, initially, a smash.

This desire for popularity has a couple of roots. Management owns stock, too, and usually has juicy stock options that aren't worth exercising if the stock doesn't go up. Acquisition-minded companies want their stock to be high in price because they can then buy other companies by offering stock instead of cash. The conglomerates, which are actually management companies that own other companies in a variety of industries, depend to a dangerous degree on the ever-increasing price of their own stock.

So, isn't it nice to have everybody pulling with you to make stock prices rise?

Below the symbols on the tape, as it zips along, you'll find the number of shares and the prices at which they sold. For example, in the above tape that leers about Sal's new bra, you see that 100 shares of General Interiors were traded at 24½. If more than 100 shares are traded at one time, it's written like the Seligman quote as "2s26"—which reads "two hundred shares at 26." Seeman traded 100 shares at 12¾, then 100 at 12⅞. Over 1,000 shares gives all the zeroes—"1,300s," etc.

The tape, as such, is not as important as it once was. You'll see it in most brokers' offices, rear-projected onto a wall. This is the "board room," where the prices of the principal stocks are also posted on the "board." It used to be an actual blackboard, with the prices continually chalked on it by perspiring young men. Although many out-of-town offices cling to this method, most big-city offices use a board on which the prices are changed electronically. You can see them go by on the tape and then—clickety-click—they change on the board. You'll also find such items as the Dow-Jones Averages, trading volume, advances and declines, and other goodies posted there and periodically registering the changing picture.

Brokerage houses are shrinking their public board rooms more and more. At most, today, they're usually a single row of seats right under the board, and a place to stand in back. If you look closely at that row of seats you'll see one reason they're getting fewer—two or three old fellows quietly snoozing the day away. This is very expensive space for such purposes. But private board rooms for preferred investors (for "preferred" read "big") will always exist.

Even the tape itself is phasing out. Reduced to the size of a large TV screen in many offices, it is being replaced by electronic wonders that do such things as providing three rows of New York Stock Exchange prices at the top, the Dow-Jones news-ticker report in the middle, and three rows of AMEX prices at the bottom—all on a big TV set. As these get more marvelous they get less readable, which is called progress.

The paper tape has vanished, together with its glass, bell-jar top; a bond ticker tape still curls up in its wastebasket somewhere in a secluded corner. And the news ticker quietly taps out its messages in another corner for those who want to check it periodically.

But the principal tool has become the Quotron, or one of the other similar devices. A desk-top gadget the size of an adding machine, it sits in repose till someone asks its buttons a question. If you want a single quote it instantly shows up in lighted letters at the top, but the most complicated information about the day's trading—the dividends, the earnings (past or projected) on any listed stock —is ripped out on a piece of printed tape before you can say "gee whillikens." Actually, the gadget doesn't know a thing—it's just a terminal for a computer that knows everything.

For unlisted stocks, you ask your broker for the "pink sheets," which show quotes on all unlisted issues.

Over-the-counter quotes are listed as "bid" and "asked." "Bid" supposedly means someone is willing to pay that much for the stock; "asked" means, hypothetically, that someone is willing to sell it for that price. The quotes are gathered by phone from no less than three houses in the afternoon of the previous day. They were accurate then— but could be a lot different by the time you read them.

Ask your broker for a current quote before you trade. Figure, on either buying or selling, that you will hit about the middle between the bid and asked, but don't count on it. And don't be surprised, ever. Be philosophical; it's an imperfect world and even Pippa passes.

You can find the most popular unlisted stocks in most major newspapers, daily. *The Wall Street Journal* (and *The New York Times,* for instance) also carries on Monday a weekly listing of less actively traded unlisted stocks. Beyond that you have to go to the "pink sheets," or ask your broker for a quote. But don't ask him unless you actually are interested in buying or selling that stock. Brokerage houses are so overwhelmed with work that they just can't keep satisfying your curiosity or casual interest. Play fair.

Don't tell me how to make the watch

That's about all you have to know about the mechanics of the stock market. A lot of the rest of it may be very interesting—how trading is handled on the floor, how "specialists" operate to keep things on an even keel, that kind of thing. If you want to know about them in detail, there are plenty of books that will make it all clear. But this isn't one of them, because this book is aimed at telling you as little as you have to know to make out.

In the advertising business (which, as you may have sus-

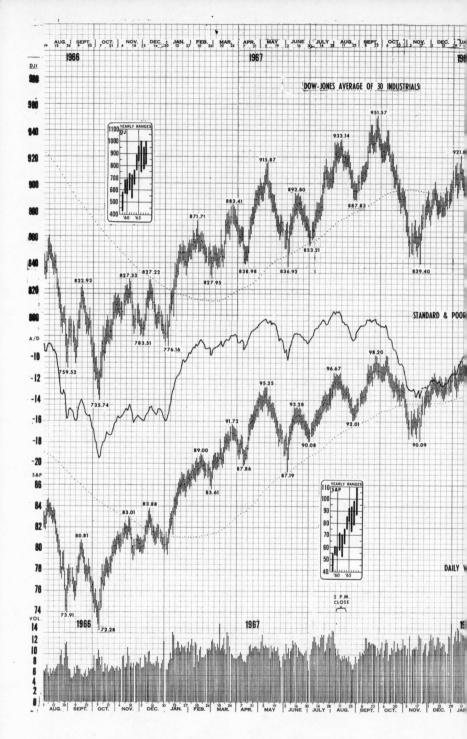

pected, gave me the money to invest in the first place) we're supposed to have a lot of Madison Avenue patter. Like, "Let's drop it down the well and see if it makes a splash." Well, I never heard anybody use that kind of jargon, but there's one I've heard that seems appropriate. "When I ask what time it is, don't tell me how to make the watch."

I remember a pitch one of my former agencies made for a big citrus growers' association account. Our new-business people produced an exhaustive study of the citrus industry, with a complete marketing plan. And the association said, in effect, "You've told us everything you know about our business, but nothing of what you know about your own business—so forget it, Charlie." Or was it Marion?

So you don't have to know what makes the market tick to know how to beat it. Once you accept that fact, everything will seem much easier. But I make one suggestion. If you don't understand something, ask about it or look it up. Then you can feel free to forget it.

Say "Howdy" to the dowdy Dow

There are only a couple more things to cover before we get down to the business of making you your first million. One of them is to explain the Dow-Jones, because we've referred to it a good many times, and so do a lot of other people.

The Dow-Jones Index, properly called the Dow-Jones Industrial Average, is the dowager of the averages. It was established in 1896 and diddled with down through the years until it's really complicated today. But, as usual, you don't have to remember how it's compiled—just what it means. It's the average of the prices of 30 leading industrial stocks, adjusted for all the splits and stock dividends through the years, so that the divisor is not 30 but some crazy number. If all 30 stocks rise one point, the D-J will rise about 13 points. Anyway, there have been a lot of more comprehensive averages compiled since then, like the New York Times Average of 50 stocks, the Standard & Poor's Industrial Average of 425 stocks, and now the New York Stock Exchange Index and the AMEX Index. The latter two average out *every* stock on their respective exchanges.

The question of whether 30 stocks can give you a reading on the whole market is no longer an academic one. For many, many years the D-J was the only average. It was like the old story of the gold miner who played the crooked roulette wheel because it was "the only game in town." But it was easy to overlook the fact that on the basis of dollar value, those 30 stocks account for 24 percent of *all* stocks on the Big Board. And now along come all these other averages and, surprisingly, they pretty much confirm the dowdy old Dow. Above, for example, is a two-year charting of the Dow-Jones and the Standard & Poor's Index of 500 Composite Stocks, which is the 425 Industrials, plus Utilities and Railroads.

So, while it's popular to pooh-pooh the D-J, there are still two things going for it, in addition to the simple fact that it seems a pretty good reflection of the action. It is the oldest and therefore has the longest tracking of any index. And it's the one that gets the headlines.

Okay, that's enough basics. You can read yourself blind on all the mechanics in some other books, but now let's us set out to make you some money.

Chapter 6

HOW TO BE A "SPECUVESTOR"

Shakespeare would have put it: "Neither a trader nor a sitter be." The course you're going to take will be dictated one hundred percent by the action of your stocks—and not by any preconceived notion as to how long you should keep them or how far you should ride them. The Little Guy who considers himself a trader is bound to concentrate on speculative issues—bound to jump in and out at a costly pace. The investor dedicated to sitting on his stocks will quite likely watch the world go by and his pile go down. Neither is being smart.

Naturally, we're talking about likelihoods, rather than remote possibilities. By hitting a lucky biggy once in a while, the in-and-outer may do very handsomely. By picking an IBM as his nest egg, the sitter may see it hatch into a sizable sum. But you can't afford to depend on the luck of the draw. You have to manage your investment. You have to combine the daring of the speculator with the solid patience of the long-term investor.

You have to be a "specuvestor."

Being a specuvestor is a state of mind. But actually the entire market is mental. Common stocks don't have a specific value, they're worth exactly what people think they're worth—no more, no less. Of course what *you* think, or some other *individual* thinks, doesn't really matter because it takes a whole lot of people to think a stock into an advance, or into a sharp decline. It's true that a stock can drift down substantially if nobody's thinking about it very much, because there are always holders who want to sell, and when nobody's very eager to buy, the price slides lower and lower. But that's just plain inaction. It's *action* that makes money—and action takes conviction on the part of a heck of a lot of people.

So, by and large, you have to tune in on people's thoughts. If you can read them correctly, and if you're nimble, you'll make money. You'll make money with any price stocks, in any industry, traded on any exchange or on no exchange. But if you can't tune in you're going to have rough going, despite all the rules and guidelines in the world.

With the small investor, this tuning-in process has to take the place of formal market research. First of all, it's the only way you can pick a winning stock. The task of selecting potential winners is a full-time job for an estimated eleven thousand very sharp analysts, complete with computers and inside tracks. For example, Chase Manhattan Bank has seventy bright young men working on this task alone—so that the bank can do its own investing wisely. And Chase is not even what you'd think of as an investment company.

Incidentally, most of those eleven thousand won't make out as well as you do when it comes to actual investing, for a very simple reason. Their view is likely to be too narrow. It is very easy to get too close to a stock or to a company. Analysts do, and so do chartists, as we'll cover later. A perfect example, provided by the amateur, is the too-frequent tendency to purchase stock in one's own company. I'm not talking about stock options that may let you buy below the current market price. Or stock purchase plans that give you a discount or let you pay over a long stretch while enjoying dividends immediately. I'm talking about the enthusiasm that makes you think your new M-4 Widget (with winch) is going to sell like crazy—so you'd better buy the stock before it goes up. Beware that kind of decision.

It's only fair, by the way, to point out that working for a company can blind you to its virtues, as well. Particularly if you see the feet of clay peeping out beneath management's Brooks Brothered shins. Like the case of one bright young VP who had a personal habit that clients and fellow workers felt to be somewhat of a reflection on the agency. I remember the day he showed up with his finger heavily bandaged. One of his more acid associates remarked that either his mother was trying to train him or he'd broken it off in his nose. Well, such personal considerations have no place in market judgment, but it's hard to exclude them from the evaluation of your own company. Little things can loom too large.

You have to take a detached view of the entire market. Take off your blinders. Open your eyes, your ears, your mind. And only after you've looked and listened a heap should you open your purse.

What's an expert, Daddy?

To whom do you listen? Your friends are full of tips, but, as a rule, that's not all they're full of. Magazines, newspapers, advisory services are packed with informed opinions. Your broker will have suggestions—which he'll try to tailor to your own needs. Of course, some brokers are worse than your friends on both counts, although most don't deserve the phrase used by one wealthy investor who asks to be nameless. He flatly calls brokers "touts with ties."

Actually, your broker is the nearest thing to an expert you're likely to find, and he has other experts at his command. So he's the one you should consult before you buy or sell. But remember—he's better at giving information than advice, because chances are he's not all *that* expert. Just having a job doesn't make a man a genius.

I remember years ago, when four of us advertising writers were penned in one office—all clacking up a storm on our Royals. One of the fellows was writing an ad that offered a free booklet on how to remove any kind of spot from anything. Well, he wrote himself into such an enthusiastic state that he picked up the phone and called the account executive. Said he'd like to get a copy of that booklet on how to remove any kind of spot from anything. "Okay," said the account executive, "just lean over and tell Larry to put in another carbon."

So don't be overawed by experts. But do learn to lean on them for what they know. Not so much what they think —just what they know. We'll go deeper into the difference in another chapter.

What expert d'ya read?

There are dozens of theories on how to pick stocks and how to handle them. You'll run into them all, and they'll baffle you till you learn to take them in stride. Here's a brief rundown on the main camps of "experts":

The random walkers. This approach is just about the same as the "efficient market" theory, which says that the market reflects, every day, the true value of every stock, with all the pros and cons and attitudes and foreign news and interest rates cranked in. So "random" or "efficient," the conclusion is that nothing that happened yesterday matters today, and, since you don't know what's going to happen today, one stock's about as good as another. You'd be amazed at the time and trouble that has gone into proving all this. But no matter how well masked it is in professional formulae and double-talk, it only means that you can beat the rap simply by picking your stocks at random.

A couple of years back, a member of the Senate Banking Committee reported that ten stocks he picked by the dart method proved to have performed, over the previous ten years, as well as several mutual fund portfolios. He had pinned the *Wall Street Journal* stock report on the wall and actually thrown ten darts at it. Then he assumed that he'd invested $1,000 in each of them ten years before. In that time, he told the committee, the $10,000 would have grown to $25,300—as good a gain as a whole list of funds had experienced in that time.

Some very serious students of the market subscribe to this dart-board theory, preferring, however, the more dignified "random walk" term. It mainly depends on the fact that inflation and the expanding economy keep the market rising inexorably, over time. But a rise by any other name smells sweet, and it's reassuring to know that the luck of the draw can make us money with good regularity. But disconcerting to learn that losing must obviously, therefore, be entirely our own doing.

Naturally, these people hold charting in great contempt. In fact, the main reason for going into this in even that much detail is to reassure you that, if you don't dig charting, you will be in agreement with the "efficient market" theorists. And if you don't believe the "efficient market" bit, then you're at least on the same side as the chartists. So you can stay stupid on both counts and make out marvelously. But not have nearly so much fun at cocktail parties.

The chartists do have a lot of fun— and they talk with greater assurance than anybody else in the marketplace (except for the real sharpies who are trying to sell you something shady). Chartists believe they can predict the future on the basis of a stock's past performance—where it went and how many shares it took to get there. This is only slightly related to palm-reading and is a considerable cut above astrology. And lots of big-time experts are quite willing to leave it at that.

64

Not only do chartists have very vocal detractors, they argue a lot among themselves. Although the most ardent of the clan use both, there is a "point and figure" camp, which charts only the one-point cumulative moves and snubs the bar-chart boys who record each day's high, low, and close. However, they do all talk the same language, bandying about "heads and shoulders" and "double bottoms" at great length. And they share something else, too —the disapproval of experts like the "fundamentalists."

The fundamentalists cling to such old, rock-steady considerations as price/earnings (P/E) ratios (the price of the stock, divided by the company's earnings), dividends and yields (the annual dividend divided by the price of the stock), and suchlike. They study annual reports and balance sheets. They believe in the logic of the market, and their touching faith shieldeth them from great harm—but sure doesn't tend to maketh them much money. Fortunately, few investors place their entire dependency on fundamentals. Most also pay attention to technical aspects.

The technical analysts try to take the temperature of the market. They can tell you at the drop of a stock whether it is a technical correction from an overbought condition, a rebound from a temporary top, or even a selling climax. They savor volume and feel the quality of the buying. They declaim that the stock is passing from weak hands into strong hands, and they are very impressive. Particularly to each other.

Some day you may decide you like one approach better than the others. All approaches attract intelligent people, all of them produce success stories. But sit loose, and pledge no allegiance for now.

Relief for the theory-weary

Your role, as a proper Little Guy, is to listen and absorb and enjoy. If you hear a chartist confide something that sounds interesting, like "Coagulated Wampum is at the resistance level on an up flag and should break out"—ask your broker what's the scoop on Coagulated Wampum. If a fundamentalist says California Cruet can double its earnings, check into it. But always remember this: *There is enough that's good about any theory to merit your attention—but not enough about any theory to warrant your devotion.*

Random walk theorists or efficient market fans tend to ignore the flexibility that is your right. To prove that ten stocks, if held for ten years, will perform thusly is meaningless, because you shouldn't hold ten stocks for ten years. Or, necessarily, for one year. You will constantly be adjusting your portfolio to conditions and to stock action. And that ain't random.

These people are in an enviable position. They can't be proven wrong, but they're a Kismet bunch who leave you with your bare face hanging out and no hint at all as to where to turn. They don't pretend to predict the market. Their position is that you *can't* predict the market.

Well, you'd darned well better predict the market. At least that part of the market that's got your money.

The chartists say you can—or at least that *they* can. They'll do it, too, and be right just often enough to keep their spirits up. Their greatest achievement, however, lies in going back over the charts and predicting what has already happened. It's somewhat like using a pantograph device—the thing with the jointed arms that lets you hold a pencil and draw a beeyootiful picture by tracing a metal pointer over another picture. It comes out just like you thought it would.

Pure fundamentalists assume that, in this orderly world, right will triumph. I suppose that it is possible for a believer in the sanctity of the price/earnings ratio to be a speculator—if the other fundamentals told him that a no-earnings company was really going to make it big. But he would certainly tend to be an Investor, with a capital "I." It's just not his bag to go in for the glamour stocks. He doesn't buy a rising issue because it's rising, but because he thinks it *should* rise—and there's a world of difference there. If money is tight and interest rates are high, that is bad for business, and the storm cellar beckons. He's got *reasons* for what he does—and he'll make them quite clear and convincing. The analysts are fundamentalists, and they lay the foundations on which hot-fund managers make brilliant guesses. But the analysts themselves don't guess; they just know what's written in the sands. They used to depend on charts, but now they count on computers, which give them the same non-answers faster and much more impressively (see "self-fulfilling prophecy," p. 172).

Man does not live by economics alone, and the fundamentalist tends to overlook the emotions, the fads, the herd instincts that sway things. He's a good man to listen to, but a dangerous one to ape, because conservatism tends only to conserve—and you're in this to build.

On the other hand, technicians are, as an old friend used to put it, a "different breed of cattle." Technicians measure the market's many dimensions, instead of concentrating on the individual stock and the economic indicators, as do the fundamentalists. Volume, for example, is of primary importance, because volume denotes interest or lack of it, and that's what moves stocks up or down. (Chartists, who are a special kind of technician, split on the volume question; bar-chartists dote on it, point-and-figurists couldn't care less.) Technical analysis resembles psychiatric analysis, because these people put the public on the couch and try to figure what makes them tick. Why are *they* buying or selling—not what should *I* buy or sell. Having satisfied themselves as to these imponderables, technicians then proceed to the unfathomable—namely what will the public be doing next? Then they act.

One technical foundation stone you had better believe is that any trend—be it of the market or an industry or a single stock—is more likely to continue than to reverse itself. In fact, that is so important a consideration that I can't bring myself to say anything snide about the technicians. Just so they stay loose and don't believe their conclusions too fervently. But that's basic to any system, to any combination of systems, or to a successful flouting of systems.

Actually, "combination of systems" is the only way to describe the operations of most analysts, professional or amateur. Few are purists even if they specialize. And the computer jockeys are winning out. Damn things can sort out the fundamentals, add in the technical aspects, and draw the charts, too. In fact, they've even been enlisted to prove that the efficient market believers are right, anyway, and it doesn't matter what you buy.

So there you stand, the Little Guy, who simply doesn't know enough to be a chartist, or a random theorist, or a technician. What do you do to pick a stock? How do you know when to buy more, when to sell? How can you match wits with these lordly experts?

Well, friend, it's trite but right to say, "ignorance is bliss." You're free to choose the individual arguments that make sense to you. And to check them against some other theory, and then to crank in your own unorthodox, seat-of-the-pants premonitions with every bit as good an expectation of gain as the rest of them.

Lucky you, with nothing to prove and nobody to answer to. Just play it cool. Pick and choose. Listen and don't argue. And make your 30 percent a year.

"Specuvesting" explained

Part of your independence will be a refusal to type yourself either as a speculator or an investor. You will be either, on occasion, and a "specuvestor" always. You will be willing to grab a low-priced, unproved stock if it seems to have enough going for it. Or you will buy the highest-priced stock with equal zest.

You will be willing to settle for a short-term profit if

indications are that the profit will be cut by waiting. But you will be willing to hold a stock for years, if it goes up and stays up and promises a further rise.

You will consider fundamentals, but be acutely aware of mass emotions. You will be daring when the signs say "dare," and conservative when they say "don't." You will sit on great gobs of your money in uncertain times, and margin to the hilt when you're doing well.

You will protect yourself from large losses but aim for stupendous gains. You will listen to the most harebrained advice, and weigh it just as carefully as the sagest words of the old hand—because neither adviser knows for sure, and either may be right.

You will, on occasion, buy even though your broker says he wouldn't, because he may know too much—and that can make a person too conservative. You will sell even when he gives you an infuriating "don't panic," because he may not know enough and you have to keep your losses low no matter what anyone says.

You will not expect always to be right, because an investor who is always right would be like a credit department that never experiences a bad debt. Neither is intelligently seeking the extra degree of risk that will produce the extra profit that's needed really to prosper.

You will sense the emotions of others, but be unemotional yourself. You will not fall in love with a stock to the extent that selling it seems disloyal. You will not close your mind to a stock or industry because of preconceived notions or past experiences.

You will ignore dividends and think only in terms of growth. You will consider gains or losses on a stock as a percentage of your investment in that stock—not in dollars—and that will free you of concern about the price level or the number of shares you buy.

You'll work hard at making your portfolio grow, knowing that, if you don't pay attention, it won't pay the mortgage. You'll enjoy the work because it's exciting. But you'll treat it as the business that successful investing must be.

And here's what will surely seem the strangest element of all in your conversion into a successful specuvestor. You're going to be a nonconformist, and, by definition, that makes you an outcast. You'll be comforted by the fact that if everyone agreed with you *nobody* could make money, because apart from the effect of inflation and the expanding economy, it's impossible for everyone to win. The winner *has* to be different. And you can only learn not to argue your point of view.

When someone says, "XYZ went up, so I sold enough to get my investment back and now I don't have to care what happens to it," you'll nod your head and say, "That's a nice-a." You'll get no thanks trying to straighten out your friend's muddled thinking. The less you find to agree with, the more surely you'll know you're making the grade as a genuine, 14-karat specuvestor.

Chapter 7

HOW TO PICK A WINNING STOCK

There are really two requisites for making money in the market. The first is to pick stocks that go up. The second is to conduct yourself properly after those selections have been made. It's impossible to state which is more important. Many a man has picked his share of winners and still come out in the hole. And yet you can't manage a winning stock unless you've got one.

So let's take first things first and talk about what makes a stock rise. This is a peculiar study and a frustrating one, because its mixture of logic and plain damned foolishness can set the serious student's teeth on edge. Just realize, going in, that the imponderables will always outweigh the measurables. In fact, I suspect that facility with a Ouija board would usually beat a degree in economics as background for the task.

There are a whole stack of reasons why stocks move up. Some of these reasons make no sense at all, but, like pretty girls, they don't have to make sense to get consideration.

Like pretty girls, too, stocks are judged by the company they keep—so a valueless firm in a popular industry can have its stock appreciate handsomely, while a fine company in a group that's out of favor can see its stock slump. *C'est le market.*

So I'm first going to jell all the reasons into one clear statement that will at least set you on the right trail. And then we can examine the niceties.

Ten words that can make your fortune

There's a come-on line if you ever heard one. But here's how you pick a winning stock: *Choose a rising, talked-about stock in a popular group.* I feel a little defensive about that rule: it's so simplistic. But it sure does clear the air and get rid of a lot of the nonsense-thinking that handicaps most people. And, in the so-important areas of cutting your risk and keeping your money moving, it is absolutely vital.

It's really not difficult at all to find a winning stock. Even in a bad market, hundreds of stocks are often rising in price. In a good market, thousands of them zoom. In fact, it's easy to get the impression that every stock other than the ones you hold is going through the roof. But how can you select the one stock that has the best chance of being a winner?

The common denominator of all winners is that they move up (otherwise they're not winners) and they get talked about if only because they're moving up. The beauty of the rule is that applying it means you will never buy an unknown stock—and that eliminates half the worthless hot tips. And you will never buy any stock that hasn't already proved its ability to get off the dime—which disposes of another bunch.

Don't get the impression that any old stock is worth buying just because it's rising and being discussed, or is in a popular group. A purchase certainly calls for more investigation than that. But it can be stated categorically that it isn't a good purchase *until* it's moving up and sparking some kind of discussion. So, before you buy, wait till those two requirements are filled. Your money is safer in your account than stuck in a stagnant stock.

72

Understand that "talked about" need not mean the stock is being featured in front-page articles. Consider it the opposite of "unknown." Chapter 17 elaborates on that more than somewhat. And, while "rising" is a relatively precise word, there are certainly degrees of movement. Some stocks jump several points a day, and others move sedately. It doesn't have to be a high-flyer to be attractive.

So there's still room for judgment, even in following that simple rule. Rather than helping guide you to the right stocks it will, in fact, serve more to steer you away from dangerous waters. If a stock qualifies on those two counts, consider it. If it doesn't measure up on those counts, stay off it until, if ever, it does.

Dishwater-dull things to look at

Fundamentalists have a whole list of things that make a stock look good. Let's touch on them. None gives you the whole answer as to whether a stock is right or not—but only time can tell you that. They are, at least, useful inches on the yardstick we'll try to build to help you get some gainers.

Earnings. How basic can you get? Every company is supposed to make money. When you buy common stock you buy a piece of the company. If it doesn't make money, you made a questionable buy. If the company makes less money than it did before you bought your piece, its stock will probably go down. If it makes more—bingo.

If a company hasn't made money and then does, or promises to, that's good. So you can buy stock of a company that has no earnings at all, if you have reason to feel it's going to make the grade (turn around). That can be a very good buy. In buying any stock, you buy the future, not the present (unless you're buying for dividend income, which is a no-no). So if the future looks good, the stock looks good, provided it hasn't already been fully "discounted"—

which means, provided it hasn't already been fully bid up in anticipation of the improvement. That, of course, is a matter of personal judgment, because the next item, which is a child of "earnings," is flexible indeed.

Price/earnings ratio. If a company earned $1 per share during the past year, and the stock sells at $10, then the stock has a P/E ratio of 10. It sells for ten times earnings. Some stocks have that low a ratio, habitually—steel, utilities, banks—very respectable companies. The Dow-Jones Industrials had a 1969 bear-market average P/E of 13.8 at one point. IBM's ratio ran about 40, Control Data's about 41—about $3.50 in earnings for a price of about 150.

If Bethlehem Steel, that billion-dollar company, with thirty years of steady dividend-paying behind it and earnings of more than $3 for each of its millions of shares of stock, is worth only ten times those earnings, what makes Control Data worth more than forty times its earnings? And it's never even paid a dividend!

Well, buster, the public makes it worth forty times its earnings, by bidding it up to that level. And there are several reasons why they do it. It's in the glamorous computer industry, which is itself growing like crazy. Its earnings, set back in 1966 after explosive growth, are now going up some 25 percent annually. (Bethlehem Steel's are Nowheresville for the past several years.) Some day the computer industry may be as stagnant as the steel industry, but if the earnings are by then some eight times as high as today's, then I suppose today's purchasers will have been right—and it can sell at a stodgy P/E of 10 without, theoretically, breaking anyone's heart. But, you see, it doesn't really matter if that happens or not. All that matters is for the stock to go up after you buy it—whether the reasons for the rise are sensible, sappy, or just so-so.

You might be interested to know that, as a rule of thumb, some experts feel that a 10 percent annual earnings gain merits a P/E ratio of 18 to 22; a 15 percent annual gain, 30 to 40; a steady 30 percent gain, 50. Me, I'll take a high

P/E every time. It shows somebody's optimistic—a whole lot of somebodys who have bid the stock up. But aside from that general statement, everything is relative. So look at the P/E ratio, nod, and say "Ayup." It doesn't have to please *you,* just so long as it's impressing a lot of other investors as reasonable, or at least acceptable.

Growth factors. Related to earnings, but also taking into consideration such entries as sales and assets, growth factors should come in for scrutiny when you're picking stocks. It's quite possible for a company to increase its earnings on the same sales by improving its efficiency of operation. That's very nice, and it speaks well for management, but what do they do for an encore? You'll want a company that is booming along in all departments—sales, assets, earnings. Even raising its dividend makes it more attractive, since this appeals to lots of people. And lots of people is the precise number we want attracted to our stocks.

No question that there can be thimble-rigging in reporting many of these figures, though the SEC is trying to impose a little more standardization in accounting practices. Some companies report, in full, sales of items on which only a small first payment has been made. The conglomerates may buy another company in December and add its sales to theirs as though they'd owned it all year. All very legal, and intentionally misleading. And another reason why the Little Guy has to act like a Little Guy. He can't possibly detect such shenanigans, so the precious fundamentals can lead him down the garden path. But not if he follows the Little Guy rules.

Book value. The assets of a company—its real estate, its holdings, its cash, accounts receivable, machinery, inventory, materials stockpile—all add up to "book value." That's what everything would supposedly bring if it was turned into cash. It's a great comfort to many stockholders when the book value of a company is equal to or even greater than the price of its stock. Which is fine if you're worried about getting your money back, but stupid if you're looking for gain. Furthermore, companies can pad book value—like adding big gobs for "good will." The myth is that book value constitutes a prop under the stock, which won't retreat much below it. But why buy it in the first place? If you want comfort, buy an electric blanket.

Expansion. If a company is content to continue making the same things in the same plants at the same rate, it can become very efficient. But what the investor should look for is a company or industry that is expanding. That's one of the troubles with dividends: they siphon off expansion money. New facilities cost like the devil, and I can't imagine how management ever gets up its nerve to expand (look at the trauma that attends your decision to redecorate the kitchen). But you want the kind of company whose management does make that kind of decision.

Being in an expanding industry makes such a decision easier—and makes a company more attractive in the first place. In fact it's one of the things you want most. That's where the action is.

Expansion can also come from outside a company's field —by acquisition. The word "conglomerate" was coined to fit that. Boy, are conglomerates great—sometimes.

Other factors. Influences entirely apart from the company's own operations will affect it and its stock. If money is tight and credit is hard to get, the stock market as a whole will tend to stay stagnant or go down. But it will particularly affect certain industries, such as those connected with building. (The term "housing starts" makes you sound pretty hip when worked into a conversation). Cement, wood products, plumbing fixtures—lots of areas are affected, in addition to big builders. Be cautious of them in tight times.

The threat of war or the promise of peace affect different industries in different ways. There used to be a vaudeville routine that went:

"A pipe burst in my kitchen last night."
"That's bad!"

"No, that's good, because it put out a fire that had chased my mother-in-law right out of the house."

"That's good."

"No, that's bad, because she fell and broke her leg and has to live with us for six months."

"That's bad."

"No, that's good, because now we can collect the disability payments."

Similarly, I never can figure out who's helped by peace and who's just flipping for more war. The defense industries will lose all that government business. That's bad. No, that's good, because you can't make much on that business . . . etc.

Strikes, strangely enough, aren't supposed to affect stock prices—evidently because the problem is such a transient one. But strikes can beat the heck out of earnings. And, conversely, a company that has just settled a contract looks just that much better from the standpoint of future earnings.

"Leverage" is a sophisticated little complication on which some investors dote. If a company has a lot of preferred stocks and bonds, which demand a fixed interest, any rise in profits may make a surprising difference in earnings on the common. Say they made $1,000,000 profit last year, before fixed charges of $750,000 in interest—leaving $250,000 for the million shares of common stock. In the current year they will make an estimated $2,000,000 before fixed charges. After deducting the same $750,000, this doubling of profits increases earnings per common share five times. That's leverage, and that's good.

Price stability in an industry can be an important consideration, too. When enough companies got into making TV tubes, it knocked the props out from under prices so that nobody—including the new suppliers—made out very well. Of course too much stability can hold stocks down as well, if it's the government doing the stabilizing. Look at the steels.

After a particular stock has caught your fancy, think it over a while. Don't be too rushed—you're not just after a couple of points. You want a big move, and if one day will make the difference you shouldn't be buying the stock. Don't get the fever. Stay cool.

You've probably become interested in a stock that someone has told you about, or that you may have read about. Well, that's good—the stock is being talked about. The more the better.

Make sure this stock is in an industry or group that is *currently* popular. For example, conglomerates (corporations made up of many companies in unrelated businesses) were excessively popular in 1967 and the early part of 1968. But then the government promised to look into the possible restraint-of-trade effects of their operations. Further, a couple of the fast-rising groupers overreached themselves, with a resulting earnings decline—and prices slipped. But the idea behind conglomerates is sound: superior management, devoted only to managing, can profitably permit satellite companies to concentrate on product development and sales. So by the time you read this, conglomerates will probably be back in favor. However, your interest in them should hinge on where they are, at the moment, in this off-again on-again cycle. Or go to some other group. Same with any other stocks. Make sure they're currently in favor.

As usual, this approach will offend the traditionalists. They like to advise the beginner or the Little Guy to play it safe—buy solid value. The idea that he should try to ride a popular wave is abhorrent to them. But in today's fast-moving market, it's stupid to seek stability. There's no reason at all why you can't benefit from the glamour stocks and ride the crazy winners. In fact it's better to make mistakes on this kind of trading than to be mildly successful at the "buy-a-piece-of-America" nonsense—because your mistakes will teach you lessons that can make you a lot of money later. But experience at investing in AT&T will teach you nothing except that you could have done as well by banking your money.

You may as well face it—if you are going to be in the market you will constantly have to make decisions. There is no grand plan that will let you invest wisely and then rest comfortably. If the institutions have to keep buying and selling—and they sure do—how can you figure to do it the easy way? You can always ride their coattails by buying a mutual fund, but don't think that's a royal road. We'll be casting some doubts on that route, later.

So, like we've said, the stock you choose *must* be moving up. There is absolutely no excuse for buying one that is moving down, and precious little for buying one that is standing still. You may be able to detect the move from watching the papers over a period of time. You may have access to charts that show it is climbing. It may be listed in the new highs—which, paradoxically, makes many inexperienced investors shy away. Or your broker may be able to confirm that it is, indeed, moving up. If it is, buy it. If not, wait.

But there is one final requisite that is mighty hard to pin down. You have to feel right about the purchase. Not just on a whim but, after considering the whole field or a good part of it, on conviction. If you don't feel right about it, wait awhile or look some more. I'm sorry to be so vague about this, but investing is not a science. It is a technique and an art. "Feel" is so important a part of that technique that I simply have to stress it.

What to do when you've found your stock

Even if you plan to buy more than one issue, which any beginning investor should certainly do, take one step at a time. Don't act like a kid in a bakery shop: "I'll take two of those and three of those and how much are these and, let me see, I've got a nickel left." Decide on one, then look for another. And then another.

You must not sink most of your money into one issue—particularly when you are just launching into a specu-vesting career. Taste the stock first. Just to give you a figure, and not because there's any magic in it, never have more than one-third of your money in any one stock. And don't even invest all of that third at once. Think of it as similar to dating a girl. You've looked her over and think she looks pretty good, but you don't walk up and say, "let's get married." Get to know your stocks before you really go all out. (Seems there was this fellow who was bored, so he said to his girl, "Let's get married or something." And she said, "We'll get married or nothing.")

Anyway, what this means is that you may be able to buy only 10 or 15 shares—or 2 shares, if it's really high priced. So buy them. With our $2,000 minimum investment at 80 percent margin, you'll have $2,500 to use. Figuring on commissions and breakage, you may want to put $800 into each of three stocks. So start with about $400 as a first purchase in each. If the stupid limitations now being imposed by some firms persist, you may have trouble making a $400 purchase. Don't let them browbeat you. If they won't take your money, find someone who will.

Plenty of people will tell you that the odd lot and minimum commissions will kill you. Well, that's not what can kill you. Overloading your portfolio with a stock that turns sour will kill you. As the littlest of Little Guys, your first job is to survive. You're like an oyster spat drifting on the tide, with every chance of being gobbled up before you can find a rock to grab onto.

You've got to start learning, which is even more important than to start winning. *And you can learn only from owning stocks,* not from playing games on paper. So buy some of a stock you like, and then work out another good purchase. *And never look back.* Never say, "I should have bought more when it was lower. If I'd put all my money into that one I'd have doubled it already." Because your task at the start is to learn, and to survive. You can't leave survival to luck, and hitting the right stock will always involve a large helping of luck. So don't plunge.

Following this procedure, your growth will probably seem painfully slow at first. But the 30 percent you're looking for amounts only to $600 on your suppositional $2,000. With provisions for commissions and breakage, you need only gain $15 a week to make it. It's worth repeating: *Dollars, as such, don't count—it's the percentage gain that makes the difference.* Ten dollars on an investment of $100 is just as surely 10 percent as is $100 on $1,000. May not be as satisfying, or as boastable, to make $10, but many a mickle makes a muckle. So don't plunge.

In this dangerous, uncertain world of investing, you will make mistakes. Instead of rocketing to riches, your progress will be more like the old math problem of the frog in the well that jumped up two and fell back one. But if you follow the simple precepts outlined in the next chapter, you will reach the top.

Chapter 8

HOW TO HANDLE YOUR STOCKS

First off, you don't handle your stocks at all. In a margin account you never see any stock certificates. Your account is what they call "in street name." That means the certificates are made out in the name of your broker, who has the right (you'll sign an agreement) to lend them to investors who want to go short. Don't worry about that, just recognize the marvelous ease this gives you. You do all your business, whether by phone or in person, with no need to deliver certificates or write checks or do anything but say when. But they're your stocks, just the same. They are simply held by your broker as collateral for the margin loan.

I can't just leave you hanging there with a bunch of stocks you've persuaded yourself to buy—that's only half the battle. The other half is managing your portfolio. Buying more or selling some or selling all or standing pat. Actually, managing your stocks couldn't be simpler in principle. Here goes another revolutionary rule which may seem almost too obvious to state:

> *If your stock goes up, buy more; if and when it goes down dangerously, sell it.*

If that sounds like motherhood, then guess again. Very few—and only the very smart few—act that way. It takes real discipline to buy more of a stock you could have picked up a good many points lower. And it takes sheer guts to sell a stock just because it's dropping—*to sell it whether you have a gain or a loss or will just break even.* But that's what I'm telling you to do.

The idea of pyramiding your stock purchases may even seem unwise, particularly if you're really impressed with the gambling parallel we went into earlier. The crap-shooter who leaves his winnings on the table and keeps on doubling up is going to get wiped out. He's got to draw down once in a while or he's dead.

But there's no sudden death in the stock market; there's always time to get out with a whole skin—or at least enough skin to leave you looking right handsome. Even in the terrible crash of 1929, the smart ones like Bernard Baruch got out in time. So play a rising stock to the hilt. Buy more as it goes up. Then buy more. Then buy even more. If you do it right, you may just about break even on your last purchase, because it will have gone up and then started down again—and you'll have sold it as it approached your purchase price. Nobody can guess a top or a bottom, so don't try.

One school of thought on this subject says to buy fewer shares on your second purchase than on your first, fewer still on your third, and so on. That builds a true pyramid and, supposedly, cuts your risk as the stock approaches its inevitable top. But, again, this may be good advice for the big round-lotter (who purchases in units of 100 shares), but the Little Guy may have bought only 15 shares in the first place. It might scarcely pay to buy fewer and fewer as the price goes up.

No, this is a matter of personal judgment, and it can change with every situation. Your first purchase is a means of getting your feet wet and getting you to watch the stock closely, and get the feel of it. If the stock looks even better than at first—if volume is rising and the talk is too—buy a lot more. As much as or more than the first time. Again, get the feel of it, and if it continues up, consider buying even more.

When to buy more of a stock

How high is up? Should you consider repurchasing after 2 points, 5 points, 10 points? That all depends on the stock. Some jump around at a great rate, delighting you one day and scaring the daylights out of you the next. Some may be priced at $2 (2 points) and would certainly merit further purchases at $3. Others at $40 or $50 wouldn't signal you anything at all with a couple of points' rise. Even percentage isn't the answer. The stock you buy at 2 isn't necessarily on the glory road at 2½, but the stock you buy at 40 sure may be on its way when it reaches 50.

The question comes up as to whether you should sell a stock that is standing still, in order to buy more of a stock that is moving up. I'd say, generally, no. If you had good reason to buy the first stock, and those reasons are still good, then you should give it a chance: Otherwise you are really churning your account. Not only will you be paying dearly in commissions, but you may move off a potential big winner. If the stock had been rising (and it had to be or you wouldn't have bought it) then it may simply be "consolidating" its gains, ready for another climb.

When to sell a stock

Don't sell any stock unless it's dropping. Then be ruthless. *Win, lose, or draw, you have to sell a stock that is going down.* The amount it must drop has to be as flexible as the amount the rising stock must climb before you buy more. Nobody can give you a figure. But you'd better start getting worried if it drops 10 percent from the highest point at which you held it. For lower-priced stocks, the percentage has to be greater or you'd be in and out of some ten-dollar stocks twice a week. But there comes a point when you have to sell it (see Chapter 16).

There is one principle you had better get clear. What you pay for a stock ceases to have any importance the moment you pay it. From that moment on, the only sum that matters is the amount that stock is worth. There is no significance whatever to the amount you paid. It's an entry in a book, and that is all.

If you buy 20 shares of a stock at 40, and it is still selling at 40, you have $800. If that same stock is selling at 50, you have $1,000. If it is selling at 30, you have $600. The stock doesn't care what you paid for it, the broker doesn't care what you paid for it. If you let it go to 20, you have $400 and you're a damned fool. If it goes to 80, you have $1,600 —and don't let it go to your head.

Paper profits are only paper money

There are no such things as paper profits or paper losses. They are just as real as dollars in a bank account. In fact they are *all* that matters because, in this course I've set you on, you're going to keep your funds in your account, so there is no such thing as real money. It's all just book transactions. If your stocks are down you're losing—if they're up you're gaining. You can't kid yourself—when your stocks drop you're getting hurt. So sell them. Ruthlessly. You never know when one is going to drop right through the floor.

This is your insurance policy. It's the only way you can protect your capital. It's your way to live to fight another day. Perhaps it will cost you money to buy that insurance policy, because stocks are perverse. The one you sell is sure to turn around the next day. Well, tell you what—if it does, and if it still looks good—you just buy right into it again. Because now it's rising, and that makes it eligible.

An example. I bought Seven Arts (which later became Warner Bros. Seven Arts) on March 10, 1967, at 28¾.

Bought the same amount again on March 28 at 31¾. The stock went to about 38 or 39, then dropped. I sold the second purchase on February 2, 1968, at 35⅞ (with a long-term gain on both purchases, it made sense to take the lesser profit). The stock then reversed its trend, after dipping only to about 34. On May 8, 1968, I bought twice as much as I had sold, paying 36¼. As this is being written, it is doing nicely at 55. By the time you read this I may have bought more, may have sold some, may have sat tight, or may have gotten out completely. Do you know what will decide me? Whether the stock rises or drops, and how much it does drop. Not sentiment, not greed, not anything but the cold, hard job of protecting my capital by refusing to watch it erode.

Daryl Industries is a relatively small producer of storm doors, sash, and suchlike. I bought several hundred shares, back in my dumb days, at 6, 4, and 2¾—averaging down like I'm going to forbid you to do. I finally sold it, when I woke up in 1963, at 2⅝ for what was then a dreadful loss. It's amazing how you watch a stock, once you've owned it, and I later saw that Daryl was being reorganized. It went as low as 1¼ and then rose again. On July 7, 1967, I bought it at 2¾; early in 1969 I bought an equal number of shares at 8.

How foolish it would have been to have held it from 1963 to 1967 at such a loss. And yet don't you know several people who have viewed their own belated recovery from a similar situation as a demonstration of the folly of taking a loss? *Living with a loss is folly—taking a loss is wisdom.* Swallowing your pride and going into a stock again at a higher price is sophistication. It makes sense, and it makes money.

How to sell your stocks

To be literal, you just pick up the phone and say "sell." Or drop into your broker's office and tell him. With few exceptions, which are covered in Chapter 22, you should sell "at the market"—which means at the best price possible when your sell order reaches the floor. Don't name a specific price when you buy or sell, because you're not in this business to make an eighth of a point—and many a purchase or sale has failed to go through because the investor missed by that eighth of a point. Which can be a very expensive piece of foolishness.

If your decision to sell (or buy) is made after the market's closing, you can put your order in to be executed "at the opening." All the buy and sell orders that come in from the close on the previous trading day till ten A.M. on the next trading day are matched up by the "specialist" and executed at the one price.

The specialist is called that because he specializes in certain stocks, maintaining an "orderly market" in those stocks by matching everybody's buy and sell orders. He also buys and sells for his own account when necessary, or when he thinks he can make a bundle by doing it.

I remember one incident involving a specialist in the advertising business—an incident that will ever be remembered by the dozen who witnessed it. Our department head's secretary was an officious young lady who always tried to rise above her very obvious femininity. On one occasion she had to get some tissue layouts mounted on illustration board, for a presentation scheduled for the next morning. The paste-up boy was swamped with work for the same presentation, and her layouts sat untouched for an hour or so.

Madame Secretary told the paste-up boy off for keeping her waiting, but he'd had it up to here with her and with the work load. So he informed her that if they had to be done right away she'd have to do them herself.

It still seems too good to be true, but she drew herself up and declaimed in ringing tones, heard throughout the office—"I was not hired for mounting purposes!"

Where were we? Oh, yes—a lot of experts advise not to put in a buy order "at the opening" because the price often drops lower later, at which time you could buy the stock cheaper. Just as many say not to put in a sell order at the opening because the price often rises later and you could get more for the stock by waiting. You can see that there's no firm pattern, and, besides, it's a situation beyond your control. So I prefer to wait till the opening and call my broker for a quote. If you're serious about selling (or buying) he'll give you the opening price or, if that particular stock hasn't opened yet, he'll get a quote—an approximation of what the opening price will be. Or he'll agree to call you when it opens, and you can make up your mind then. Naturally, too, you can be at the board room at the opening and see for yourself. Incidentally, don't pester your broker for quotes if you're not going to act; he's a busy man.

If you want to, you can put in a "stop" order, which authorizes the sale of your stock if and when it reaches a certain price. The reasons against using "stops" or "limit orders" are given later. Unless you are going to be totally unable to check stock prices for a long period of time, don't use them. Period.

Long term vs. short, and who cares!

There's a tax ruling that causes a lot of confusion and inspires a lot of wrong thinking. That's the one on "capital gains" (properly called "long-term capital gains"). Profit on an investment that you hold for at least six months plus one day (long-term) is taxed at a special low rate. Profit on an investment held for less than that (short-term) is taxed as regular income. Current tax reform tries may change that.

The long-term capital gains tax is, to all intents and purposes, one-half your regular tax—at least that's the way to look at it. Actually, you pay your regular tax on one-half of the gain, which is not quite the same thing. The most you can pay on your long-term gains, no matter how big they are, is 25 percent, which you don't have to think about unless you're in a bracket over 50 percent. Of course, this tax, like others, is increased by the surtax, if there is one at the moment.

Obviously, you save a lot of money if a gain is long term (over six months). But don't let it overwhelm you, the way it does many people. Never hesitate to take a short-term gain, for reasons explained in Chapter 32.

The one time when it pays to be extra careful about long- vs. short-term gains occurs when you want to sell *some* of a holding you have built up over time. If you have bought blocks of that issue at different times, be careful which you sell first. You can specify which shares are to be sold by telling your broker to "sell *x* number of shares against" the specific date those shares were purchased. Your thinking as to which to sell first should go like this. (And don't consider it too complicated. It's very simple, but just takes a lot of words to explain. After all, the instructions for Parcheesi take several pages, but kids play it.)

Let's say, for example, you have two purchases of 100 shares of the same stock, but at different prices:

1. Why are you selling? If the stock is dropping, and you are protecting yourself, it doesn't matter (except from a tax standpoint) which block you sell because both are worth an identical amount at the moment of selling. If you are selling to get money to buy something else, then it still doesn't matter which you sell, for the same reason. Now how about that? You'd be amazed at the percentage of Little Guys who will *always* take the profit because it is psychologically difficult to take a loss—so they'll put it off. Or they'll automatically take the *biggest* profit first because it feels good. But it's often better to take the loss first or the smaller profit. Taxes are the deciding factor.

2. Are all of the shares long-term? If so, all gains are long-term capital gains, and the only consideration is the price at which you bought the various blocks, which will determine how much profit you have on each. Whether you take the bigger gain or the smaller one may depend on how well you've been doing that year. The chapter on taxes goes into the business of offsetting losses and gains.

3. Are some long term and some short? If they are both, you have to examine the profit picture:

a. Do both have a profit? Then sell the shares that are long term. Maybe the others will reach six months before you want to sell them and you'll save on the tax. It can be a lot. But if one profit is much bigger than the other, and both are long term, take the smaller profit first. See page 251 for a year-end exception.

b. Do you have a long-term profit on some and a short-term loss on the others? Then take your loss. Remember, you're only selling part of your holdings in that issue. If you sell the shares on which you have a profit, you'll pay a tax and your loss on the other will either become greater, or will turn into another profit (on which you'll pay taxes). But if you sell the ones with a loss, you can use the loss to offset other gains, and your profits on the retained shares will either shrink (in which case you pay less tax) or the stock will go up and you may not sell till some other year. Rule of thumb: *Short-term losses are as useful as long-term losses, in reducing taxes.* But long-term profits are one heck of a lot better than short-term profits, in keeping taxes down.

c. Do you have a long-term loss on some and a short-term profit on the rest? Then you're off your rocker. You must have been "averaging down," so read Chapter 19. But take your loss and let your profit run. And don't do it again.

d. Do you have a loss on both blocks? Again, you've been naughty. You probably shouldn't have bought more of a stock that had gone down—unless it had dropped very little and was recovering before your second purchase. *You should have sold the first block, not bought more.* At any rate, if you're close to even on both, take your short-term loss—the long-term loss may turn to a profit. If you're sharply down on both, sell both and protect yourself, unless the stock is rising again—in which case hold it all, for crying out loud.

Above all, don't hesitate to take either a profit or loss—whether short term or long term—if selling is indicated. The action of your stocks is what dictates selling what you have or buying more. Unless there are very few days left before your six months is up, grab a short-term profit that is slipping away. Thousands of investors feel "locked in" by profits and losses. But the specuvestor knows the key. *Protect your principal.* If you have to pay extra taxes later because you cautiously realized a short-term profit on a slipping stock, just consider it another insurance payment on that growing portfolio of yours.

Later on I've slipped in a formula for figuring how much a stock can drop without hurting you, while waiting for a short-term gain to become long term. You'll want to use it, but remember the reasons given there why *you should not wait.*

How many issues should you own (and how long is a piece of string)?

Abe Lincoln's answer to the question, "How/long should a man's legs be?", expresses it pretty well. He said, "Long enough to reach the ground." As far as the proper number of stocks is concerned, the right number is the number that makes sense to you at the time. There are a couple of angles to consider.

If you buy a lot of issues, you'll be spread thin and won't make much on any of them. So you won't make as much, in toto, as you would on a lucky buy of a couple of stocks. On the other hand, if you put all your eggs into too small a basket, you may drop them all.

If you buy several, you may not be able to keep track of them all comfortably—it may take more time and attention than you're willing to give it. *But if you don't buy a good many issues you will not learn as fast.* And for at least a couple of years, learning is more important than earning.

If you buy many on a small investment, the minimum and odd-lot commissions add up pretty fast. But you have to get used to handling several holdings, toward the day when you'll have a lot of money in the market.

I've held as many as sixteen issues. Yet, at this writing, with five times as much money in the market, I hold only eight. Why so many then? Because it seemed right. And it feels right to have fewer today. Tomorrow I may be up to sixteen again.

In our system of tasting stocks, you're bound to hold more issues at one time than at another. And there is protection in holding a fair number at any one time, since a tumble in one won't hurt you badly. Not sixteen, with only $2,000. But don't hesitate to hold as many as four with that small amount. Find out for yourself how many you can follow with comfort.

And this is as good a place as any to suggest that, if you plan to add regularly to your investment, don't feel you have to buy a different stock every time. In fact, don't feel you have to buy anything at all, just because you have cash in your account. Let it sit there till you really know you should commit it in a particular stock—either adding to your current holdings or going into a different stock altogether.

As you gain knowledge and confidence—and that all-important "feel"—you'll probably concentrate your holdings into fewer issues. Well and good. But, even then, I strongly suggest your initial investment in any issue be relatively small. And, although a refusal to hold a plummeting stock will protect you from severe losses, it will never be good specuvesting practice to put too large a portion of your equity into a single issue. How large? Up to you.

92

Be precise in your instructions

I must emphasize that you should make your instructions crystal clear at all times. Have your broker repeat them back to you. If he doesn't understand them that's your fault, not his—even though he'll correct the mistake through the firm's error account and you won't lose by it. Above all, don't ever claim you said something else to cover up an unfortunate move you made. It's disgusting how often otherwise decent people pull that trick. It is absolutely fatal to a business conducted on good faith.

Obviously, honest mistakes do happen, but a little error can make a big difference; so be sure.

Chapter 9

SPLITS, PUTS, AND OTHER SIREN SONGS

You'd better be familiar with all the mysterious offshoots and byways that will beckon to you as you march bravely down the road to riches. We've covered shorts—and you should be knowledgeable enough by now to wince at that minor play on words. Chapter 25, in the "Twenty Rules" section that follows, will scare you a little more on that particular brand of Russian roulette. There are other aberrations, too, which offer big gains but harbor big risks. For example:

Puts, calls, spreads, and straddles

There's probably a lot of money made on "puts and calls." But most of it is made by the dealers who handle this peculiar business. Because puts and calls are bad medicine, psychologically—and too expensive to boot. As evidence of how good a thing these are for the dealers, however, many brokerage firms that used to look down their noses at the trade are now going after it.

Basically, these devices are simple—mighty attractive, too. Their joint name is "option," due to the option the purchaser has of whether or not to "exercise" it. Oh-oh, I said it was simple, didn't I? Well, it really is.

You pay a stipulated amount that permits you to sell 100 shares (usually) of that stock any time within a given period at a stated price. You buy a put when you think the stock is going to drop. Any time within the thirty, sixty, or ninety days (or six or twelve months) specified, you can sell that 100 shares (which you will first buy at the cheaper, market price) to the dealer for the higher price. It's just as though you had gone short at that price, but it didn't cost as much to do it. Your profit will be the spread between that price and the price you actually pay for the stock—minus what you originally paid for the put.

A "call" is the opposite. You buy a call when you think a stock is going up. It gives you the right to buy 100 shares of a certain stock at a stated price, no matter how high it goes during the life of your option. You buy it at the call price (not to be confused with the "call price" on convertible preferreds—oh, brother) and sell it at the market price or hold it for a further rise. Your profit is the difference between the price you pay for the stock and the price you sell it at, minus what you paid for the call. And rots of ruck.

Obviously, the appeal of all this is that you can participate in a stock's action by committing only a fraction of that stock's actual cost. Look at the Puts and Calls ads on the financial pages and you'll get a clearer picture. There's a list in front of me now, in a Sunday paper. Avnet closed Friday at 30¼, so I would pay $3,025 plus commissions to buy 100 shares. But for $225 I can buy the right to purchase 100 shares at 31⅜ any time during the next thirty days. I could break even if the stock goes to 34 and make money if it goes higher. Well, add a point for round-trip commissions. True, to exercise the call I have to put up some money, but I can sell it immediately, so my money isn't tied up. And I only risk $225.

Understand, the first-person pronoun is figurative, because I don't use puts and calls any more, and lost far more than I gained on them when I did use them. In all likelihood, you will, too. Chapter 25 tells why.

Just to help you keep them straight, here's a mnemonic device I made up (haven't devised one yet to help me spell "mnemonic"). Think of a telephone; you "call up," then you "put down" the receiver. Buy a call when a stock is supposed to *go up*—a put, when it's supposed to *go down*. Only don't buy either, ever.

To make things even more complicated, you can buy a "straddle," which is a put *and* a call—both at the current market price. Then you make money no matter which way it moves, if it moves far enough. Or you can buy a "spread" —which is the same thing, only cheaper. That's because the call point will be a couple of points above the market and the put point a couple below, which means you have all the farther to go before you break even or make money. Theoretically, you can make money on both ends—selling when the stock goes down, buying when it goes up. You should be so lucky. Not satisfied yet? You can buy a "strip," which is a straddle with the put part good for 200 shares, or a "strap" with the call part doubled up, instead. Strip, strap, straddle, spread—stay away or you'll lose your bread.

Splits—or one and one makes one

There's a lot of wishful thinking about splits, and a lot of confusion. Contrary to what it seems, you do not buy one and receive two. Look at it this way: A share of stock is a share of the company (bonds, in contrast, are loans to the company). Therefore, let's say you own 100 out of the 1,000,000 shares issued by that company. The company announces it's going to split its shares two for one—no, let's really make you deliriously happy and split *five* to one. Presto! Now you own 500 shares. But out of a new total of 5,000,000 shares! Earnings are then divided (adjusted) by the new total number of shares.

Net gain is actually zero. You still own exactly the same

percentage of the company. Technically, each new share is worth one-fifth as much as the old shares. Same pie, smaller pieces. So what have you gained?

Well, for one thing, you've gained negotiability. If you wanted to sell 20 percent of your holdings, previously, you would have had to sell an odd lot—20 shares. Now you sell a round lot and save perhaps $25. That's worth something. With more stock out, there will be more stockholders, more supporters of the company, more talk.

Then, too, a split is most often accompanied by a dividend hike, so that you get a higher yield. The per-share earnings are divided by five, of course, so a higher dividend on your new fifth-sized shares does return more money. While you didn't buy the stock for its dividend, the raise does make it more attractive to the majority.

But, most of all, the effect is psychological. It works in two ways. First of all, most investors shy away from high-priced stocks. As a stock approaches the hundred mark, it gets less and less attractive to more and more people. Sure, some stocks sell well over that and have for years. IBM, even when it splits, never gets down to 100. But most of them split around 100, or even lower. Not the preferreds, mind you—the common shares. People don't like high-priced stocks unless they're hot-as-a-pistol glamours. The NYSE recommends the 30 to 40 range as most popular. So splitting makes shares easier to trade and it makes for bigger volume. Companies like their shares to trade in volume.

The other psychological factor is related to the first. People like to own a lot of shares. The man with 20 shares of a $100 stock may have a good investment, but owning 100 $20 shares feels so much better. And if he could end up with *500,* he's Mr. Wall Street, even though he's gained nothing tangible. But stocks never split as low as $4—or even $10. That would put them in a class with the cats and dogs and the psychology would work the other way. Which shows how crazy it all is.

So why isn't a splitting stock a dandy buy? Because you'll

be too late. You're just plain not going to hear about it in time to get in on the action. No matter what the SEC does to crack down on insiders, word will out. And when it doesn't, conjecture will take its place. The sophisticates will smell a split and the stock will edge mysteriously upward until—bingo—the announcement comes. And then it's too late. Even if the stock doesn't sell off, it won't rise much farther, as a rule.

Since you must not go into an issue with the expectation of small gains, you must not buy on news of a split. Not unless there's something else going for the stock, too. Often there is, which explains why a stock sometimes continues to rise appreciably after the announcement, and why the new shares may go up after the split actually occurs. It's seldom the split alone—though the split may call attention to a good situation. In fact, it wouldn't have had to split if it hadn't gone way up—and unless management thought it would stay there. So don't hesitate to buy a stock that is about to split or has just split—but don't buy it on those grounds alone. Even though it probably qualifies as a "rising stock that's being talked about," look for some added reason before you buy. Splitting may make it more attractive, but it isn't the big criterion.

Why a stock dividend can be better

Strangely enough, people don't get nearly as excited about a stock dividend as they do about a split, and yet the stock dividend is exactly the same thing and is often much more truly a bonus. In fact, sometimes it's called that. A company doesn't have to ask its stockholders about a stock dividend; they do about a split. But they have to hold enough "treasury stock" to cover it.

Companies have a great deal of latitude in declaring such a dividend, which is too bad, because some of them purposely play on the confusion—just giving you what's already yours anyway, and acting like Santa Claus about it.

Sometimes they do work it so that you get more stock of the same value as your original shares—which isn't ever the case with a split.

Such stock dividends are usually 5 percent or less. In fact, the New York Stock Exchange rule says anything over 25 percent is a split, not a dividend. Over-the-counter terminology has no holds barred. In any case, the cash dividend is usually not increased, because if you get the same dividend on the additional shares that's extra money.

A company may issue "rights" to their stockholders instead of new shares. This is usually done when a new issue is being brought out, which would "dilute" current holdings. You trade in a fixed number of rights for one share of the stock. Or you can sell the rights. In fact, you can buy and sell rights just as you do shares, but there's a trap there. Rights expire at a certain date, usually after only a couple of weeks—so you must sell them, turn them in, or lose it all. They rise in value only if the stock rises, and they go down if it does. Remembering that it's bad business to buy stock that has to be sold at a certain date, you can see that rights have this problem built into them. So don't trade in rights.

What this all adds up to is that you should be grateful if a company whose stock you hold declares a stock dividend or a split or issues rights—because it couldn't hurt. But don't lose your cool over it and buy just because of such a piece of news. By itself, it's no big deal.

What are "warrants," anyway?

Well, whole books have been written about warrants, and the publisher of one hardy perennial is still acting as though he just discovered them. They can be very good, very bad, or very nothing.

Warrants used to be attached (literally) to certain bonds. Now they're more likely to be issued with a new preferred issue. They're designed to sweeten the offer; you buy one bond or preferred and you get one warrant as well. So the interest can be lower with less annual drain on the treasury. That warrant entitles you to *buy* one or more other shares of the stock at a stipulated price, within a stipulated period of time—usually several years. Not trade it in for one, but buy one at the set price. In fact, warrants are really only "rights" that are exercisable over an extended period of time, some being perpetual.

You can see that if the stock goes above that stipulated price, then the warrant is worth money, because it will let you buy the stock below the market price. But if the stock goes below the stipulated exercise price, does the warrant become worthless? Heck no. There's always a chance it will go up again and literally be worth something again. So it always has a speculative value, which causes it to sell "at a premium."

Since they always, therefore, have a value, warrants are traded just like stock. But if the parent stock is traded on the New York Stock Exchange, that doesn't necessarily mean the warrants are, too. Trans World Airlines stock is on the Big Board, the warrants on the AMEX. Okonite and its warrants are both on the AMEX. National General Corporation is on the NYSE while one type of its warrants is sold over the counter and another entirely separate National General warrant is sold on the American, the Midwest, and the Pacific Coast Exchanges. Very interesting.

The reason warrants are a favorite speculative tool is that you can usually participate fully in a stock's rise at a fraction of the stock's cost. So your percentage of gain is greater. In fact, in a turnaround situation, when a stock has been selling well below the exercise price of the warrants, the gain in the warrants can be explosive. To make that clear let's take a hypothetical example.

Let's say Kontinental Kumquat warrants would enable the holder to purchase the common for $16. Because of a bad infestation of Kumquat beetles, the company has experienced a poor couple of years. As a result, the common

100

has been selling at 12. Naturally, the warrants sold off, too; at 2 they were commanding a premium of $6. (The $2 you'd pay for them and the 4 points that would be required to raise the common from 12 to 16). When the common did reach 16, the Kumquat warrants would still seem to be worth nothing, but, for reasons I'll make clear, would actually have begun to be very valuable.

Finally the research and development department at KonKum (as it would undoubtedly be affectionately called) discovers what they should have guessed. The Asiatic Kumquat beetle is terribly susceptible to yellow fever. With a controlled epidemic wiping the squishy things out, KKQ begins to go up—and the warrants rise, too. In fact, they rise point for point with the common. Because, assuming the premium of 6 points holds, the warrants are actually worth $1 more for every point the common goes up. So, with the common at 16, the warrants are at 6. The common finally rises to 24—and the warrants rise to 14.

That means that, while someone's equity in the common doubled, your equity in the warrants would have gone up 700 percent. And that's Dreamsville.

While the Kumquat caper is oversimplified, these things do happen. One of the famous examples of that kind of growth is TWA. That airline's common stock went from a low of $7\frac{1}{2}$ in 1962 to 101 in 1966 for an appreciation of better than 1,300 percent. At the same time, TWA warrants rose from $3\frac{1}{2}$ to $82\frac{1}{2}$, for a gain of better than 2,300 percent. And that's a very mild case of the leverage warrants can give.

Even when the common is above the warrant's exercise price, the warrants will be cheaper and will rise point for point with the common. So they will be a good investment if the common does rise.

Unfortunately, that's the chief danger with warrants. They go down point for point, too—so you can *lose* your money faster in that particular vehicle. However, since as a good little specuvestor you won't follow the price down but will sell before you lose too much, by all means consider warrants. Don't necessarily go looking for warrants, but if a stock you like has warrants, try them.

I'm dying to work in another advertising story, so I'll seize on that phrase "follow the price down" to tell you about a misadventure on one of the early TV shows with which I worked. In the advertising business, by the way, this type of lead-in is referred to as the "just as, so too" lead—as in "Just as Man O'War won every race he entered, so too does the Pfister Transistor lead the field." It's very bad writing, but what the heck.

Anyway, the program was "The Stork Club," which took place in a phony room above the phony eatery itself. It was a low-budget variety show with only two cameras, one or the other of which was usually dollying around groping for its next shot. The opening sequence was always a waiter coming through a door toward the camera, carrying a huge tray on which was a beautiful lobster, surrounded by all sorts of fancy goodies. All in all, a gorgeous culinary creation—which was carried to the table of the week's principal guest as a suave way of bringing him on.

Well, one night the waiter stumbled. And the tray tipped forward, slipped off his flattened palm, and headed for the floor. The cameraman, unfortunately, was usually assigned to sporting events, and he kept that tray centered on camera all the way to the floor and stayed there as the whole mess exploded and settled back again. While the technical director screamed into his earphones to get off it.

Unfortunately, when the second camera found something to focus on, it was the late Sherman Billingsley's horrified face. Obviously, the program never again reached that peak of melodrama. As a matter of fact, it expired after a few months of comparative dullness.

Which gets me back to my subject as gracelessly as I left it—because one caution about warrants is that they, too, expire. On a certain date their value vanishes entirely, and, as you approach that date, the premium erodes as time for further growth evaporates. After that date, they're wallpaper. So know the expiration date of any warrants you buy, and be sure you don't hold them too long.

Bonds and preferreds are definitely not

We might as well dispose of bonds and preferred stocks right now. They're the backbone of Amurrica, so I won't say anything really bad about them. But they're not for the specuvestor because they're an income vehicle.

There are lots of kinds of bonds—debentures, collateral trust bonds, general mortgage bonds, income bonds, convertible bonds—all of which I'd have to look up in my reference books, because I couldn't care less. Every one of them represents money that somebody loaned to the company some time, and they pay interest (not dividends) at a fixed rate, based on the principal amount (almost always $1,000). Each matures on some specific date, at which time the then holder will get his thousand back and thank you very much. So, with the exception of convertibles, they do not keep up with inflation. In fact, since interest rates have gone up sharply in recent years, earlier issues wouldn't give you nearly the return that more recent ones do—and have, therefore, gone down in price to the point at which they're competitively priced. So you lose three ways. Inflation makes the $1,000 worth less, the percentage interest you get is below current payments, and the price of the bond goes down because of it. Geest!

You look at the "New York Stock Exchange Bonds" columns in a big evening newspaper, or in *The Wall Street Journal,* and you'll see evidence of that. Almost without exception, these are $1,000 bonds, with the prices expressed in units of 100—yet some sell in the 50's. AT&T, for example, has ten separate bond issues, maturing at dates ranging from 1971 to 1990—and prices ranging, at the time of this writing, from 62 to 92¾. The latter, with an interest ticket of only 2⅞ percent, is selling close to par because it will mature in a couple of years and the buyer who gets it now for $927.50 will have his 2⅞ percent interest for those years, plus the $72 needed to bring it up to $1,000.

Straight "preferred" issues are in the same category. Unlike bonds, however, they do represent a hunk of the company. They may be issued when one company wants to buy another (although today the straight preferred is rare, being supplanted by the "convertible preferred"). Instead of paying all cash, the company offers a new issue of preferred in trade for the other company's stock. Or they may simply want to raise money, for that matter.

Unless they're "convertible," preferreds have no relation to the common of the same company, and they won't go up in price even if the company gets ten times as prosperous. "Preferred" simply means they get first crack at the earnings, so the common can't get any dividends till the preferred dividend has been taken care of. "Cumulative" preferred issues even provide for getting first dibs on following years' earnings if this year's aren't high enough to pay their dividend, so the back dividends accumulate until the company can pay them off—sometimes for many years. They are nice and safe, but nonproductive as far as you are concerned. So forget them.

A slightly better deal is the "participating" preferred. This type of issue lets its holders get a little of the gravy when dividends on the common are increased. But it's still a dodo unless you really decide to live on the income. Like I say, wrong book.

Convertibles with the top down

Then there are "convertible preferreds." These used to be great speculative tools, but somebody's always taking the fun out of things. In this case it was the Feds, trying to cut down on speculation. They cut the legs out from under a most surprising gambling tool that used to make the advantage you get from margin look like a pale shadow.

There are two methods for "borrowing" money in the

stock market. One is strictly legit—margin. The other is semi-legit—borrowing to buy convertible preferreds, or, more accurately, borrowing on the convertibles you buy.

Just to get your attention, let me state that until 1967 you could buy convertibles by putting up only 25 percent of the cash. The rest was borrowed from a bank, with the convertibles themselves as collateral. Even today you need put up only 60 percent for bonds, but the broker is authorized to lend the remainder, so no bank is needed. This killed a business for the banks that totaled $800,000,000 in 1967.

Convertibles are called that because you can trade them in at any time for the common shares of the company that issued them. Especially in times of rising stock prices, a company that wants to issue a preferred stock often makes it more attractive by putting in that convertible provision. To make it more confusing, the company might issue a convertible preferred, which is a stock, or a convertible debenture, which is a bond and was just barely mentioned a couple of pages back. Either is convertible into the common, the holder receiving a certain number of common shares for each $1,000 preferred. I swear it's time for another anecdote, but I don't know any that might even remotely fit.

Naturally, the CvPfd can go up and down in direct relationship with the common. In that way you get a good income and, at the same time, participate in the growth of the stock (or the shrinking, mind you). The simple, easily forgettable fact is that if a convertible goes up point for point with the common, it will go down point for point with the common. Then the leverage that its borrowing power gave you will help you lose your money that much faster. There are no one-way streets in the market.

Notice that I say "if" it goes up point for point. That's by no means automatic, for the simple reason that a convertible always sells at a premium (because of its income-generating value) when the common is selling below the conversion price. It won't really start to boom along until the common reaches the conversion price. Then it can move very fast.

However, convertibles have a call privilege—meaning that the company can force you to convert them into the common. They're not going to do that until the common is well above parity (the conversion price) because they may want to sell another issue some day, and nobody would fall for that kind of a shuffle twice. But if the common has had a nice rise, and the bond or preferred stock can be converted into more shares than the original price would have bought, they may very well call the convertible in. This is done to save paying the interest ticket it carries— since the common pays only dividends, if any, which come out of earnings, if any. Like the man said, somebody's always spoiling the fun.

So convertibles are fine, but you really shouldn't buy them except to use the leverage they give you by their loan value. They're basically for income, and are fine for people who want that plus a chance to participate in the company's growth. Talk to your broker about it and then make up your own mind.

Dollar cost averaging—the "sure thing"

There's really only one "system" that works in the market, and that one shouldn't be of interest to you. But you might run into a discussion about "dollar cost averaging," so let's give it a few paragraphs.

Because of the economy, plus inflation, the trend of the market is inexorably upward. And so this system is a winner. It consists of putting the same amount of money into a specific stock at regular periods—every month or every quarter. When the price of that stock is down, your money buys more shares; when it is up, it buys fewer. The New York Stock Exchange has established a Monthly Investment Plan (MIP) for investors who want to put in a minimum of $40 every month or every three months. Under this you sign a contract with your broker and at the agreed-upon intervals you put in a fixed amount of money and he buys as many shares or fractions of shares as that will cover. You can actually own fractions of shares under the MIP, and when a dividend is declared, fractions of that dividend are credited to your account. As one writer put it, it's like buying a dollar's worth of gasoline—you get whatever that pays for, including a final fraction of a gallon.

Once (parenthetically) when I worked on a gasoline account, a co-worker ran up against that particular practice. The brass had considered it a good idea to lease a service station so that we could all learn the business first hand—and a dirty hand, at that.

On my friend's first day on the pump island a car drove up full of tough young punks. The driver, in fact, looked more like a hood than the front of the car did. As pump jockey, my friend said, in the approved manner, "May I fill it up with Super Shell, sir?" And the kid just gave him a look and, without a word, held up one finger.

The way the chariot had snorted and rumbled as it eased up to the pumps told even my untutored friend that the powerful beast wouldn't go far on one gallon, but he wasn't going to argue. So he put in the gallon, took the dollar, and was counting out the change when off they blasted.

When the manager heard about the magnificent tip they'd left, he patiently explained they had meant one dollar's worth, not one gallon. Then he packed my friend off home before they could come walking back with bicycle chains and garrison belts swinging.

And that's the way stocks are sold under MIP—a dollar's worth at a time. And it's probably a good way to get shaky feet wet. Over the long run it is almost impossible not to register a gain on your investment. But, of course, it is utterly foreign to the approach you must use to get the most out of the market. You can't afford long-term, sink-or-swim commitments because you can make far more by following a more active course.

I must, however, point out the irony of a situation that now follows years of service for these tiniest of investors. Because of their own inefficiencies, many brokers are now refusing small accounts, restricting low-price purchases, and otherwise harassing him. Not the first instance, of course, of the wooed getting scrooed.

Mutuals, the swinging nursemaids

An "investment trust" is a company that pools money from a lot of people and invests it. There are several kinds of investment trusts, and they're popularly lumped under the common name "mutual funds"—even though all of them aren't. Basically, there are closed-end investment trusts and open-end trusts (which are the ones more properly called "mutuals").

When a closed-end trust is started, a specific number of shares is sold at a set price. That is all the money that particular trust ever gets. All its investments are made from that total sum and whatever gains it accrues. The shares themselves are sold on the open market, just like other commons. Tri-Continental Corporation and Lehman Brothers are two that are traded in this way on the NYSE. When you buy their stock, the money goes to the previous holders of the stock and not to Tri-Continental or Lehman Brothers. As the fortunes of a closed-end company rise or fall, as their asset values (net worth divided by number of shares) increase or decrease, the stock goes up and down. So, instead of you worrying about which stocks to buy in which industry, you just buy Tri-Continental and they do all the worrying. Plus paying a nice dividend and, every so often, a capital gains distribution as well.

So what's wrong with buying stock of a closed-end trust? Nothing, except that I believe you can do better making your own investments—and I *know* I can.

Open-end trusts, or mutuals, are something else again. Their popularity bespeaks a strong sales force more than it does a strong performance record. This heresy is covered fully in the scurrilous Chapter 27, in which I fearlessly attack these great institutions. But I'll explain them enough here to register the fact that you should steer clear.

Like the closed-end trusts, mutuals do your investing for you. But while closed-end companies work with a finite sum, mutuals sell more and more of their shares and constantly increase the amount of money they have for investing. Unlike the closed-end trusts, they sell shares directly to the public and buy the shares back directly from the public. What you pay and what you get when you redeem your shares depends on what the total value of all investments and cash held by the fund amounts to at that time. Thanks to computers, this is figured out a couple of times a day.

The trouble with mutuals, put simply, is that you pay too much in salesmen's commissions and management fees —and they don't consistently do that much better than the general market to make the cost worthwhile. But they do have slick salesmen and high-powered support from certain brokerage houses, attracted by the fat 6 percent commission and a you-scratch-my-back attitude I'll explain later.

After all, if I spill it all now I'll have nothing to say on the subject in the "Twenty Rules" section. So let it go at that. Mutuals may not be bad buys, but they're not good enough to give up your freedom of action for. And that even goes for the go-go funds that rack up tremendous gains at times. And fall right on their fat faces at others.

Investment Clubs—or mystery loves company

You've heard about investment clubs. You and your friends or fellow workers get together and form your own mutual fund. That's what a club is, really. Everybody kicks in so much a month and you invest it in a club portfolio. The idea has been so attractive that there are now an estimated

50,000 of them, with portfolios totalling $900,000,000, according to an organization called the National Association of Investment Clubs.

Investment clubs, like bridge clubs, are often more social than practical—but they do have a practical side. They are particularly useful to the novice who, through them, can join in discussion of the market. Of course, to think that ten heads are better than one at making investment decisions is more a testimony to the appeal of democracy than to the difficulty of such decisions. Actually, a club should not be a substitute for your own portfolio. Use it to get yourself interested or a little more knowledgeable—or to get your spouse into the picture. But do it with extra money you would not otherwise put into the market. The intermittent nature of a club makes sufficient flexibility difficult, and gain correspondingly more elusive.

There are many ways to run such a club. Some have a committee appointed to investigate stocks and make recommendations. Others are catch-as-catch-can, with anyone who comes across a hot tip bringing it in. The one I've belonged to for years assigns a man each month, according to the alphabet, to study and recommend suitable issues. Then we vote by secret ballot as to whether and what to buy.

It works pretty well, although the desserts provided by the distaff side are perhaps as great an attraction as the gains we've made. The difficulty is that a club is a cumbersome apparatus in a very fluid element. Viewing the market once a month is like looking at every hundredth frame of a motion picture film. It's kind of hard for anyone really to get a feel for what's going on.

Since its beginning, seven years ago, each couple in our club has put in a total of $2,600, in installments that have grown from $20 to a current $40 a month. At this writing, our portfolio is worth $4,050 per couple—a rate of growth beyond me to calculate because of varying amounts invested, but still not discouraging.

During that period, we have also consumed a couple of hundred chiffon pies, two dozen orange cakes, and a plate of cannoli. Plus which, the friendship of the six original couples has survived, intact. It must be admitted that one sword member (bet you didn't know that was the opposite of "distaff") decided he couldn't take any more fresh pies and canned wisdom, so he withdrew that family's funds. But he had the good grace to do it just before a severe market decline, so we paid him with some gains that we very soon wouldn't have had, anyway.

Anything that will get people intelligently interested in the market is a good thing. So, if you feel like combining sociability with a small part of your investments, write to the National Association of Investment Clubs, 1300 Washington Boulevard, Detroit, Michigan 48231 for information on how to go about it. I'd rather see you put $40 a month into such a club than into MIP, good as that operation is for the timid.

The new-issue nonsense

If ever there was a get-rich-quick area in the market, it's new issues during a highly speculative period. Because of its apparently sure-thing nature, these can be a real danger to you—since the sure-thing aspect will be denied you.

When speculation is running high in the market, there's nothing that gets more attention than new issues. That's the time when all the dogs come out to bay at the moon; and many of them are in a fair way to reach it, too, before they finally burn out. The companies can be virtually worthless. They may never have made a profit—in fact may never even have made a product—yet they're snapped up like a plum in Jack Horner's pie.

It used to help if the name had an electronic, computer, or nuclear ring to it. The name-dreamer-upper can be more important to a new company than its scientists or production people. But today there's a new craze—franchise companies. All these companies have to do is hit the street and zowie—the stock is off to the races.

Weight-Watchers International was issued at 11¼ and hit 37 the first day, and it's still fat at this writing. Four Seasons Nursing Center of America was first offered at 11, doubled the first day, went to 44 in three months, and is now at 80 after a two-for-one split. In a typical week in the spring of 1969, 26 new issues came out and 22 of them ended the week higher—one of them, Information Machine Corp., jumping from the 7½ Wednesday introduction to 31 bid at Friday's close.

Now there's no reason on earth why a confirmed specu-vestor shouldn't get in on this madness, as long as he "keeps his head when all about are losing theirs." But you're going to have the devil of a time getting in at the start of a new issue. First of all, your brokerage house will have to be part of the underwriting team—that is, the group that con-tracts to take the stock off the issuing company's hands and sell it to the public. No broker will try to get you shares of a new issue before it hits the market, unless his house is bringing it out. That's because the underwriters are re-sponsible for the situation's being as described in the stock prospectus, and you can sue them if it isn't. So no broker-age house that hasn't thoroughly investigated the situation can take a chance on getting in on the original deal even if shares were available. That is, not for you and me, the Little Guys, anyway.

Even if your broker is on the team, you'll hardly get a smell. These issues are in such great demand (and there are usually so few shares) that you'll only get five or ten shares, if you're that lucky. And, sorry, they won't let you open a new account to buy a new issue, so that ploy won't work.

The appalling thing is that these things take off so fast that by the time you can buy them on the open market the bloom may well be off the rose. And if you chase after them you stand a good chance of getting your head beaten in when they take the almost inevitable tumble. After all, the companies bring their stocks out at the highest price they can justify. If they could get more they would. Who's kidding whom?

It's really a scandal what happens to many of these stocks after the ball is over. By that time, the insiders and their friends have unloaded their stock on the gulls who have been attracted to the thrashing of the bait fish. But it was fun.

The SEC recently studied 504 companies that went public from 1952 to 1962. No fewer than 60 of them had disappeared without a trace—and if the SEC can't find you, you ain't no company. An additional 216 had gone under —dissolved or gone into bankruptcy. Of the remainder, 130 had reported a loss on their latest statements. That means a total of 98 were breaking even or operating at a profit in 1968. Rather risky, wot?

But let's suppose you can take care of yourself. Let's assume you'll know enough to get out when the roller coaster starts to drop. Should you go into new issues? Heck, yes. As long as this madness continues—and it may once again be quiescent when you read this—you may be able to get some gains out of it. But recognize that it's a wild gamble, in many cases. It's a pure example of the "bigger fool" theory—you're counting on somebody bailing you out higher up. And every con man knows there's no easier mark than the man who thinks he's cheating the other fellow.

If there's no new-issue fever going, then these stocks can be marvelous buys from the standpoint of solid potential value. You will look into them carefully and decide, on judgment, that they're going to be a good investment. And you won't be buying them just because they're—hot dog! —a new issue.

THE NEW ISSUE

The stock that draws attention—that the plungers all adore—
Is the one that no man living has ever seen before.
The charm of the unknown, surrounding this superb new issue,
Supports its price with all the strength of dampened toilet tissue.

Chapter 10

TWENTY RULES TO HELP YOU MAKE IT IN THE MARKET

Investing in the stock market is obviously a very complicated business. The most difficult task of all is to cull the harvest of words, the hundreds of aphorisms, the thousands of disjointed pieces of advice—and come up with a sensible program of action. As a result, the Little Guy is lost, and even the professional is likely to hop happily from thought to thought and tip to tip, like a sparrow in a barnyard.

Whatever the market level, at any one time you can find the doomsdayer advising caution and the tub-thumper predicting an upswing. The only thing that changes is that they trade the word "continuing" back and forth according to what the previous market move has been. No less an authority than a leading financial weekly has missed entire bull markets with its pessimism. And a certain well-subscribed advisory service is so hipped on the gold shortage—and has, therefore, been wearing sackcloth for so many years—that they've really fallen on their ashes.

Sooner or later they'll be right because, as the fellow says, even a stopped clock is right twice a day. But your own fortunes can't be allowed to hinge on what paper you happen to read or what broker you happen to choose. You have to claw your own way through the wilderness and plot your own course to Fatland. But I'm going to help you along.

I'm going to list twenty rules that will help you make a good thing out of the market. Notice I'm not even ducking behind the word "can." They *will* help you to build your equity. They've doubled my money every three years since I started to formulate them. Admittedly, that was not a century ago, but before I learned them I lost. Today I win. Like Sophie Tucker once said, "I've been rich and I've been poor—and, believe me, rich is better."

"Rich" is a comparative word, but there's no reason you can't become rich, *no matter how little you start with* if you keep investing long enough. And if you follow these rules.

With the exception of a rundown on record keeping and tax lowering, the rest of this book will be taken up with explaining the whys and wherefores of these rules. But, before you go beyond the next pages, *read the twenty rules five times.* So far we've covered enough of the basics so that every one of these rules should make sense to you. If you can nod your head to each, you're halfway home.

The Twenty Rules

1. MAKE YOURSELF AND YOUR BROKER WORK —and everyone else's, too.
2. GO FOR GAINS. They're the only thing that counts in the market.
3. THINK BIG—ACT SMALL. Stay worried and you'll stay solvent.
4. DISREGARD PRICE. It's potential, not price, that counts.
5. BUY ONLY ON THE RISE. Stocks and the market have momentum.
6. SELL ONLY ON THE DROP. You have to let your profits run.
7. BUY TALKED-ABOUT STOCKS. You'll never make it on your own.

8. BUY ON MARGIN. It immediately multiplies your money.
9. AVERAGE UP—NEVER DOWN. Throw good money after good.
10. KEEP TASTING STOCKS. Small investors should take small bites.
11. TAKE SHORT-TERM GAINS, rather than watch profits slip away.
12. BUY OR SELL "AT THE MARKET." Never use "stops" or "limit orders."
13. DIVERSIFY. Put your precious nest egg in several baskets.
14. BEWARE THE BLUE CHIPS—you need bigger gains than they give.
15. DON'T GET FANCY or you'll just get hurt.
16. DUCK DIVIDENDS—they give *everyone* your money.
17. KICK THE MUTUAL CRUTCH. You'll get farther on your own.
18. DON'T FOLLOW ADVICE. Just use it intelligently.
19. NEVER TOUCH YOUR STOCKS or the money they make.
20. DON'T BE AFRAID TO PANIC. Gains are better than guts.

Read 'em again. Then let's see how they parse.

Chapter 11

Rule Number 1: MAKE YOURSELF AND YOUR BROKER WORK

I've given you the generalities: Investing-is-hard-work-and-if-you-don't-want-to-work-hard-at-it-get-out-of-it. Now, just what is it that you and your broker can do? What can you expect from him? How can you use *other* people's brokers? What free services do the various firms and the exchanges offer? What services should you buy?

First of all, let's define "work." As far as I'm concerned, you need only give one-half to one hour a day to your investments. Just enough to follow your stocks, to do some occasional phoning, to skim *The Wall Street Journal* and glance at whatever other business publications you run into. And to talk a little—which doesn't count.

Naturally, this doesn't have to be evenly spread. You don't have to say, "Gloriosky, I haven't devoted my daily half hour to the stock market. Whatever will Mr. Owen say!" This isn't like muscle-toning—you can usually ignore the whole works for a couple of days, without affecting your pot. Especially after you've built up the kind of rapport (and size of account) that lets you count on a call if your broker sees something funny happening.

There is such a wealth of material available, you will have to pick and choose to some extent. You won't want to follow many stocks, so scanning the stock reports can be a very brief matter. In fact, it's almost a matter of self-discipline to keep the number of stocks you follow at a minimum. The problems caused by tape-watching, which we talked about earlier, are related to those caused by getting too interested in too many stocks.

You can jolly well take it for granted that there will never be a time when some other stocks are not doing better than the ones you hold. You will almost never have the biggest gainer and you will absolutely never have *all* the biggest gainers. What counts most is what's happening to your own stocks. Watching other people's stocks should simply be a low-key means of preparing to decide where you might shift your money if one of yours goes really sour. So you not only don't have to, but really shouldn't follow a lot of them.

You will want to read in the daily and Sunday reports the reasons the gainers are gaining and the losers are losing. This is necessary to get the all-important feel of the market. In addition to the stock reports, glance at the financial news in your daily paper. The wire service items—AP, UP, and the like—are often helpful, because they deal with things of national importance and the market is national—in fact, international. But, particularly in papers outside New York, local items are seldom much help unless, of course, the company involved is of national importance.

That sounds so stuffy I'd better make it clearer. Local pride don't butter no parsnips in the market. Like it or not, New York is the bellwether—just as it is in the advertising business. Plenty of money is made elsewhere, but you ought to play the percentages. The advertising man adrift in Cleveland may have made out fine when he was wooed out there, but he'd have more of a continuing chance in New York. Similarly, the local industry in Van Nuys may just possibly make its stockholders rich but the specuvestor would probably, in the long run, do better with stocks that have meaning nationally. And in the market "nationally" focuses on New York.

Thus, an item on Pabst Brewing will get a very big play in Milwaukee. But so might one on Noname Industries or Bloops Department Store. This is not said patronizingly, but the reader in Twin Cities had better learn to spend his time (and money) on Pabst rather than on the other big, local newsmakers. The bigger the market for his stocks the better off he is—and there's a bigger market than just the local one.

The columnist's curse

The syndicated columns, almost without exception, are very little help in the kind of investing you're trying to do. A column is a fragmentary thing. It cannot build a state of mind, so it usually settles on day-to-day trivia. That is its curse. It cannot select out readers fitted to a bold course and advise them, without performing an absolute disservice to the conservative oldster. So it treads a safe, conservative path.

Further, there are too many influential people looking over a financial columnist's shoulder. He can't tell it the way it is—or the way a skilled cynic might suspect it is. Financial columnists are not supposed to excite anybody, one way or another.

Most financial columnists devote their space to answering letters about specific transactions, or about a puzzling experience with a broker. They try to choose letters that will have significance to a maximum number of readers, but steady reading discloses a wearying sameness as well as a depressing conservatism—the natural result of being denied a focus. Remember, this book is not written for everyone, so I can afford a definite viewpoint. Daily columns can't, because they are written for everyone. Except thee and me.

I must name an exception, and it's going to be very unfair to do so because I haven't read every columnist and the implication will be that he is alone. But it would be more unfair not to mention that Gerald M. Loeb does a fine job with broad basics and incisive advice, as contrasted to the "I bought 100 shares of Litton" school. He wrote *The Battle for Investment Survival* mentioned earlier, and will probably welcome these plugs while disagreeing, violently, with some of my own points—like buying on margin.

So scan the columns if your paper carries them, but by and large you won't suffer if it doesn't. And if it does you'll quickly learn to skip over the twentieth explanation of how commissions are charged.

Skimming the financial press

The Wall Street Journal, for which this book sounds like an ad, is a must. It gives all the stock prices on the New York, American, and regional exchanges plus the principal over-the-counter stocks. But it also reports briefly and clearly everything that's happening to the companies themselves—from earnings to personnel changes. And on its next-to-last page it manages to explain, more logically than most, how those changes affected yesterday's prices.

The *Journal*'s language is remarkably clear and the editors are constantly aware that new investors may not understand the terms used. It is refreshing, for example, that every mention of a short sale is accompanied by a one-sentence definition of what such a sale is. You will understand this paper. And you'll enjoy its nonfinancial front-page stories on widely ranging subjects.

It shouldn't take more than ten minutes for you to cull what you need out of the *Journal,* if you don't count your engrossment in those lead articles. Try it for a few months, at least.

Barron's is a weekly, tabloid-sized paper which the Little Guy can take or leave alone. It's loaded with more information than you need, written more for the Street than for you. And, unlike the *Journal,* it indulges heavily in opinion, rather than merely reporting the news. This is not said critically, because that's what it sets out to do. But it is harder for the Little Guy if he gets so many conflicting opinions. And *Barron's* often does conflict. Again, try it.

Business Week, U.S. News & World Report, Time, Fortune—they can all be helpful, so skim them whenever you get a chance. But the day is too short for the small investor to spend it reading all there is to read on the subject. Much better to keep your ears open for mention of some item or article and then buy the issue. Or wander into a public library once a week and flip the pages.

Years ago I attended a client lunch at which the conversation turned to a current best seller. I made some comment on it, and one of the men asked if I'd read it, "No," I said, "I read the review in the *Times* Book Section, so I just pretend I read it."

A colleague leaned forward and solemnly declaimed, "You ought to read the *Times* review, the *New Yorker* review, the *Saturday Review of Literature,* and *Time* magazine—and *then* you can pretend you read the book."

While I acknowledged his superior phoniness I did have the feeling that it would probably be quicker just to read the book.

However, you do have to take shortcuts or you'll be spending too much time at this business. And don't forget, your aim is not to be your own research department, but just to keep in touch. You can do that casually.

How to use a bunch of brokers

What I'm about to suggest may not suit your temperament, but it really isn't underhanded or unfair, so give it plenty of consideration. My advice is to take advantage of all the offers of help that will be given to you by rival brokers. In this day of computerized mailing lists, once you get on somebody's list you're on everybody's. So you'll get some fearful and wonderful offers.

Your mail will bring offers of literature; you will be invited to seminars on investing; you will receive offers to review your portfolio. You will be wooed with offers of lists of stocks about to split, or emerging industries that can make your fortune by 2069. So bite.

Go to their seminars; listen; eat their cake and drink their coffee. You might learn something. Believe me, you might not, because some of the brokerage firm lectures are pathetic. But even then it's hyacinths for the soul to realize that you know more than the broker. And it keeps you from being too awestruck by them, as a class.

Fill in the card for their literature. You don't know everything and you never will. Maybe it will supply just the missing chunk that will make something fall into place for you. Brokerage houses spend millions researching and preparing this material. Merrill, Lynch alone has a department of 300 working on it. Make them feel good—put the staff to work. All firms offer items ranging from a 200-page paperback to forms on which to record your gains and losses. Read their brochures and stock rundowns. Send them your holdings for review and analysis, if they ask by mail or in an ad (but take their reactions with a grain of salt and don't get shook by their clucks of concern; remember, they're selling).

Answer newspaper ads that offer all these goodies. Get on their lists. There's only one price you'll pay. Someone will phone you or at least write you, and solicit your business. *At this point terminate it,* unless you really are considering a change of brokers. When a man makes a personal contact, it would be unfair to continue to take his time. Brochures and analyses were made to be distributed, so you're entitled to them. Lectures are far more successful if they're crowded, so you're paying your way by being there. Even the analysis of your portfolio, while borderline because it's personal, is fair game since both parties know the broker is merely chumming the waters.

But don't lead the poor guy on, once he phones you, man to man. Don't accept a *personal* offer to go over your portfolio unless you may actually change brokers. Don't let him come spend time with you. Don't go to see him.

He'll appreciate a quick turn-down so he can graze greener pastures. I find the one best approach is to say, "I really couldn't change brokers because mine has done very well, and, besides, he's a personal friend." End of discussion. I stumbled onto this because mine is, but it works beautifully, and it's a kindness to the solicitor.

One·more thing. When one asks what you thought of his lecture, and you thought it was a lousy lecture, just tell him it was very helpful. You can't change him anyway, and he won't take your poor opinion well at all. Just as I said about your friends. Don't try to straighten them out; it's tough enough to keep your own head above water.

A foolproof, painless way to amass information is to visit the board rooms of various firms. Each has a rack of literature. Just walk in and pick what you want. If someone asks if he can help you, just say, "No, thank you—I just want to see what you have this week." This implies that you're a regular and you'll be left to do your selecting. Or, at worst, offered help. But usually no one bothers even to look up.

The literature you find there is surprising in its variety and excellence. Among the most helpful items are the research reports on various stocks and industries. They're very good. But you'll also see suggestions for tax switching, special rundowns on convertibles—all kinds of information. It's there for you to take. Take it. You'll never want to read it all, but make like the kid at the Boat Show. You will find some of it useful. *P.S. There is no charge.*

This is the most important contact you'll have. Let's assume he's good. You'll want to get the best out of him, and one way of assuring that is to be sure you don't overwork him. He has to make money and he can't spend all his time being helpful to you. That means no idle questions, for which you can get answers elsewhere. It means you can't call him for quotes unless you really plan to buy or sell. It means, in short, you can't tie up his phone, or his time, or the chair by his desk.

But he is, unquestionably, there to be of service to you. Prepare him to be of service by making clear what your investment objectives are. If you really buy the principles of this book, the best description is: you want gains in stocks with good fundamentals, with no restrictions on price. You want special situations in which there is some reason to expect large gain. You want only those stocks that are already moving (including those hitting new highs). You don't care which exchange or even whether it's listed.

You may have a couple of provisos of your own to add. Might even tell him you've read this book, to which he may reply, "Oh, that nut." But don't let him talk you out of following the principles established here—at least until you've tried them for a couple of years. Everybody has a pet theory on one phase of the market or another, but we're trying to establish a course of action all the way from picking stocks to selling them to buying back in again to getting rich.

There's a very good reason for my stressing this in a chapter on working with your broker. I want you to argue with him. Remember, I said don't bother to try to straighten out your friends because that's a thankless task. But do argue with your broker on points of investment practice.

Actually, "argue" is too strong a word. Don't become a pain in the neck, challenging his every statement. Don't question his opinions in front of other brokers or his other clients. But make him explain his theories and his particular recommendations. And listen.

Your aim in this is to learn, not to convince. If he says something you don't understand or with which you don't agree, question it. A very important part of using your broker properly is to avoid taking what he says at face value. It's up to you to do this with enough sensitivity to keep him from becoming angry.

What you must establish is best described as rapport. Not as between bosom buddies, not just as between salesman and customer, but as between a reasonable, intelligent person who wants to earn while he learns and an expert who can make some money while teaching him. Mutual self-interest, to coin a phrase.

Part of the process of getting the best out of your broker is to ask him for back-up material when he makes a recommendation. This does two things. It makes him think before he recommends—and that isn't necessarily automatic. And it disciplines you to applying reason to your moves. Stock market advice and stock market moves should never be casual. The act of Xeroxing a research report or news item—in fact the responsibility for *having* material to support his recommendation—will make your broker a more reliable source of advice. And dependence on the printed word will keep you from going off half cocked quite as often—even if you don't know what to do with the material when you get it.

Make sure he puts you on the mailing list for their regular reports. Some firms get these out weekly, some less often. And ask, every three months or so, for a copy of Standard & Poor's *Stock Guide,* the 250-page book that's packed with information on some 10,000 issues.

A question that bothers some people and never even occurs to others is whether to reward your broker when he "gives you" a good winner. Just remember that the broker doesn't give you a stock. You pay—oh boy, do you pay. There is absolutely no need to share your good fortune with your broker. He's already shared it and has, in fact, profited from your bad fortune as well. A box of cigars or a bottle of Pepsi would be a gesture you would both enjoy. But it is not necessary, nor is it expected. The holidays of a good year might call for a bad tie or perhaps a discreet Bentley—but it's strictly up to you and is not customary.

And if you find he's not doing what you consider is a good job for you, change brokers. You'll be doing yourself and him a favor.

Chapter 12

Rule Number 2: GO FOR GAINS

Those three words probably tell the entire story, but a fuller explanation is in order. Since this is the most basic rule of all, it could probably also be called the most important. But it would be unwise to assume it is also the most obvious.

Strangely enough, the cult of growth and the preoccupation with gains are relatively new in the market. Only since World War II has such overriding emphasis been put on getting someplace fast. There has always been speculation. But pursuit of gains is not exactly the same thing as speculation, although they're certainly related.

The New York Stock Exchange glossary, *The Language of Investing,* says a speculator is "one who is willing to assume a relatively large risk in the hope of a gain. His principal concern is to increase his capital rather than his dividend income. The speculator may buy and sell the same day or speculate in an enterprise which he does not expect to be profitable for years."

That, of course, is as myopic a view as could be taken. It tars anyone who doesn't want dividends, and also muddies the water rather completely. For example, it's obviously possible both to "buy and sell the same day" stock in a company you don't "expect to be profitable for years." This is no quibble on my part. "Speculator" is a dirty word to many people, including, from time to time, the Federal Reserve Board, SEC, and other august bodies. So we'd better get our semantics straight.

"Speculation" defined

For our purposes, you "speculate" when you buy a stock in the belief something is going to happen in the future to make it rise. You "go for gains" when you buy stock in a company that already has reason to prosper and is prospering.

If you buy stock in a silver mine because you think the price of silver is going to go up, that's speculation. If you buy stock in a sulphur-producing firm that has just announced a new find, you're going for gains. I don't care if this isn't a black-and-white matter because few things are, but you must understand that "speculate" may be naughty, but "gains" is apple pie and Mother. Gains and "growth" —they're Ammurican.

The key word in the specuvestor approach is "reason"— "reason to prosper." That's why you question the tips and challenge the tipsters—to learn if there's a reason behind the advice. That's why you examine the fundamentals. Your best specuvestment is a stock that is rising like a rocket *because of some specific circumstance*. You can make money on pure speculation—lots of it—and you'll be indulging in it from time to time. But don't build your portfolio on it because speculating is unnecessarily dangerous. Let me give you an example of the difference in the two types of purchases:

In 1963 my broker told me about a kookie company called Radiation Research, whose stock had already gone from just about nothing to $60, over the counter. A couple of engineers in the Army Signal Corps laboratories had developed a process for coating anything with just about anything, through a process of ionization. Having set up their own business, they had fabulous developmental contracts with leading firms in packaging, rubber, fabrics, plastics—crazy, man.

No one had been able to make the process work commercially; there had never been any earnings, and assets were in the low thousands. But the possibility was there, and I rode it from 60 through a five-to-one split, buying it all the way up to a top of 96 (480 in the old shares). Then I rode it halfway down in blind faith, but that's another chapter.

Radiation Research was a speculation, and a successful one. Its rise was built on faith, hope, and a little investor charity. It's now around 12.

In early 1968 I learned of an outfit with the unlikely name of General Numismatics (since become Franklin Mint) which had the only private mint in America. They were all set to start producing "coins" for a game our petroleum client was going to test, but the principal appeal was a most aggressive management with some tremendous promotional ideas.

At a time when gold and silver prices were trembling on the launching pad, they were selling commemorative sets of medallions in precious metals to collectors (hoarders). And they were preparing a series of sterling medallions, honoring the American Revolution Bicentennial. Buyers would have to contract for one nine-dollar medal a month for the next two hundred months. From a 22-cent loss in 1965 they had progressed to a 5-cent loss in 1966 and had turned a 50-cent profit in 1967. I bought at 18. Then when it rose, I bought more at 23.

They sold 10,000 sets of the new series, for an eight-year backlog of $20,000,000 or $2,400,000 a year (after total 1967 sales of only $2,700,000). I bought more at 60. In October, 1968, they announced third-quarter earnings of 91 cents and projected around $2.50 for the year. I bought more at 110. They declared a 100 percent stock dividend at 120, and have since split two for one, again.

General Numismatics (Franklin Mint) was not a speculation, it was participation in a growth stock. The fact that it was little known had nothing to do with the case. It rose on solid accomplishment. (P.S. If it is down by the time you read this, I will have sold it, so don't stick out your tongue at me.)

IBM has been *the* growth stock because it has been *the* growth company. This may end some day, but morons have been predicting the tumble for many, many years—while others reaped the benefits.

Brunswick was a growth stock till the bubble burst. Mohawk Data Sciences looked like a growth stock, but earnings that soared from 29 cents in 1967 to 58 cents in 1968 couldn't very well sustain that. However, the gains were there—6⅜ to 99¼ in 1967. And further earning increases are lifting it back again.

You can get gains from pure speculation or from solid growth. In fact, there's a lot of speculation mixed in with every growth stock, but that doesn't mean the difference cannot be quite distinct.

Some out-and-out speculations

Gale Industries was a rank speculation for its stockholders —though very likely something else for its management. At one time in 1967 Gale was, according to its chairman, "completely insolvent"—so badly off that it was paying 18 to 24 percent for temporary financing. On January 31, 1968, liabilities topped assets by nearly $750,000. Nevertheless, the stock rose 1,000 percent, from 1¾ to 21⅝ by October 19, when trading on the AMEX was suspended. When it was reopened on the AMEX the price had dropped to 13⅜—down 8¼—and it has since been delisted. What had bumped it up so sharply? A well-spread story about supposed inventions, featuring a way of causing glass to conduct electricity so that its entire surface becomes a heating element. No facts, no sales, no agreements—just "talks with several manufacturers" about this secret process. And speculation about it.

A warning to you, in the gravest possible tones. There's nothing burns so badly as being caught in the fire of an SEC investigation. To have a stock that's soared so beautifully shot down so cruelly must be a bitter blow, indeed. Then it's not a case of selling and taking your medicine, it's a case of not being able to sell at any price until the clamps are off—then often with a 60 to 80 percent drop from where it sold before. But it's no one's fault but your own if you get trapped in this way. Nobody is innocent who buys those soaring shares, because he either knows he's on thin ice or he's committed the even greater sin of not examining the situation.

Cameo-Parkway Records went from 2⅛, early in 1967, to 76⅝ in February, 1968. Its president had quietly bought 297,000 shares at $1.75 in July—which was nice. In the first six months of 1967, turnover had been 135,000 shares. The next month alone saw 263,000 shares traded with only 240,000 outstanding. (That means all but the 240,000 shares were closely held, and one month's trading exceeded that number). From August, 1967, to February 15, 1968, volume was nine times the number of shares outstanding, which is just a bit much. Trading was finally suspended on February 16, not to be resumed over-the-counter until September. At that time it reopened at 15 bid.

All this furious activity hinged on a $1,500,000 loss in fiscal 1967 and talk about a merger with a company wholly owned by the very man who was president and controlling stockholder of Cameo-Parkway.

Hindsight tags Cameo-Parkway as a speculation. But don't you think you could have given it that name any place on the way up? Without one single, solid basis for gains—with only vague statements to feed it—this unprofitable little company was suddenly worth $47,000,000 (the price of 76 multiplied by the 620,000 shares issued). You can be that greedy, but not that dumb.

So speculate when the spirit moves you. But, when you

do, recognize it. And when things get so crazy they look crooked, get out even without waiting for that drop in price I keep insisting should be your only sell signal.

Let's hope a healthy respect for fundamentals will keep you clear when someone's hand gets caught in the cookie jar. Speculating is for the strong in both stomach and pocketbook. But the search for growth and gains is a legitimate quest—the only logical reason for risking your money in the market.

Wall Street's mud-colored glasses

How do you find potential gains? Well, if you believe everything you read, you'd think every stock offers them. Market opinions are always couched in the most ambiguous terms, just in case the writer turns out to be wrong. The deceased *New York World-Telegram & Sun* used to give three opinions every day—three expert views carefully selected from the flood of releases and statements issued by the very vocal investing community. One would state that the market was going to rise, one would predict a drop, and one would see it staying in a narrow trading range. Nobody knows what the market is going to do. Nobody knows what a stock is going to do. Educated guessing is the best you can expect. Educated guesses and muddy predictions.

It's hard to find a stock for which somebody doesn't claim a gains potential. "The shares have considerable longer-range appreciation possibilities" is about the lowest rung on the ladder of forecasts. You'll come across double-maybes like "—we expect it to participate in the probable growth of medical electronics." Or the neck may go way out with "—we suggest a dollar-cost-averaging approach for patient investors willing to assume above-average risks."

You'll note the fail-safe in all of those: "longer-range" can be thirty years; "expect it to participate" gets the writer in about as deep as his shoe soles; "patient" puts the monkey on *your* back if you're so foolhardy as to sell this side of 1980. Everybody writes that way—it's the true art of Wall Street. Standard & Poor specializes in gratuitous and muddy evaluations. They put out periodic information sheets on just about every stock, which are very helpful. Most of them end up with a faint recommendation of some sort. But they've never yet stated that a stock stinks. Some of them do stink. Will Rogers said, "I never met a man I didn't like." The writers for Standard & Poor feel that way about stocks. At least they're forced to write that way, probably for legal reasons. It would be better if they dropped the semblance of recommendations and just gave the facts.

The wonderful world of "capital appreciation"

Obviously, in the imprecise world of Wall Street, growth is an extremely flexible word. Like "beauty," it is in the eye of the beholder. You and I are certainly as entitled to use it loosely as the experts are, but let's try to clear it up a bit before we proceed to look for it.

What we want to achieve is "gains" or, to be properly stuffy, "capital appreciation." These gains can be achieved by buying the stock of a growth company, or by buying what I choose to call a growth stock. In an orderly universe, these would always be one and the same thing, but many a director of a stodgily successful company has gloomed over the realization that they are not.

You'll find some pretty complicated definitions of what a "growth *company*" is. These deal with percentage of compounded earnings increase, the price/earnings ratio in relation to (*a*) other industries and (*b*) other companies in the same industry, the annual increase in percentage of retained earnings—all sorts of very deep stuff that is undoubtedly as right as rain. So I'm going to sound very much the country boy when I tell you that for your pur poses a "growth *stock*" is a stock that's rising, has som reason to rise, and looks like it could continue to rise.

The specuvestor is interested when he learns about a growth stock and delighted when he learns about a growth company. He's perfectly willing to buy the glamour or the technical situation that may make a so-so stock rise, but he'll treat that holding differently from his investment in a company that has everything going for it. He'll be more sensitive to down-turns, less likely to pyramid his holdings, quicker to sell. But he'll gladly buy into such a situation.

The search for growth companies and growth stocks is, of course, a very large subject. Whole books deal with it, whole departments carry it on, whole businesses thrive on it. We have our usual Little Guy advantage here—we can oversimplify things. All we need know is enough to understand what the experts are trying to tell us. We're just going to listen and watch and read a little, and finally do what a lot of other people will be doing, too. On this you can make a fortune? Bet your sweet life.

So let's take a very brief look at the anatomy of growth —the stuff of which good gains are made:

The turn-around. Among the best of the moving-up stocks are those that have spent a long time in the cellar because of bad earnings. There are no greater favorites on Wall Street than these "turn-around situations." When a company has been losing money or suffering from greatly decreased earnings for some time, only a few cents on the plus side can cause a gold rush. Sometimes it seems just plain silly that a stock selling at 20, while the company's losing a dollar a share, should soar to 50 when it suddenly earns a nickel a share. But yours not to reason why—yours to act the Little Guy. If people say it's a big deal and back it with their own cash, feel free to join the bunch. As a matter of fact, it all depends on projections for the following years, which, in such a recovery, will usually be quite handsome.

You'll find this kind of action usually attends a stock that has been a good earner and a big favorite and has fallen on thin times. An extraordinary write-off such as airframe manufacturers sometimes have to swallow, or a fouled-up sales situation that's been corrected, will have the well-informed watching for a recovery and ready to buy in when it takes place. It won't take more than a solid token increase to get the buy orders coming, with great confidence that more earnings growth is inevitable.

The earnings jump. Naturally, the same thing applies to a company that sharply increases earnings over those of previous years. But this is usually all over before you hear about it because, unless it's a really big boost and looks like a permanent move, a few points will equalize the price/earnings ratio. And one day or two will run it out. You can't win much on that kind of gains. In fact, the price usually drops when the news is published, because everybody knows ahead of time.

Even a big earnings boost may not move a stock much. It depends on how popular it is in the first place, how much talk it creates or interest it arouses. When Roan Selection Trust raised annual earnings from $1.42 to $2.21, it was quite a jump, but full many a rose is born to blush unseen. How can you work Roan Selection Trust into a conversation? The stock did move from 9⅞ to 10¼, but then settled back into its customary doldrums. By mid-1969 it had struggled up a few more points but was still at a sizzling P/E of 5, after a split.

Consider it as a sign of health to add to other considerations, but don't buy just because of an earnings increase.

The management. Not at all unrelated to turn-around situations and earnings jumps are changes in management. Don't ever lose sight of the importance of management to a company's (and a stock's) success. One man can make the difference—and his advent or departure can signal drastic action in the market.

There are dozens of evidences of the importance Wall Street places on the individuals in management. Fairchild Camera and Instruments stole Motorola president Charles

L. Hogan. Fairchild jumped several points the first day and went up another handful when other Motorola biggies followed him. Motorola dropped sharply in the same period and promptly sued for unfair business practices.

Group management—the philosophy and the caliber of the entire upper echelon—can be the deciding factor in lifting a company, too. A youthful, in-depth team such as that built up at Litton Industries is worth many, many points on the weird Wall Street scale. But that stock's drop from 77 to 48 when the government roasted Litton's Jones & Laughlin acquisition shows how sharply a heavy thumb can change a stock's delicate balance.

The new product or industry. I probably won't have to get beyond Xerox—or at least no farther than Polaroid—to convince you that a new product or line can make a lot of money for a lot of people. But it doesn't have to be as basic or as revolutionary as electrostatic reproduction or instant photos to do the trick. In fact, if you want to be snide about it, it doesn't have to be much of anything, as long as enough people get the hots on the subject.

Most important of all, grasp the fact that the stocks of companies that are suddenly in the news for new products (or most other reasons) almost always go up too high and then settle back or plunge. Thiokol made a big splash a few years back when its solid fuel for rockets seemed the ultimate in glamour. It subsequently dropped from 72 into the teens in which it wallows today. With earning of a little over a dollar all these years later, you might say its stockholders got pretty badly burned on reentry. They're down to earth, now—but those who got off while it was still in orbit did fine.

We discussed Brunswick, with its automatic pinsetters. The bowling boom went bam, but a lot of money was made on the stock before the alley foreclosures began.

In later years TV picture tubes were in short supply, and wowee! About the same time transistors and other little widgets became a profitable craze. Birth control pills, nuclear energy, computer services, and data devices of all kinds, all have gotten a big play.

Today they're talking up things like oceanography, pollution control, learning aids. Look into them, then sit back and see what moves. Know why it *should* move, but wait till it's on its way—then hop on board.

Here's that roller coaster again

But keep your head in all these ventures—most particularly when you're buying gobs of the future. The chartists describe the various phases in a stock's rise as "Accumulation," "Mark-up," "Distribution," and "Mark-down." Here's what they mean:

1. Accumulation. The long period near the bottom, when the insiders and knowledgeables are quietly acquiring the stock because they know something you don't.

2. Mark-up. The period in which the demand exceeds the supply and the public is beginning to hear things carefully spilled. This is the period of sharp rise.

3. Distribution. The time when the public has been attracted to the flame. High volume accompanies a slacking off in the climb rate. The inside trackers are taking profits, selling to the great unwashed.

4. Mark-down. Continued profit-taking by the insiders, with the supply exceeding the demand, panic setting in, and the stock in ever-weaker hands.

You are the public. *Yours* are the weak hands. What can you do to beat this roller-coaster effect? Well, you can't be an insider, but you can be a very smart Little Guy. Chapters 15 and 16 govern your behavior in these circumstances. I bring it in here because you must perceive that there is accelerated risk in buying for gains, and the more you move from company growth to mere stock gains, the more alert you have to be.

There are fads in stocks, just as in anything else. It would be folly to buck those fads, and, in fact, it's good sense to take advantage of them. If the whole chemical industry is in a slump (which it has been for the past several years), it will take some doing to raise any chemical stock appreciably. With steel in the doldrums, any steel stock has an uphill fight for a good gain. But a small company with a good, new desk-top computer terminal device gets a running start from the fact that computer stocks, in general, are getting a play.

In fact, merely being in an industry that has achieved glamour status has boosted many a mediocre stock to rewardingly high levels. Witness the new-issue craze that has goosed the new stock of many completely unknown companies just because they have names with "electron" or "data" or "computer" in them. Glamour companies usually do become popular as groups. And when they do, you should try to participate. It's fascinating to see the waves spreading outward from the big companies, lapping over all the medium-sized ones and then the little-bitty ones as investors frantically try to find one that hasn't "participated" yet. But that's forcing things. Go ahead and buy the fringe companies if you feel they're solid and not just riding the craze. But look into them closely first because they go down fastest. Better to get one with a proven record, buy in, and average up. Not as exciting, but far less chancy.

A new product that affects just one company has to be *some* product to influence earnings appreciably. The bigger the company the truer that is. I just read about a new self-defrosting rear-view mirror one company's going to market. Gee, great—but it would have to be a mighty small company for that to be a big deal. On the other hand, winning the contract for the "Air Bus" moved Lockheed stock at least 10 percent, although it couldn't hold the rise. Big as the company is, the prospect of selling an estimated

1,000 of the $15,000,000 craft has long-term implications—and they ain't bad.

A new drug—such as a cure for cancer, for example—can absolutely send a stock through the roof. Syntex, with its birth control pill, shot from 15 to 90 (adjusted for some of those delightful splits) in less than six months. More than the actual earnings potentials are involved in such a rise. The amount of talk generated is even more important—certainly birth control pills were on everybody's tongue. (Sorry about that.) You'll see some prize silliness running around, masquerading as glamour. Let me recite you a little fable:

Once upon a time there was a rather staid company called Deep South Utilities. If anyone asked what they did for a living (which few ever did), they might have said, "Oh, we fool around with sewage treatment systems—we purify sewage and waste water that little towns and big companies pump out all the time. You know." But nobody did know. Or care much, either, judging from the stock action.

In 1964 Deep South made a fine, fat 36 cents a share and, after an acquisition, 42 cents in 1965. But still nobody really paid much attention. Then one day one of the officials at—what was its name?—Deep South Utilities was reading an article about how important it was getting to be to fight pollution, and how we were lousing up our whole world and upsetting our entire environmental balance. So he put an old piece of pollution into the magazine as a marker and went and looked up the word. And he said, "Heck, we're not fooling around with sewage treatment systems, we're saving our entire environmental balance."

So he talked to their financial people and they brightened up and said, "I wouldn't be at all surprised if we're one of those Emerging Industries everybody's talking about."

So they decided to Emerge.

By that time it was 1966 and earnings were down to only 3 cents. But that would only give them a better spot to

Emerge from. So, as a first step, they changed the name of the company, and it was only fit that they should honor the word that woke them up to their real mission in life. "Environmental Science Corporation" certainly sounded better to the board—and it kind of made a hit with the financial community, too, because they had heard about this Environmental thing and how it was going to be very big.

Even a slight earnings drop to a deficit of 4 cents in 1967 didn't discourage people from bidding the stock up from 10 to 24 before the year was out. You see, you had to have faith in a company with the word "environmental" in its name, in an industry which was clearly Emerging.

Besides, there were fine rumors that they would earn from $10 to $20 "in the next few years"—which was precise enough for any analyst. And it was widely reported to be a "potential $100 stock." Also, the company was "planning a lot of acquisitions." Well, you couldn't hardly pass up a chance to participate in an operation like that, even if one unkindly expert did call it a "conglomerate of small companies with prosaic products."

After all, a press release said that good old Emerging Environmental was trying to find the "lowest-cost answers to all of man's environmental requirements," such as the proper handling of air, water, garbage, and power. And they were reported to be very, very big on Motherhood, as well.

In 1968, the stock reached a tidy 66½, about the time the president of the company said they were "building things that have never been built before." He added, excitingly, "We're working on a half dozen new things, but I can't say what at this time."

But they did propose a 2½ to 1 split so that they could acquire a maker of heat exchangers that listed among its attractions a net loss of $379,000 in the first six months of 1968. Though by the time that was voted, the stock had eased off close to 20 points, possibly because even the very nice 40 cents earnings that this fine little conglomerate

140

generated in the first six months didn't look enough like pie in the sky. In the meantime, a big brokerage house insisted that "the overall pollution-control market may be developing into one of the most rapidly growing segments of the economy. Therefore, the potential for companies in the industry appears to be highly promising. Most observers believe that the market will double in five years—others believe that it could do so in just three." And they didn't seem to find anybody at all who said it could also take ten.

So the outcome for little Environmental Science Corporation remains to be seen, even though it has flushed all the way down to 15, by the latest bacteria count. But the moral is clear: If you see a bandwagon passing by, hop on it and start tooting your horn. Chances are somebody will pay attention. For a while.

Some other growth hormones

You can't be your own research department. Heard it before? You'll hear it again. The finds will be found for you. All you have to do is recognize in them some of the growth factors we've discussed and a couple more very obvious ones that can mean a lot.

Like "thin issues." Stock action will be in inverse ratio to the floating supply of shares. The fewer shares the more action, up or down. A growth situation with a small float will be explosive. Always ask about the capitalization (number of shares issued) or look it up in Standard & Poor's monthly *Stock Guide*. Then find out how many are held by officers, by underwriters, by controlling stockholders who won't want to lose control. The fewer left over the better—if it's action you're looking for.

Solitron Devices had only 750,000 shares outstanding in 1967, with much of it closely held. It went up 17½ points one day, and down 13 the next. A five-to-one split has since calmed it down. It can happen to companies whose stock numbers in the millions, too, if the "float" is small. Digital Equipment, with over 3,000,000 shares, rose from a 1967 low of 29⅜ to an early 1969 high of 188. Management held 17.5 percent of the stock and another company held 60 percent, so there were only about 400,000 shares available for trading.

Franklin Mint had 337,000 shares, of which all but an estimated 100,000 were so closely held that they were not considered available to the market. (It has since split.) A purchase or sale of as few as a hundred shares moved the stock up or down a point or so. The sale, on one day, of 2,500 shares dropped the stock 8 points, on another, 300 raised it 9. The word is "volatile"; with the earnings growth I described earlier, the scarceness of the stock made it all the more attractive. All the more dangerous, too— don't forget.

A small float can be an invitation to manipulation, a dirty word that pops up now and then despite the best efforts of all regulatory bodies. In 1967 a Federal Grand Jury looked into six American Exchange issues that seemed to have acted in a decidedly fishy way. The average number of shares outstanding, of all six suspect stocks, was only 650,000. Remember, Little Guy, you're not playing with kids.

One thing about thin issues, the large brokerage houses will never tell you about them. Not officially, at least, though your own representative may pass the word along. The reason for the restriction is obvious; with several hundred or even several thousand representatives talking about the same scarce commodity, that firm's customers would simply be bidding against each other—and if it fell sharply there could be quite a wave of discontent. All firms have a responsibility to help maintain an orderly market and if they don't take it seriously the SEC does—sometimes very publicly, which is bad for image. In many cases, if you want to buy a stock, particularly one below $4, which is in short supply or has had a sharp, unexplained rise, you will be asked to sign a paper stating that it was your idea.

This Pontius Pilate position used to be forced on the brokerage houses because they had no real house rules against such trading. Today, however, some firms will simply refuse to execute a buy order on any stocks below $5, while others keep such transactions at a minimum by refusing their representatives a commission on these low-price buy orders. They do, however, give commissions on sell orders in these same stocks—presumably on the theory that they're better off in someone else's portfolio in some other firm.

Well, to be pragmatic about it, gold is where you find it, and you can't afford to worry about the position you put the broker in, or whether your trade is good for the economy as a whole. If you have good reason to buy a stock and your broker won't buy it, don't transfer your account. But do draw out enough to buy it somewhere else. And then, if it goes down the drain, take your medicine like a man.

This matter of ethics and morality is something you will have to decide for yourself, whether it involves your business dealings or the stocks you buy. Many people won't own stock in liquor companies, others in tobacco companies. There's a company called Resorts International, formerly Mary Carter Paint Company, which sounded as though they mixed the colors for Grandma Moses. They have big gambling holdings in the Caribbean and may not be nice people at all, for all I know. But I'll bet some of their stockholders are ministers.

Jumping on the cycle

"Cyclicals" are stocks that periodically rise and fall as a group. Metals, machine tools, building supplies of all kinds —these are cyclical industries. Their fortunes tend to depend, not on their individual efforts, but on the tides of the economy, of foreign competition, even of public tastes.

Some stocks within any group rise higher and more swiftly than others, when they are doing well—and some drop more swiftly when things turn down again. To that extent you must pick and choose among them. But don't choose any at all unless they're firmly on the way up.

Your broker will make these categories clearer, but the principle is very simple. These stock groups sit in the cellar for long periods of time and they are not, then, a good specuvestment. The building industry, for example, is usually held down when money is tight, because mortgages cost so much and are so hard to get that private citizens and business alike hold off new construction. That hurts cements, lumbers, steels, and other involved companies, as well as builders. But when interest rates go down or some other factor overbalances that one, the lid is off and great gains can be made in hundreds of issues as a result.

You'll hear about those moves. Fireworks go off when a cyclical group is turning. Jump on, by all means, but not till they start to climb. You can't afford to have your money sit in the cellar of a building boom. Incidentally, just because your town is all over steelwork doesn't mean there's a building boom going on. When there is, you'll be told.

Look for the green thumb

A very simple point. Into the equation that is finally to end up "buy," add plant expansion. You want a company whose plants are growing (nothing worse than being caught with your sales up and your plants down). That doesn't mean you buy a stock just because the company is expanding. In fact, overexpansion has put many a firm under. But the upbeat company that is building new plants and opening new branches is the one that deserves your close attention. When you buy stock you buy futures. That future is compounded of yesterday and today. With stocks it's not only a case of "What have you done for me lately?", it's also "What are you doing right now?"

Chrysler is a good example of foresight that paid off. They spent fantastically on plant expansion—not only

144

because they needed it then (you can always hold off a couple more years) but because they believed the car market was going to expand. You can call it a gamble or an investment because these are always closely allied, but it has paid off extremely well. And the beautiful part is that *you* wouldn't have had to invest a penny till it did start to pay off. Then you could have ridden it from the 40's to the 70's in 1968 before it backslid so grievously.

You've heard it before: it's better for a stock if a company plows earnings back into the business, rather than pays them out in dividends. Chrysler, of course, pays a good dividend—close to 3 percent even at the $70 range. But not at the price of expansion.

In this chapter we've talked about some of the risks of speculation; touched on a couple of questionable operations; dropped a few other warnings that I believe belong in a discussion of growth and gains. But to help you maintain perspective, so that you see the market as the honorable arena of opportunity that, with marvelously minor exceptions, it truly is—let me touch briefly on pension funds. These are what you might call sacred trusts, because it's the worker's money and you can't fool around with that.

The company fund committees and the big banks that usually handle these enormous hoards are under considerable compulsion to show good growth every year from capital appreciation. More and more they are putting as much as their own rules permit into common stocks—and are striving to have the permissible percentages increased.

To get an idea of the magnitude of their holdings, in 1967 they held more than three times as much in common stocks as was held by all the mutual funds combined. Largest of all is AT&T's—with $1,500,000,000 in commons.

Why do they put these vast sums into risky, iffy common stocks instead of holding it all in nice, safe bonds and government securities? For the fabulous gains available. Your own private pension fund should surely follow suit.

Chapter 13

Rule Number 3: THINK BIG—ACT SMALL

This chapter departs even farther from the tangibles and deals wholly with a state of mind, an attitude.

Inside every investor's mind, there is an impression of himself and his role in the market—his market ambitions. And no one need have small ambitions in the market. It can be very good to you. Depending, naturally, on how much you'll put in and how long you'll keep it there, investing can not only ease your retirement—it can retire you. It can put your kids through college, and it can endow a scholarship, if that's your bag. It can buy you a yacht and also the estate next to which to dock it.

It can also put its hand in your pocket instead, and take a good percentage of what you've already got.

Much of the outcome will depend on your attitude going in. Recognize, first of all, that you *are* master of your fate. You can't control the market, but you can and must keep your own participation in it under control. No one else can make your decisions. You can be sure no one else will shoulder your losses, so don't ever think they deserve the blame. You get the credit; you get the blame.

The worst attitude of all is a modest ambition. "Make no small plans." *Think big,* and let the force of circumstances tone things down if need be. Let's examine the significance of this first half of our maxim—"Think big."

The fundamentals of thinking big

Start with a look at the opposite aim—"Think small." This is the approach that would have you seeking dividends, and there's a whole chapter (26) to dissuade you from that. Thinking small would have you hiding forever in defensive stocks like utilities and foods—the kind that "don't go down much" when the market turns sour. Or up much either, with exceptions that your attitude would probably deny you.

Thinking small would have you grabbing the 10-point gain because "a bird in the hand . . ." and all that nonsense. It would make you weigh each commitment till the bloom was off the rose. It would have you buying stocks at their lows because "they're cheaper at that price"—and spurning stocks at their highs, because "they've had such a run-up."

It would make you concentrate on lower-priced issues under the insane delusion that you're "not running as big a risk." It would make you steer clear of the over-the-counter market because you "never know about those stocks."

The small thinker holds a stock no matter where it drops to, because he can pretend he doesn't have a loss. Then, when it finally recovers, he'll sell it at his going-in price and glow because he got his money out, while the issue screams on to new heights.

He'll watch a stock double and then sell half—and gloat that "it doesn't owe me anything." Exactly as though he'd put something over on the stock.

He'll buy more of a stock that's dropping because it will give him a "lower break-even point." But he'll never buy more of a stock that's rising because he "could have had it 10 points lower."

The small thinker is a defeatist. He's negative. And his results probably will be, too. All those phrases in quotes are lines I've heard a hundred times, because the Wall Street woods are full of small thinkers who get small results, if any. You've heard them, too. In fact, you're blushing.

Go into the market with the simple aim of making as much money as you can as quickly as you can. To all the well-meaning conservatives who quiver with shock or even rage at that charge, I say this: "How stupid it would be to figure on making *less* money than you can, as slowly as you can." And that's not just playing word games.

Climbing the money mountain

Attack the market like a mountain climber. Go for the top. Either determine to be bold or stay off the cliff. Know what you're doing before you take each step. Have an escape route all planned. Hey—don't look down.

Brokers like to pretend that the market is a neat beast, not only housebroken but trained to roll over and fetch and bark at prowlers. So they like to talk about "objectives." "What is your objective in that stock?" (Meaning how many points do you expect it to rise?) Or "It's reached its objectives, so I advise selling." But an objective by any other name is a limit, not a goal. And how foolish it is to set limits on what you expect to gain. Aim for the top of the mountain. And no one knows where that top is.

Think big. Don't go into a stock for which you don't have great expectations of gain. And, for heaven's sake, don't limit those expectations. More money has been "lost" by getting out too soon than by getting out too late. And that's the money you can least afford to lose. You need that big money to cover all your little losses, and if all you have is little gains you're dead.

Think big. Don't weaken your resolve by viewing your stock market funds in terms of "things"—a car, a vacation, a summer home. Don't even view them as money. Very few of us are so accustomed to handling large sums that we can calmly buy 50 shares of a $100 stock if we think of it as $5,000. It simply has to be 50 shares of a $100 stock. That is one of the reasons for never touching your stocks or your money (Chapter 29). If you have to write checks and make deposits whenever you buy or sell, you will never lose the small view that money gives you.

As you already know, I recommend caution. But that caution should not be inflamed by equating your investments with the good things in life. Pay now, fly later. You'll go around the world instead of just to Hackensack.

Think big. Don't be diffident about your investments. Your money is as important to you as a million dollars is to Onassis. You know how he'd swing his weight around for a million dollars. Well, don't apologize for the size of your little bundle. Handle it as though it were a good ten times its size. Within reason, demand for it the same kind of thinking on the part of your broker. Not the same amount of attention, because business is business. But the same *quality* of attention.

Your broker's attitude will be a reflection of your own. If you're serious about your investments, he will be, too. If you're actively interested in improving your position, he will be, too. You can't keep pestering him and never making a move; you can't keep him off balance by constantly changing your mind; you can't whine and complain when a buy goes wrong. But if you act decisively and in an adult fashion he'll delight in helping your account grow. He's human, too. Feel as though your account is ten times its size. And eventually it will be.

Think big!

But act small

How do we make this paradox ring true? Most of the remaining chapters in this book are devoted to it. The small investor has to conduct his affairs with a precision far beyond that required of the large investor. To a far greater extent he must protect his capital. He has to depend more on himself. He must be a follower in the market, rather than a leader. A copier, rather than an innovator.

The Little Guy has handicaps, and he must adjust to them. If you live in a house, you don't have to be nearly as concerned about windstorms as does the fellow who lives in a tent. That doesn't mean the tenter packs up every time it starts to blow, but he sure perks up and pays attention. In the market it's too often just the opposite. The small investor thinks he's safer because he doesn't have as much to lose. Or he thinks he can't do anything about it, anyway. Or, even worse, he thinks there's no difference between his position and that of the big investor.

There's a big difference. But here's the funny part: If the big investor would use the principles expounded in this book, he might do better, too. If he'd drop his investment manager or take discretionary powers away from his broker, and devote his own half hour or so to the market in the way we're outlining—he'd get his 30 percent, too. The difference is, he doesn't have to. He'll survive massive stupidities and wholesale foolishness. But you won't.

Don't shoot the piano player

So act small! For one thing, don't get cocky. Don't get the feeling you know it all—or that you know much of anything, for that matter. Keep that healthy concern that something is going to happen to steal it all away. Retain a proper awe for those who make a business of the market, while weighing their pronouncements as any prudent man would. Never feel annoyance or contempt for those of them who call the turn wrongly; like the sign in the saloon said, "Please don't shoot the piano player; he's doing his best." You need those piano players.

I'm just full of vapid quotes. Like, "He who fights and runs away . . ." That's your role in the market, Little

150

Guy. Get in there and throw that punch. But when you and a stock are taking a beating—backpedal. Don't brazen it out—sell it out. You'll live to fight another day.

Don't ever get over that fear of being clobbered. Remember the Johnstown flood, and when that crack appears in that big earth dam don't stick the thumb in—get the heck out. `

Act small!

Chapter 14

Rule Number 4: DISREGARD PRICE

Guess what the difference is between a $10 stock and a $100 stock? That's right, $90. And, as far as you're concerned, that's the only difference. There may be, and probably is, a tremendous difference between the two companies. But the stocks themselves—just $90 difference.

Stock A isn't better or worse because it costs a hundred. Stock B doesn't have better prospects for appreciation because it costs only ten. Where each stock has been makes a difference. What brought them to today's prices makes a difference. Thousands of things make a difference. But the price doesn't.

Therefore, whether you buy 10 shares of Stock A or 100 of Stock B must not hinge on whether you'd rather hold 100 shares than 10. That must have nothing to do with your decision. All things being equal, the difference in commission between odd lot and round lot might be a tiny factor. But all things are never equal. There have to be more important considerations.

Your aim in buying a stock is to increase your equity—not just the 30 percent we've set as a goal, but as much as possible. Percentages are all that count, because, whether high price or low price, we'll assume you're going to invest a certain sum in the stock—not buy a certain number of shares, but invest a certain sum. The $50 stock that rises 5 points appreciates as much as the $10 stock that rises 1 point. And, if you choose correctly, it's just as likely to make that gain. No more likely, I insist, but just as likely. Therefore, whatever sum you invest will increase 10 percent in either.

The fatal blind-spot

There's only one reason for spending this much time on a truism. As obvious as it is, many small investors incline toward low-price stocks and resist higher-priced issues— simply because of a blind spot in this area. Because of this attitude, all kinds of promoters can float all kinds of phony-baloney stocks. It helps fan the new-issue craze that doubles low-price stocks on their opening day and the hell with six months from now. And it keeps millions of Little Guys skirting the edges of solidity and safety while they take big chances on little stocks.

Mind you, it works both ways. There are thousands of fine companies whose stock sells for ten points or less. And, parenthetically, the specuvestor can even find profits in the rising stocks of companies that aren't so fine. So don't snoot this group, either. Buy any stock on the basis of its merits and pay whatever price it has at the moment.

Don't, above all, buy a stock just because its price has dropped to whatever you consciously or unconsciously feel is your buying area. When choosing a commitment, use all your skill and knowledge—and ESP, if you can bring it into play—but always remember there's no such thing as a "high"-priced stock or a "low"-priced stock, except in relation to where that price has been and where you think it's going.

Chapter 15

Rule Number 5: BUY ONLY ON THE RISE

Start with the precept that your money is better off sitting quietly in your account than it is sitting quietly in the market. The dreadful itch to get funds working probably causes more losses than fraud does. Resist it. Don't just do something—sit there. This does not mean that you should sell a stock just because it isn't moving up. But it sure means you should hold off *buying* a stock because it isn't moving up.

The alternatives, of course, are two. You can buy a stock that's standing still. Or you can buy one that's going down —a mania called "guessing bottoms." Since one of the phenomena of the market is that stocks simply don't stand still for long, a temporarily stagnant stock is going to move one way or the other. Why not wait to see which way it goes? If it goes down before it rises, you'll get it cheaper. If it goes up, you'll have your buy signal and can make your move.

It's obvious that this kind of tactic will keep you from getting in at the bottom. You'll miss that warm glow of accomplishment, and you won't be nearly as impressive to your friends. But you'll make more money, more consistently. And that's not a bad substitute.

The points you give away by exercising caution don't cost you one red cent. The points you can lose by going in too soon cost you exactly one dollar per point per share. I've talked frankly about the gambling aspects of investing, so look at it in that light, if it helps. You'll agree that buying a stock that is sitting still or is actually moving down is a sucker play—like drawing to an inside straight. There's more chance you won't make it than there is that you will. In a favorite Wall Street phrase, "the risk is all on the down side."

Chartists refine the admonition. They don't consider it a buying opportunity when a stock merely moves up—not until it breaks through a "resistance area." Stated simply, that means it goes up past the highest point it's hit recently. What they are trying to do is define the exact moment when the stock becomes a buy. But the basic element there is that the stock must be moving up.

What is most difficult to grasp is that sitting on your money is not only the most comfortable but often the most advantageous position of all. When you buy a stock, you automatically make it necessary to make other decisions— to hold, to sell, to buy more. A plus balance in your account requires no decision whatsoever. Eventually you will have to put it into a stock that seems to have all the elements you're looking for. But you can't lose a dime until you do. True, you won't make anything either—but don't rush it. Wait till the stock you're eyeing moves up.

Stocks and the market have momentum. They tend to continue in the direction they are going. Naturally, they don't go down forever and they don't go up forever. But it's better than an even bet that they'll do tomorrow what they did today. People who buy for the long term, who buy a stock and put it away, can afford to scoff at day-to-day action, or month-to-month action. To the extent that their approach is right, their scorn of a stock's swings is right. But, in specuvesting, taking advantage of a stock's momentum will give you a valuable extra edge over the man who tries to get in at the low.

A fatal viewpoint is commonly held by the uninitiates. You'll hear it expressed as, "I wouldn't buy that—it's gone too high already." Or, "It's already had its run-up." I can't imagine anything more stupid than to reject a stock because it's hitting new highs. In fact, I can't imagine a better clincher in the debate about buying a particular stock than the fact that it *is* at its high.

Naturally, it can't continue to hit new highs. One of Wall Street's favorite wise-guy sayings is, "No tree grows to the sky." But when it breaks through its old barriers and hits its high, whether it's all-time or for the year, sit up and take notice. And when it continues into that new ground there's a good chance that it will keep going for a good rise.

You don't have to be a chartist to learn when a stock is at its highs. Papers with good financial sections publish lists of "New Highs" and "New Lows." And the stock comments often mention them, if the company is at all well known.

Again, a new high cannot be the reason for buying a stock, but it is definitely a reason for looking into it—and absolutely not a reason for not buying it. Always remember that a stock is worth only what large numbers of people think it is worth, and a new high is a pretty good expression of confidence.

Use caution, of course. The first new high after a long, long sell-off and recovery cycle will prompt a lot of selling from people who have just been waiting to get their bait back. The stock will often stumble after it first touches that point. But a stock can stumble any time, and it's got a better chance of fast recovery when it's riding high than when it's just pooping along some place down the scale.

A little extra caution is suggested after repeated new highs, too. But it all depends on the stock and the reasons for its climb. Actually, if the fundamentals look good you should be willing to buy at any place on the upswing. We'd all like to get in at the beginning, but we rarely will. Half a loaf is not only better than none, it is absolutely essential to survival.

And, incidentally, there's a siren song your broker may sing every once in a while. It's called:

IT'S IN A BUYING RANGE

The stock, bedight with promise bright, is brought you on
    a cushion.
Of all the lot, with all they've got, this is the one he's
    pushin'.
It's sound, it's bound to turn around. He urges purchase, so
You say, "OK, but by the way, why has it dropped so low?"

    O-o-oh, it's in a buying range.
    Why do you find that strange?
    Nothing grows high till it reaches the sky.
    This one's all set now to change.

    It's getting ready to turn.
    Think of the money you'll earn.
    You'll sure be smart to be in at the start
    When a stock's in a buying range!
              (REPRISE)
Good stocks never fall, never tumble at all,
They descend to a buy-ing range!
    (ENTER FAIRY GODMOTHER, WHO WARNS)
Go to Bowie or Preakness, but don't buy on weakness
Down in that old——buy——ing——range!

Chapter 16

Rule Number 6: SELL ONLY ON THE DROP

At this point we enter the great unknown. Having made a commitment, when do you unload? It's bad enough having to decide what to buy and when to buy it. But the devil himself invented the problem of when to sell it.

There are many schools of thought on that one. There's the grab-it-and-run school that sees any gain as a delightful bonus that must be seized immediately. There's the buy-'em-and-hold-'em group that ascribes virtue to the inability to handle stocks properly. There's the I-can't-lose club, which sells enough of a rising stock to get their money back, then gleefully pretends the remainder doesn't matter.

None of these positions stand scrutiny. You really mustn't be surprised when your stocks make a gain—that's what they're supposed to do. Instead of getting more and more nervous as they continue up, you should feel more and more comfortable. I used to brag to my wife that a certain stock had gone up so many points. Her reaction was always a very logical, "When are you going to sell it?" It was years before I hit on the right answer: "When it starts to go down."

The eagerness to sell is based largely on a misunderstanding of the relative roles of paper profits and realized profits.

You have to accept the fact that they are, as I've pointed out previously, one and the same. A profit is a profit is a profit. A loss is a loss is a loss. You do not have any reason to realize a profit on a stock until that profit is threatened. There is only one thing that threatens profits in a stock— a drop in price. Bad news doesn't threaten them, a drop in earnings doesn't threaten them, a strike doesn't threaten them. Any or all of these may cause a drop in the stock's price, but it is only the decline itself that should pull the trigger on your sale. Nobody in the world knows what effect any piece of news will have on a stock or on the market. Educated guesses are the best you can expect, and there are too many educated losers in the market to make that an attractive reason for action.

Be a stock holder

The grab-it-and-run schools fails to recognize that good winners are few and far between. When you get one you have to let it run! It has to pay for all your losers, plus its part of the big 30 percent you're looking for.

Their opposite numbers, the buy-'em-and-hold-'em people, simply don't want to make money, or don't know how to. Or, possibly, don't have the guts to. I would have no argument at all against this approach if all stocks were Xeroxes or IBMs or even General Motorses. But they're not. Many stocks are U.S. Steels—which hit $108\frac{7}{8}$ in 1959 and ten years later is holding nicely in the 40's, thank you. Many are Motorolas, down almost a hundred points from the 233 it hit in 1966. KLM soared above 150 in 1966, but closed out 1968 below 70, after struggling back from a desperate 44. Transitron's glamour took it to 60 in 1960, but wore off all the way down to $3\frac{7}{8}$, three years later. It's way back to 12 as I write this. You can't just hold stocks forever. Not and have a good chance of making money. Remember the 85 percent who don't make money in the market? A good percentage of them are sitters.

The I-can't-lose club is more to be pitied than censured. The flaw in their approach is so obvious. In the first place, these are potentially the most successful investors of all, because to apply their peculiar psychology they must have winners. Given a stock that has risen appreciably, there are only two possibilities—it will continue to rise or it will fall. If it falls, this deluded investor is willing to risk a good portion of his gains in the fond belief that it isn't costing him a thing. If it rises, he ends up with a fraction of the gains he would have had—*and has the problem of finding still another successful vehicle for the portion he has pulled out.*

There is no better place for his money than the stock he's just sold. He should never have pulled out penny one until it went down enough to constitute a serious threat to his gains.

Understand, if a risen stock falls, it is perfectly valid to sell part of it. In Chapter 8 we discussed which of two or more purchases in the same issues should be sold, based on buying prices and long-term/short-term aspects. Let me now add that it is probably perfectly good sense to feel your way out of a stock, even if you bought it all at once. You may wish to protect the major part of your equity and still keep a commitment. *I, myself, don't sell part of a single purchase because a part of my investment is as important to me as all of it is. If I think it's seriously threatened I'll pull it all out and either hold it while watching the issue for a recovery or put it into something else.* But you do what feels most comfortable, as long as you remain acutely aware that what you leave in is your money, too.

But do sell!

Let's move from "Don't sell a stock *until* it drops" to "Sell it *when* it drops." Think of your money as hitchhiking. It gets aboard a vehicle, and, when that one turns off on a side road, it gets off and waits for another one that's going in the right direction.

You cannot stand by and see your money vanish. *Your money*. Remember, the current price of every share you own is your money. If you buy a stock at 50 and it goes to 40, you've lost $10 a share. But if it goes to 60 instead, you've gained $10 a share. If it then *goes back to 50, you've lost $10 a share and you'd better believe it.* Did you think you'd broken even? No such thing. Too many people think paper profits are an illusion. The real illusion is to think you can let a stock drop from *any* point and not have it cost you money.

Here's your arithmetic homework for tonight:

Johnny bought 1 share of Dennison Manufacturing for $45 on March 4, 1968. Johnny sold his 1 share of Dennison Manufacturing for $47 on November 8, 1968. How much money did Johnny make?

Answer: Johnny lost $33 in the transaction because Dennison Manufacturing had been to $80 in the interim.

No matter what you say, and the Internal Revenue people say, if you've let a stock drop under you, you've lost that much money.

Warning: don't fall in love

A word of caution. It's easy to fall in love with a company or product that seems to hold bright promise. Then it becomes an act of faith to hold the plummeting stock when things don't pan out. I reluctantly recall a company I've mentioned before, Radiation Research, the one that has patents on a weird process that coats all kinds of materials with all kinds of materials. When I bought it at 60, oodles of big companies had it under development contracts—to line beer cans, bond rubber to metal, produce stain-proof fabrics. It shot up and kept splitting, while I kept buying and had tripled my total investment when it began to drop and I sold out. But then I couldn't stand being out of that swell little company, so I bought in again lower, and bought more all the way down to a point where I had to face reality and get out just about even on the whole, fool deal. And all that was long after I had learned better, I might add.

Visions of the future are dangerous. Ride the new products and industries, but keep your head. Most of the stocks will fall way back again, so only involve your money, not your emotions. If it dips and you sell, and the stock goes back up, buy in again for another ride. It's your stock, not your baby. And it really doesn't care a hoot who owns it.

The *Boston Transcript* once wrote about the Harvard crew, "Win or lose, their speed is marvelous." Such loyalty is touching, but in the market it can be disastrous.

The grim story of the Odd-Lot Index

Of all the Little Guy's areas of ignorance, the timing of purchases and sales is the biggest and blackest. Testimony to that is the *Odd-Lot Index,* which reports his transactions. Wall Street is happiest when he is selling, on balance (more than he's buying), because history shows it means the market is going to rise. And when the odd-lotters are buying, the knowing ones batten the hatches, because the market's riding for a fall.

It would be different if he just bought for the long pull and nobody ever heard of him again. That could be hailed as a virtue of sorts. But to be so consistently and thoroughly wrong in his buying and selling is an absolute disgrace. Every day *The Wall Street Journal* and others publish the sad little story of his strivings. And the big fat people look and nod their heads and reach for the phone.

Actually, of course, I'm overdramatizing it. But the principle is absolutely correct. The odd-lotter—who is the Little Guy at his littlest—finally gets up courage to buy just when a stock is ready to top out, finally is convinced he's done it again, and sells—just before his stock starts to recover. His are the "weaker hands" into which the capable investors pass their stock when they take profits. His are the hands from which they take it back in time for the next rise.

No picket lines protest this unfair treatment because he does it to himself, through ignorance, insensitivity, and sheer stupidity. But he needs help. Join the fight to louse up the odd-lot index. I'm doing it by writing this book. You do your part by taking its lessons to heart. We'll start a group called "FOOLS" (for "Fight to Overcome Odd-Lot Silliness"), and our slogan will be "Succor the sucker."

Chapter 17

Rule Number 7: BUY TALKED-ABOUT STOCKS

In all our childhoods there were dreams of being explorers who discovered unknown wonders in distant lands. Or scientists who discovered the secret of something very secret. Or just plain us, digging up pirate treasure. All my life I wanted to find an arrowhead. I could have bought one for fifty cents in any of a thousand shops, but I wanted to find one that would be mine—my personal link to an almost unimaginable past.

We carry that longing over into stocks. Somewhere there is a stock nobody knows about, that's just waiting for my nod at $2 a share. Oh, it's well within the rules if my barber knew about it first—just like it would have been okay to find a rough map of the pirate treasure trove pressed in an old book. But it's no fun if my broker told me about it—in fact, to make it a real triumph, he should try to discourage me.

Well, it's a great way to lose money. The fewer the people who know about a stock, the less likely it is to move, unless the few people are really inside, or are getting set to buy in stock-moving quantities. All moves, whether prompted by earnings or schemings, start behind closed doors somewhere. But you, the Little Guy, just plain cannot expect to get in at the start. Forget it.

The stock you should buy is the stock that's being openly talked about, at least to some extent. It doesn't have to be in the headlines, or featured in a *Barron's* article. But you can't dream its attractions up all by yourself. *Somebody* else has to know *something* about how wonderful it is, or how the heck is it going to move? If you think it's good and nobody is showing evidence of sharing your enthusiasm, watch it but don't buy it. *Unless* you see it rising sharply, even without the slightest fanfare. Then move in, gingerly.

Even if it's just that somebody told you about the stock or the company or its products—that qualifies it somewhat. But it isn't enough. Ask where he heard the tip—try to assess how widespread the knowledge is. Don't be delighted if nobody else knows; be hesitant.

Always ask your broker about the stock and the story. Have him check his research department for their opinion. Even if you read the item, discuss its meaning with him (again, it's not for advice but for information). Don't be afraid you'll miss the boat by waiting to check up. If the rise is going to be all that brief, you don't want the stock anyway. That's *money* you're throwing around, and it's a lot scarcer than hot stock tips.

Big gains are just a lot of talk

There's an old saying that "money makes the mare go." But it's talk that makes a stock go. You may think increased earnings make a stock move. You may think new product developments make a stock move. But it's people that make a stock move. *People talking and reading and buying.*

And what you know doesn't count at all unless and until somebody else knows it—a lot of somebody elses. That's one difference between you and the big investor.

You don't get inside news first, so if it's news to you and it isn't common knowledge to a lot of very competent investors, then it probably isn't worth much.

Oh, once in a lifetime of investing you may stumble, early, on a genuine bit of inside information. But even then the wise move is to hold off until you get some evidence that the news is actually going to boost the stock. The evidence of that will be that it starts to move.

Forgive me if that prompts a burst of song. It's to be sung slowly, with feeling—ending up with a rousing chorus:

SOMEONE MUST KNOW SOMETHING

It happens sometimes, that a stock of which you never heard
Gets thrust into the limelight in a manner most absurd.
The company it represents may almost be unknown,
But it begins to burgeon with a life that's all its own.
It paints the tape while brokers gape, its symbol on all lips,
In undertones they tell the phones this hottest of all tips.
But if a customer should ask just what it's all about,
The dulcet murmurs vanish and you'll hear the fellows shout:

> *O-o-oh! I understand an acquisition's just around the bend, or*
> *It's one a leading service is about to recommend, or—*
> *I'm told that their new process will really take the cake.*
> *Hold on, please, while I look it up to see—just—what—they—*
> *make. HEY!*

Yessir, sometimes a stock gets talked about just because it's going up. Get aboard that kind, if you want to—but realize that it can soon get itself talked about again by going down just as sharply.

And use caution about "chasing a stock up," the broker's term for eagerness to get in on a stock that has shot up unusually fast. A prime example was one over-the-counter issue called Energy Conversion Devices. They were a small, unknown producer of electronic components who had a very quiet run all the way up to 57 bid. Then on Sunday,

November 10, 1968, the papers broke a story about a new development of theirs that would turn cheap glass into transistors and suchlike. The release envisioned TV sets that would hang on the wall like pictures.

The stock opened at 105 bid Monday morning—up 48 from the previous close. It hit 150 during the same day (up 93), then dropped to 70 (down 80), then closed at 85 bid. Wouldn't you have loved to chase that one? And just where do you figure you would have caught it? That's right —150. The stock, at this writing, is at 67 bid.

What constitutes legitimate talk?

Back in Chapter 7, on "How to pick a winning stock," we talked about some of the reasons for buying. Like increasing earnings, a good P/E ratio, steady expansion, other solid growth factors. These all cause favorable talk and provide underpinnings for steady gains.

Now let's cover some of the things that cause a gust of talk—the kind that can blow a stock a good many points up the ladder in a relatively short space of time. Most of these were covered earlier, but repetition is the soul of learning (remember, you heard it here).

New inventions. Gale and Energy Conversion Devices demonstrate what this kind of talk can do (1968 was certainly the year of electronicized glass). But there are plenty of examples of lasting benefits gained from such developments. New processes, new drugs—try to get evaluations of the chance these developments have for permanently improving the company's position. There is a lot of difference between news that gives a stock a goose and news that heralds true company growth. That difference may not be discernible at first, but try. It's important in dictating your own conduct as an owner of the stock.

If it looks like a flash in the pan, move more quickly to

sell when it drops (but still don't hesitate to go back in if it recovers). If you and whatever experts you believe feel that it's a solid development, be willing to ride it down a little farther on a decline. And be even more certain to repurchase on a good recovery. It's all a matter of degree, because the rules still apply, but it can be an important degree.

Splits. As we discussed, while you can revel in a split when it happens in a stock you hold, you're foolish to buy a stock on the strength of an impending split. The couple of points that the news will inspire will have been posted by the time you learn about it. Buy a splitting stock or the new issue for its own sake, if you like it. But remember that the two shares together aren't worth any more than the single. Stocks aren't amoeba, you know.

There are sometimes "reverse splits," which give you one for two on a low-priced stock. Or even one for five. Sometimes an exchange will force a company to reverse split so as to raise the price of its stock, on threat of de-listing. I can't think how this would ever present a buying opportunity, even though it will, indeed, cause talk.

Mergers. Usually the same thing applies to buying a stock because of a proposed merger or attempted take-over. A company will publish an offer to buy in or swap stock at something more than the market price of the shares of the company being pursued. That company's shares will then rise to around the offering price—but you're usually too late. You just can't afford to chase a finite price increase. That's one of the penalties for being a Little Guy.

However, if it looks as though the company that's sched-uled to be eaten doesn't like the idea, or if some third com-pany has been angling for it, then the stock may go well over the initially offered price. Nothing like a good fight to stir up the investors. It's like a poker game—see you and raise you five points. Oh yeah, well I'll just see you and raise *you* three points. Don't just dream those situations up, though. Talk to your broker.

A chase history

Abex, formerly American Brake Shoe, was a company so unglamorously tied to railroading that its stock consistently sold at multiples of around ten. That means the stock usually sold at about ten times the annual earnings (price/earnings ratio of 10). At 30, where it usually dwelt, the stock was lower than the actual book value of the company, which ran to about $34 a share. That's how much a stockholder would supposedly get if the company was liquidated, and it's the kind of situation the corporate raiders dote on. They get control of a company and drain its assets for more than it cost them to buy it—then, perhaps, sell and howl on.

The wolves started snapping, and Abex ran for cover, arranging a favorable take-over deal with Illinois Central Industries, a conglomerate with its own railroading history. By the time you and I heard about it, the stock had eased up to 37 (after being briefly higher). With the offer at about $50 in various fancy stock dealings, Abex opened the next morning at 40½. The question was—could a Little Guy still get some good out of it?

The word was that the raiders might still be on the prowl, so with that possibility and a cushion of several points before it reached the offered price, I opened my squeaky purse and bought some at 41. Sure enough, North American Rockwell (the raiders had retreated) made a higher bid, and this was answered, in turn, by Illinois Central. Having bought again at 47¼, I sold it all at a comfortable 52 after the IC merger went through.

But let me make a point. I'm really not in favor of going into a stock for a *limited* goal. I didn't want either Abex or the surviving company as an investment, but the prospect of a 25 percent gain with very little downside risk was sufficient to get me in. Could it be that I was extra sensitive to it because a friend is an Abex official and had talked about the company for so many years? You bet it could. I felt familiar enough with the situation (though the rat didn't tip me off in advance) to be comfortable in it.

I spend so much space on this transaction because it's typical of the limited opportunities often available. Look them over, but, as a rule, don't tie up your money for the possibility of the few points' gain offered by most merger deals.

An acquisition-minded company, however, can be a good bet. Better, as I pointed out earlier, in times when conglomerates are popular than when they're not.

So mergers generate talk and do offer possibilities for gain. But every deal is different, so study them carefully before you buy on the strength of it.

Management changes can be among the most talked-up events in the market, and they can certainly spark marvelous developments for a company and its stock. Often this is tied to acquisitions. Listen to what a new viewpoint did to Great Western United, just as an example:

GWU (not to be confused with Great Western Financial) has always been a big producer of beet sugar and flour, and that was about it. Along came William M. White to shake things up a bit. In 1968 they got rid of three unprofitable flour mills, bought a residential developer, opened a chain of steak houses, bought a manufacturer of artificial Christmas trees, and opened negotiations for several other acquisitions. The stock went from 69 to an all-time high of 158 before it split and settled in at around 70 on the new shares until the 1969 bear market.

"Special situation" is a term used when your broker can't find a better basket to put a promising development in. It covers everything from a proxy fight, in which an individual or group tries to get control, to the liquidation

of a business. Broadly, anything we've covered qualifies as a "special situation," since it usually applies to only one company rather than a group or industry. But the more specific the more helpful, so let's break it down even finer.

Stock holdings. Company A holds a big block of Company B's stock. Company B's stock rises. Talk, talk, talk that A will rise, too.

Spin-off. Company A owns Company C. The courts say that's a no-no. Restraint of trade and like that. Company C is split up among Company A's stockholders. Nice, complacent talk, and maybe a very big deal.

Tenders. Company A wants to control Company D, or put a man on its board. Offers *x* dollars for all D shares on the open market—a sneak attack. Since offer will be above market, D shares will rise. But not a whole lot, in all probability.

There are endless possibilities for generating talk and for presenting opportunities. The big point is simply that (*a*) something must be happening, and (*b*) somebody must know about it.

Obviously, you have to evaluate all this talk, to try to figure what it will mean in terms of stock movement. Sheer volume certainly isn't always the most important consideration. It's what's being said that counts.

I remember once, at an advertising presentation, when a colleague of mine forgot that this is usually the case. He was running on, well over his allotted time, so I caught his eye and gave him the familiar television signal for cutting it short—which consists of drawing the forefinger across the throat. To my amazement he stopped short and his jaw dropped—then he stammeringly concluded and sat down in absolute confusion. I found later that he was totally unfamiliar with the signal and thought he must have said something truly dreadful to have prompted such a vicious gesture. Anyway, consider content as well as volume.

The self-fulfilling prophecy

But before we leave the subject, I must present "The self-fulfilling prophecy." This is the ultimate demonstration of how talk moves stocks.

Item: Airline profits slip despite the unexpected economy of jet operation and a great increase in seat-miles. *Wall Street Journal* says investors are getting uneasy. Prices promptly slide.

Item: Merrill Lynch's research boys unearth a solid citizen. The advisory goes out to its 3,000 registered representatives in its 167 offices across the land. They reach for the phones and recommend the stock. It goes up.

Item: A closely followed issue has traced a perfect "head and shoulders" on 10,000 charts. Ten thousand chartists watch to see if it breaks through the support level—a sure sign of further decline. It breaks though. It declines sharply.

Those are facts of investing life. It's *The Wall Street Journal's* job to report developments, and they'd be remiss not to add what those developments mean. Merrill Lynch is in the business of watching companies and reporting on them to their customers—and they certainly have to let them all in on it. The chartists have a right to believe their charts and to act on them when the squiggles finally say something.

But I know of a proofreader for a big news magazine who always proofs their business section. And he's done extremely well with the two-day jump it gives him.

Merrill Lynch acknowledges the force of its own recommendations by forbidding any employee to buy or sell a stock for his own account within forty-eight hours of their issuing a new report on it.

Anyone not an ardent chartist will refuse to say whether the market makes charts or vice versa.

But, as a Little Guy, you can happily run with any of these recommendations, if the rest of the deal looks good. After all, you can use all the help you can get.

Chapter 18

Rule Number 8: BUY ON MARGIN

I've done the arithmetic for you before. If margin is set at 80, multiply the amount you want to invest by 10 and divide by 8. That gives you your buying power. Working it the other way, to buy a specific amount of stock—say $1,000 worth—you have to put up only 80 percent of the money, or $800.

You should use margin because it is a quick, painless, and relatively cheap way of extending your buying power. When you hear what nasty things I have to say about the 1½ percent management charges on mutual funds, you'll wonder why I call 8 to 10 percent interest "cheap." Well, the difference is that margin gives you extra buying power —on which you hope to make far more than 10 percent. The mutual fund charge is right out of your pocket for "services." More later on that touchy subject.

Your borrowing power keeps pace with your equity. At 80 percent margin, my $1,000 gives me $1,250 to invest. That stock then doubles in value—and, without putting up another dime, I have an additional $300 in buying power. This can be used in any way I see fit, even withdrawn in cash if I wish (naturally I pay interest on it if and when I use it).

While it is less attractive a deal at 80 percent than at 50 (or when the interest rates reach up to 10 percent), it is still worthwhile. The Federal Reserve Board regulates the margin requirement, moving it up when they feel that speculation is running rampant. Strangely, there are few experts who feel this has much of a dampening effect. Since 1934, the margin requirement has ranged from 40 percent to 100 percent (in effect a cash transaction). The record is as follows: 1959, requirement 90 percent; 1960, changed to 50 percent; 1963, raised to 70 percent; 1968, raised to 80 percent. The increases in margin do not affect current holdings, but only further purchases.

In a much more logical move, the Federal Reserve Board has also been attempting to clamp down on "unregulated lenders," who used to loan up to $90 on a $100 purchase. These lenders include groups, individuals, and even cash-rich corporations. Strangely, the people who advance such 1929-type loans often get their money from banks—who would throw you out if you tackled them, direct, for any such deal. In 1967 the Feds imposed a limit on these sources, too—moving them under the margin rule. Also, as mentioned before, they have toned down the lending on convertible bonds. The exchanges themselves occasionally slap a 100 percent margin requirement on individual stocks that are going wild. In the highly speculative fall of 1968 there were forty of these 100-percenters on the American Exchange. Over-the-counter stocks aren't usually margin-able.

How you open a margin account

Most brokers require a $2,000 minimum for a margin account—and this is why we insist that the Little Guy start with a minimum of $2,000. To open a margin account you must agree to have your stocks "in street name," made out in your broker's name and left in his custody. They are collateral for the loan he gives you. This is nothing to make you nervous, because they're safe with him, and, even if he goes under for some reason, the exchanges and other brokerage firms will take care of you. They have too much at stake to let you down. The worst that will happen is that your stocks will be tied up for a couple of months, and that's a remote possibility.

You will also be asked to sign a couple of agreements that let him lend your stocks to short-sellers and pledge them as securities for loans. Again, don't fret—you'll never even know when it happens, and you'll *never* find it interfering with your transactions.

Keeping your stocks in street name makes so much sense that I won't brook any arguments. There is no reason to subject yourself to the bother of handling your stock certificates—they are an expensive nuisance. A friend lost a certificate and laid out $35 to replace it so that he could sell his stock at 12 instead of the 18 that had sent him searching for it in the first place. And even if you don't lose them, do you really need to cart them around and mail them back and forth?

In these days of back-room turmoil, when everybody's running late on deliveries if they make them at all, enjoy the luxury of a street-name account, with buying and selling made as easy as getting service from the local Dial-a-Chicken.

That ole debbil "margin call"

Memories of the crash somehow linger on—even in those who weren't born at the time (a phenomenon into which geneticists are delving). And the most fearsome echo of all is the clarion call of the margin. That was the call that had the big plungers taking the ultimate plunge, and the little investors hocking their spats.

Well, leave me state that I've never yet had a margin call and never expect to have one. Let me explain why.

The New York Stock Exchange, which kind of rules the

roast,* says the *current* market value of all the stock in your account, minus the amount you owe your broker, must be no less than 25 percent of that total current market value. Most brokers make it 30 percent. If your stocks are worth $10,000 and you owe your broker $3,000, the remainder (your equity) is $7,000—or 70 percent of total value and you're okay. Your equity would have to drop to about 30 percent before you got a margin call under those rules. The only way you could make your equity drop that low would be to ride your stocks down drastically—which you are not going to do. Or else have such a succession of losers that you'd better sell out anyway while you still have your gold inlays.

Keeping monthly records, as you will be instructed in Chapter 32, you will know where you are at all times. And, believe me, you will never come close to a margin call, specuvesting.

Maintaining margin is something else

There is one aspect of margin that will confuse you. While you will never get a margin call (which requires you to put up more money or sell some of your holdings), you will run into adjustments made to "maintain margin." These take place when you sell something. All of a sudden you find that some of the money you supposedly received on the sale vanished. All very legal and necessary—but confusing.

So, okay, let's take an example. Say you bought $1,000 worth of stock under a 70 percent margin requirement and the next day the margin requirement was raised to 80 percent. That wouldn't affect your previous purchase; you wouldn't have to put up more money or anything. But say you then sold that holding, breaking even on the deal

* No, Chester, "rules the roost" is a corruption. The saying referred to the master of the house, the head of the table. Sorry.

("and did I need it!"). You realize $1,000, $300 of which you owe to the broker. Under the increased margin requirements you cannot then buy $1,000 worth of stock, but only $875 worth (your $700 times 10, divided by 8).

It feels like you got gypped, but it only means your debt is reduced. He's simply lending you less money, not taking some of yours.

This also happens when your stocks go down and you are fully invested—you inadvertently are on your broker's books for more than current margin requirements permit. You don't get a call. But when you sell, he takes back enough of his own money to bring your loan down to the legal limit. You won't have as much to reinvest, but you'll owe him less. So don't get shook.

But there's a cozy little exception to the rule. The broker doesn't have to adjust your account *if you reinvest the sales money during the same trading day*. You can use the entire $1,000 to buy another stock that same day. This rule is a throwback to the pre-computer days, when it took overnight calculation to figure where you were with your account, and your account was "marked to the market" only once a week, unless you traded. Today your broker probably gets your account and every one of his other accounts printed out for him every morning, and he can figure your current status in five minutes. But nobody's pushing to change that rule.

The reason is simple. The broker doesn't make any money by reducing your loan. His company likes the interest on the higher loan as well as the commissions on the extra couple of hundred they'll let you invest. So if you buy another stock the same day, you can spend it all.

Now, that's fine if you have another stock that you're panting to buy. But you're foolish to rush into a purchase just to help enrich your broker. And it doesn't cost you a cent to "lose buying power" by having your debit balance reduced. So lose it, rather than risk making an unwise purchase—particularly if the entire market is trending down.

There used to be a neat way of eating your cake and having it. You'd buy a bond with your $1,000 that same day. Bonds don't fluctuate much, and they draw interest. Also, the commission is very low. So, when you eventually decided to buy something, you sold the bond and made your purchase, retaining all your buying power. The SEC decided to cut down on credit, though, and now if you buy a bond it has to be done in another account. That means your balance has to be adjusted before the money leaves your margin account, so that door is closed.

Today, your broker may suggest that you immediately buy some very conservative stock, such as a utility, to maintain your buying power at a minimum risk. The trouble is, you'll have a round-trip commission, plus taxes to pay on the whole $1,000 deal—and the stock may go down a couple of points. And that really is losing your money, whereas, you recall, just having your debit balance reduced is not losing money.

Let me give you a couple of specifics. On August 1, 1968, I sold 200 Ogden Corporation because it was dropping. I didn't want to reinvest it right away, but I didn't want to lose any buying power. So I bought Long Island Lighting at 28¼. A little over a month later, to go into Abex, I sold LILCO at 28. That fulfilled my mission—to maintain buying power by buying a stable stock. Result? A loss of $243.25 in commissions, transfer taxes, etc., on the transaction. Of *my* money, not my broker's.

Don't go for that holding action. Don't buy any stock except with the definite conviction that it is going up. Let your buying power drop a couple of hundred dollars. It's better than losing equity, 'cause that's money.

You'll need a cash account, too

One final confuser. If you have a margin account, you will require a cash account, too, because you can't buy most over-the-counter stocks on margin. That also applies to

National Exchange stocks and many Regional Exchange stocks. Specific American Exchange stocks, at your broker's option, are not marginable, and the American Exchange itself frequently puts high-flying stocks on 100 percent margin to cool them down, but all these will be purchased in your margin account for some obscure reason.

You have to transfer funds for the other cash purchases from your margin account to your cash account—losing about a third on the way over (but not *your* money, sonny, they just don't let you transfer the loaned part). However, when you move it the other way they margin it again.

And be of good cheer. You don't do the arithmetic, they do.

Chapter 19

Rule Number 9: AVERAGE UP—NEVER DOWN

Let's go through this very simple proposition again slowly. I will first be Mr. Average Q. Investor listening, perhaps, to my broker. I have bought 100 shares of United Grape Haulers at 40. It drops to 30, so I buy 100 more at that appealing number because, I am reminded, it need only go to 35 and I will have broken even on the entire transaction. And indeed I will have, if it goes up.

But it goes down and, not illogically if you grant the wisdom of the first move, I buy another hundred at 25. This is really a fortunate move because UGH need now rise only to 31⅝ for that great break-even day instead of all the way to 35 or 40. Of course I now have two and one-half times my original investment in good old UGH, but I'm protecting that original investment, aren't I?

I aren't. I'm compounding my original mistake, that's what I'm doing. Why shouldn't the stock keep dropping even farther? Why this mania for breaking even? Why is a bad stock worth such a large part of my funds? And a stock that is dropping is a bad stock.

Do you know what I, Mr. Average Q. Investor, say at this point? All together now—"I can't afford to sell, I've got too much of a loss." Boy, am I mixed up. You can *always* afford to sell—it's "buy" you often can't afford to do. Selling doesn't cost you any of your own money; it may keep you from making some or recouping some, but it doesn't cost you anything you haven't already lost.

Don't "average down." Don't buy more of a stock that's dropping. You watch it like a hawk, and if it keeps dropping you sell it. Even if you think it's going to turn around tomorrow, you sell it. Then buy in again after it turns around, if you still think it's good.

Now let me be Mr. Enlightened Q. Specuvestor. I buy 100 General Energy Elimination at 40 (anything with "energy" in it has to be great). Indeed it is, so I get another 100 at 50. And another at 55. GEE goes to 67, then drops back to 60. There I sell the lot purchased at 55, but hold the others back. Reasons: (*1*) take your smaller gain first (remember all three lots are *worth* the same, they simply represent different profits). (*2*) A recovery might give me six months on those held longest, so that I could benefit from a long-term situation. (*3*) There was still hope for a recovery, so I didn't want to close out my position.

No recovery, however. After hovering around 60 and moving back up to 62, GEE is no longer a whiz; it starts to slide and I get out completely at 58.

In that venture I did two things that should be usual but are strictly un. I bought more on the way up. And I refused to ride the stock down. If it had gone to 120 without serious setback, I would have held it all the way and probably bought more en route—but when it dropped, so did I.

Let's count up my gains, even though they're hypothetical. Lot A: bought at 40, sold at 58—that's a 45 percent gain (minus commissions, etc.). Lot B: 50 to 58—that's 16 percent. Lot C: 55 to 60—that's only 9 percent, but in a rather short time. Your money compounds quite nicely if you can make 9 percent every month or two. As a matter of fact, 9 percent every three months comes to over 41 percent annually.

Wrassle yourself and win

There are two reasons people don't like to buy a stock again at a higher price ("average up," if you don't mind a phrase no one ever uses). Since both are purely psychological, I even hesitate to use the word "reason." Firstly, you don't feel smart paying more for something you could have bought cheaper. Secondly, it's obvious you'll make less money with your second purchase—and even less with a third—and that seems like a questionable deal.

Neither argument holds water. You're not in this to feel smart, but it certainly is smart to put money into a stock that has *proved* to be superior. You have to invest in something, and here's a stock you *know* is good. If you have to fool yourself, pretend it's a tip from somebody else and you'll jump at it.

As for making less money, that's counterbalanced by the fact that it will be tied up for a shorter period of time before the stock peaks out. I've just demonstrated how time means money—how 9 percent every three months beats the heck out of 25 or 30 percent in a year. And you'd sure grab 25 or 30 percent a year.

Wrestle with yourself next time a stock of yours moves up. What better investment beckons than that very stock? Keep buying it till you just break even on the last purchase, or even lose a little. Then don't ask yourself why on earth you didn't leave well enough alone on the last turn—instead, figure how much more you made in toto than if you'd just sat on your first purchase.

Incidentally, I'm using round lot illustrations simply because it helps my arithmetic, which is very bad. Naturally, it all applies to odd lots, too.

Wall Street has it all wrong. When a stock drops, they like to call it a "buying opportunity." If they mean a good chance to make money, they should call it a buying opportunity when a stock goes up, instead.

Chapter 20

Rule Number 10: KEEP TASTING STOCKS

There's not an odd-lotter in the world who wouldn't rather purchase round lots. Now I'm going to tell you to buy odd lots purposely, even if you have the buying power for a hundred shares. There are good reasons.

1. You never really watch a stock unless you own it.
2. There's never any way of knowing, in advance, what a stock is going to do.
3. If you buy in large quantities you tie your hands.

We've covered the fact that you should hold a limited number of securities, so I'm not suggesting you dabble. But do follow a policy of getting your feet wet before you plunge. In later days, when you're dealing in large sums, do your foot-wetting in round lots if you wish, but still keep the initial investment proportionately low.

It's obvious you can't hold all the stocks that are going up. I hope you're adult enough not to worry if someone else is making money faster than you—next time it will be your stocks that are beating his. And even if the rest of the investing world should somehow be doubling its money annually, I hope you'll be content resting on your fat little 30 percent.

So don't ever be afraid you'll miss out if you don't rush in and corner the market. Take small bites.

When an issue interests you, go into it. When it works out, buy more. Feel your way, so that when you're wrong you don't get hurt but when you're right you do get rolling.

There's always a big debate about whether you should be fully invested at all times. Well, of course not. You can't let buying power burn a hole in your pocket. But there's no sense letting it sit idle if there's a good specuvestment around. Use it to buy more of a holding that is already doing well. Or use it to taste another issue you've had your eye on.

In a good market you'll want to be more fully invested than in a bad. When the entire atmosphere is bearish, let your funds accumulate as you sell off your sliding issues. Remember, you never lose buying power once it's in your account—even if they raise the margin requirement or the value of your holdings drops. Your broker can tell you at any time what that buying power is as of right then. You don't pay interest on buying power in a margin account. Let it sit till you have a conviction about one stock, then taste it.

Don't worry about the commissions on these small purchases. I once read about a baseball pitcher who dislocated his arm swatting a fly. Maintain perspective and you'll see that your main task is not to keep expenses down but to keep losses down—and profits up. Your best approach to that goal is through tasting your stocks before you really bite.

Chapter 21

Rule Number 11: TAKE SHORT-TERM GAINS

Let's get one thing clear. That doesn't mean grab them and run. It means, if a stock is dropping, sell it whether you'll realize a long-term or a short-term gain. I've seen too many good profits slip away to have any illusions that it pays to wait. Naturally, I've seen cases where it would seem to have paid to wait, where the stock dropped very little for months after a sale. Just as I've seen plenty of cases where the stock should have been held, not sold at all, because it turned right around and went back up.

But run your portfolio on percentages. And the percentages say that when a stock is dropping it keeps going. You'll be right in the majority of cases, by far, if you sell willy-nilly, regardless of whether it's long or short term.

If you're close to the wire, and it's only a couple of weeks to the six-months' break, then seriously consider waiting. But many a man has found to his sorrow that he's solved the problem of paying high taxes by letting time eat away all his profits. That's bad for the soul and doesn't do much for the wallet, either.

I've made up a formula to help me figure how much profit I can let slip away while letting a short-term gain mature into a long-term gain. It goes like this, and I'm proud of it:

A = the amount of long-term profit that would net the same amount as your current short-term profit.

B = 100 percent, minus your tax bracket (approximate income tax percentage you pay Uncle).

C = 100 percent, minus half your tax bracket.

$$A = \frac{\text{profit} \times B}{C}$$

For example, if you have a profit of $1,000 and are in a 30 percent tax bracket, it works out like this:

$$A = \frac{\$1,000 \times 70}{85}$$

$$A = \frac{\$700}{85}$$

$$A = \$823$$

In other words, if you're in the 30 percent bracket, you'll net as much with a long-term profit of $823 as you will with a short-term profit of $1,000. That means if you have 100 shares with a 10-point gain you can lose 1¾ points and net as much. If the $1,000 gain was obtained on 10 shares, you can lose 17¾ points. Naturally, the spread is wider as your tax bracket goes up (if your bracket is above 50 percent, the divisor stays at 75 because the tax stays at 25). So, if you're in the 70 percent bracket, you can actually break even by holding only 4 points of the current 10-point gain (work it out). I hope that, with my help, you get there, too.

But if you're in that 30 percent bracket and your 100 shares drops 2 points, instead of the 1¾, then you've lost money by waiting. *And here's the point most people miss —you've lost the use of your money while you waited.*

Let me state that proposition in relation to the other rules we've covered. You wouldn't buy a stock that was dropping. You definitely would sell a stock that was dropping. The reason is that stocks have momentum, and a sliding stock is more likely to keep sliding from any point than it is to go up from that point. So why, in the illustration given above, would you take a chance on the stock recovering before it slipped that fatal 1¾ points more? Very early, I stated that you must not make decisions based on any considerations but market considerations. Since neither the company whose stock it is nor the market itself will know or care whether you pay 30 percent tax or 15, it is definitely not a market consideration. So dump the stock unless you're right on the edge of the period, or your tax bracket is a high one. Then you may want to sweat it out.

Now consider the other negative—you lose the use of your money. When you set out to make your 30 percent, don't necessarily expect to make it all in one stock, or in a couple of stocks held for the entire year. You might do that or even better, but it's just not likely. It would be a lucky group of selections that, held for a year or more, would deliver the gains you need to cover any losses and still end up that much ahead. So the specuvestor is in and out of stocks all the time—not because there's virtue in trading, but because his rules dictate such movement.

Funds held in a sinking stock (say that fast, I dare you) are not only not being properly used, they are in jeopardy. Funds held as buying power are in no danger whatsoever and are immediately available for further growth.

Chapter 22

Rule Number 12: BUY OR SELL "AT THE MARKET"

There is a fatal fascination in stealing half a point or so. It works on buyers and it works on sellers. The quote is 24⅞ bid—25¼ asked; the sharpshooter will say, "Put me in for it at 25." The rug merchant will say, "Put in a sell at 25⅛." Both of them think they're being shrewd, but they're just being stupid. The market is enough of a gamble, but at least it's for high stakes. Here are these two fellows trying to make a trade, and they may not both make it.

If the stock goes up, the sharpshooter draws a blank. He may never buy the issue, or may have to pay a point or considerably more extra, later. A characteristic of those who put in a bid at a specific price is that they are stubborn; they'll be determined to wait till it gets down to that price again before they buy. Then, if that does happen, they buy into a declining situation after missing what may have been a marvelous run-up.

If the stock goes down, the rug merchant doesn't get the sale off. Who knows where it will drop to before he gets his ego under control sufficiently to try again?

Of course, they may both get their way. Stocks fluctuate

enough to make that possible. But why take the chance. If he gets his way the sharpshooter will save $12 on a multi-thousand-dollar transaction. The rug merchant will net that same fabulous sum—all at the risk of not making the trade at all.

Don't put in a specific bid or offer. Buy or sell "at the market." Your broker and the floor men representing his firm at the exchange are bound by law, honor, and their Boy Scout oaths to get you the best deal they can. *And* you will be sure of making your trade. If the stock is so precarious that half a point or even a full point will make or break you, stay out of it. If you're already in and want out, don't let a few dollars stand in the way of your decision. Get out.

On exchanges other than the NYSE, or on over-the-counter stocks, there is some reason for stipulating a price. Ask for a quote (let's say it's "20 to a half") then buy or sell at "20¼ or better." This gives you control, usually without delaying the trade.

The myth of the "stop-loss"

You have a profit in your stock. You want to protect that profit. You put in what you blithely call a "stop-loss" order. And you're kidding yourself. Take an example:

You bought Gaines-Galore at 30, it's now at 42. You tell your broker to sell if it goes back to 40. No matter what you ask for, that's what you get—not necessarily 40 but an order to sell when the stock touches 40. There's really no such thing as a "stop-loss" order; it's a "stop" order. And it doesn't stop anything except your freedom to handle your own affairs.

Gaines-Galore drops to 40. This triggers your "stop," which now becomes a *market order* to sell your stock at the best possible price. Not only does that not necessarily mean at 40, it may get off many points below 40—and won't you be surprised!

190

Your stop order gets into line behind all the other stops on that stock at 40 received by the specialist up to the precise moment when your broker puts yours in. When Gaines-Galore touches 40, he starts matching up orders, starting with the first order on his 40-stop list. He may or may not get that one off at 40. Meanwhile any market orders that come in take precedence over any stop order he has. So yours gets shoved even farther back. The retreat may become a rout, and you may finally get 35 or even 30 for your stock. And it's all perfectly legit and logical.

The specialist's job is to "maintain an orderly market." To do this he will trade for his own account, so as to smooth the fluctuations. But no rule says he has to go broke doing it, so when a stock really wants to dive, he has to stop the trading or let it dive. And a stop order puts you in a position where it can land on *you.*

Remember this: *A stop becomes an order to sell a stock at the market price, as soon as the stock touches the stop price.* The price may go up or down before your sale goes through. Believe me, it usually goes down. There is, however, a device that makes sure you don't get sold out for less than you expected to get. This is called a "stop-limit" order. If you put in a stop limit at 40 on Gaines-Galore, the stock would not be sold unless you could get 40 or better for it. A stop-limit order does not trigger a market order, *but you may not sell your stock.* A stop-loss order triggers a market order at the stop price and you will very definitely sell your stock, *but you may not get your price.* Neither eventuality is a great comfort.

Stops placed *above* the market price are called "limits." Gaines-Galore is at 38; you decide to sell if it hits 40, so you put in a limit order at 40. If the broker can't get 40, he doesn't sell. It's foolish to put in limit orders, because you are guessing that if the stock reaches that price it will go no higher. You can't guess tops or bottoms. Let the stock decide what it wants to do.

There's a chain reaction in stops. They trigger each other, and, in turn, the decline causes traders to put in sell orders that trigger more stops, and so forth. This being a country run by the decimal system, such rushes are particularly noticeable around the ten figures and, to a lesser extent, around the fives. Semismart investors therefore shun the point itself and put their stops in at an eighth or so above or below, according to which direction the price must go to reach it. But really smart investors don't use stops. And they're glad, when the stock rebounds sharply from the artificial selling pressure imposed by this triggering effect.

Your broker's no baby-sitter

The use of a stop or limit to prevent a loss is identical to that which supposedly protects a profit. As I keep saying, it makes no difference to the market if you have a gain or a loss, so the same system pertains. And my same advice, too. If you want to sell, sell. If you're worried, watch your stock and sell when advisable.

Don't make your broker a baby-sitter; he's simply not set up to change diapers. The system that has been established is almost a shrug of the shoulders. It's mechanical, unthinking, and often a failure at protecting you. But it's all you could expect. There's only one person who can give you personal service and that person is you, personally.

There's an unofficial pipe dream called the "floating stop," which is an order to your broker to keep moving your stop up, say, 2 points behind the stock as it rises. You should live so long. After you have your first million, maybe you can find some untalented bloke to play nursemaid that way, but meanwhile you're on your own.

When limits are acceptable

As always, there are exceptions. If you're going to be completely out of touch for a long time, talk to your broker about putting limits (stops) on some of your holdings. But be prepared for disappointments when you get back.

Incidentally, anywhere in this country is not "out of touch." While you shouldn't abuse it, long-distance reverse-charge calls are completely acceptable (note clever phrasing) to your broker. Make them brief and infrequent, but do make them if you're worried or if one of your stocks is wobbling. Tell your broker in advance that you're going away, so that he will be prepared for such a call and may just possibly watch your stocks a little more closely. Mind you, he doesn't have to, and you can't fault him for failure to do so. But he will if he can, because he'd like to help you make money. For that matter, since the telephone is a completely adequate means of communication, many investors use brokers hundreds and even thousands of miles away. It's better than using a local man you don't believe in.

The New York Stock Exchange is very orderly, and a market order is relatively safe there. In other words, if a stock is 21 to a half (that's the way quotes are reported; you interpret it "21 bid–21½ asked") you can be fairly sure of selling at 21 or better, or buying at 21½ or lower. The American Exchange (sorry, fellows) is a little wilder, and it goes downhill from there. The over-the-counter market is Nutsville, as far as quotes are concerned, so in all those markets use a little caution. When buying on those, since a quote is not at all binding, you might tell your broker to "buy at offer or quote." When selling you might say "sell at bid or quote." Then you don't take a hosing. He is duty bound to get you the best price, so if he can beat the bid or offer price he will. But if he can't make the trade at the bid (when you're selling) or the offer (when you're buying), the "or quote" part of your order means he has to call you back with another quote. Then you can move it up or down to fit the new quote, but still keep control.

You may think this contradicts what I said in this chapter, about saving fractions, but it doesn't. It applies mainly to the wide-swinging stocks and mainly to over-the-counter and the smaller exchanges. Its purpose is not to chisel half a point but to protect you and maintain control. And, by the way, the "spread" in those instances can be several points—which is really cause for concern.

There are several kinds of limit order, among them "today only" and "good till cancelled" (GTC). When you plan to be away and are protecting yourself, use the GTC. Otherwise make it "today only" and don't even let the trading day close without acting. If your broker doesn't call you by half an hour before closing, you call him and find out what's happening. This is the one time you do have a legitimate demand on his time. If you've decided to make the trade, don't let fractions of a point deter you. This means you have no reason for using the other forms —"good this week" (cancelled at Friday closing), or "good this month" (cancelled at the close of the last trading day of this calendar month). Unless some such date coincides with your return from a trip, it's better to make it "GTC" and then call in and cancel. Gives you a good chance to discuss what has transpired in your absence.

"Good this week" and other examples of that type of precise nonsense amuse me. Despite all the statistics about year-end rallies and sell-offs prior to extended holidays, it's never yet been demonstrated that a stock knew what day it was.

Chapter 23

Rule Number 13: DIVERSIFY

If you could put all your money into one real winner you'd certainly be better off than if you scattered your shots. Now turn the coin over; if you are so unlucky as to put all your money into a real loser, you can be in serious trouble.

Do you need the extra profits that concentration in one or even two issues might give you? No—it would be nice to get them, but you can't say you *have* to have them. Can you stand the severe loss that concentration in a couple of bad stocks might give you? Absolutely, categorically, no— you have to protect your capital.

That's why you diversify—not because you make more money that way, but because it spreads the risk and helps prevent fatal mistakes. If you accept that premise, then you can go on to the supposition that diversification might also help you to make more money in the long run because it helps you find winners in which, then, to concentrate.

Specuvesting policy certainly calls for having more money in some stocks than in others. But you build up that imbalance as the winners start to emerge; you don't decide in advance that one stock or two stocks deserve it all.

Time out for an English lesson. I wrote a letter for a local organization to send out, and one of my friends objected to my starting a sentence with "and." It simply wasn't good grammar. I told him I believe you should write the way people talk, and that he himself didn't try to use proper sentence structure when he talked. "But I don't start sentences with 'and,'" he replied. End of very human story.

There are two kinds of diversification; simply buying several different stocks or making sure they are in different industries as well. While it would be bad practice to concentrate everything in a single industry, there is nothing wrong in having two or three issues of your entire portfolio in one industry. The stock market is like any other auction. Today, if you had your choice between selling three Tiffany chandeliers or an assortment consisting of one chandelier, a spinning wheel, and a horsehair sofa, you'd be wise to choose the chandeliers. Maybe horsehair sofas will be very big tomorrow, and there's a nice market for them right now—but Tiffany gets the play today. In the market you buy only to sell, so don't hesitate to buy more than one fad piece. That's often better than putting all your fad money in one issue. Remember, though, buy some unrelated industries, too.

My current portfolio

Take a look at my own portfolio. To play fair, I'll give you my holdings as I write this. I've held more balanced proportionments in the past, and I've held more lopsided ones. But here's what specuvesting has prompted me to hold:

ISSUE	INDUSTRY	% OF PORTFOLIO	
Daryl	Building supply	4.4	
Warner Bros.-7 Arts	Entertainment	18.9	
Franklin Mint	Coinage	40.5	
MITE	Data Transmission	3.4	
Stelma	Data Transmission	5.4	11.5
Astrodata	Data Transmission	2.7	
Abex	Industrial Parts	21.6 (special situation)	
Cash		3.1	

196

Understand, this does not reflect my investment in these stocks, but my current equity. A table on invested amounts is somewhat deceptive, since they were all bought at different times and some several times, so they at no time represented a percentage that corresponds to the amount invested. However, it would read like this:

ISSUE	% OF INVESTMENT	NUMBER OF PURCHASES	FIRST PURCHASED
Daryl	3.1	1	7/ 7/67
Warner Bros.-7 Arts	26.1	3	3/10/67
Franklin Mint	21.3	3	3/28/68
MITE	6.7	1	8/ 1/68
Stelma	7.7 } 18.4	1	10/22/68
Astrodata	4.0	1	11/13/68
Abex	31.1	2	9/12/68

Don't try to relate the two tables. Look at them simply as an example of random diversification based on what I thought individual stocks would do and on what they subsequently did. The first table represents sizeable gains in several stocks, satisfactory progress in several, and a loss in one.

Not one of these holdings is the result of consciously deciding to find a good stock in a specific industry. It is significant that my biggest investment at the time was in Abex, explained earlier as a move to get a relatively small gain at relatively low risk.

Keeping monthly rundowns as prescribed later permits me to go back over seven years of records. Only once have I held precisely the same amounts of the same stocks two months in a row. I claim no virtue for this; it just happened as a result of stock action. But I assure you it's not restlessness but flexibility. I would much rather hold a stock than sell it.

For many years I have never held fewer than eight issues or more than fifteen and I notice that the bigger my account gets the fewer issues I hold. A better man than I (oh, surely there must be) will have to figure out which is cause and which effect on that one. The key, as stated before, is to hold as many issues as is comfortable. Not a specific number, because with our system of tasting stocks, adding to winners, and dumping losers, you have to stay flexible. But there's safety in numbers, and tremendous opportunity as well. With luck and good judgment you'll always be in the position of holding small quantities of a new winner to which you'd like to add.

Chapter 24

Rule Number 14: BEWARE THE BLUE CHIPS

Sometimes good isn't good enough. Not when better is within reach—and you can do better if, by and large, you stay away from the blue-chip stocks. Blasphemy it is, but leave them to the pension funds and institutions, which need large gobs of respectability and solidity to keep everybody off their necks. You, Little Guy, cannot afford the limited gains their relative safety usually offers.

I will quote another definition from the NYSE's *Language of Investing*. They say a blue chip is "Common stock in a company known nationally for the quality and wide acceptance of its products or services, and for its ability to make money and pay dividends in good times and bad. Usually such stocks are relatively high priced and offer relatively low yields."

I could not have stated my case better, for you know by now that specuvesting does not permit much interest in long-term stability or in dividends. You must try for maximum gain—and the blue chips usually don't supply that. When they do show life, as in the fall of 1968, you'll hear trumpet blasts and can buy into them for the rise, if you've a mind. But normally their good, solid virtue has to be its own reward.

Nobody can really damn the blue chips (nobody can even define them, for that matter). So I retreat to my rather feeble position that, even when they are at their best, you can do better. To demonstrate this I will take the period from January 2 to November 15, 1968, and compare some blue ones with some growth ones. And remember, this was a kindly stretch for the upper-crust stocks, with the D-J Index rising from 910 to 965, despite an early spring drop.

Random blues vs. me

Since there'll be criticism of any selection I make, let's just pick all the bluest among those stocks called "American" something. Nobody'd better carp at my growth selections, though, because they're the ones I held during most of that period. (I've left out some over-the-counter stocks I held, so the picture will be clearer.)

So here's the way the two groups looked:

RANDOM BLUE CHIPS

ISSUE	PRICE ON 1/2/68	PRICE ON 11/15/68	% '68 GAIN (LOSS) TO 11/15	ALL-TIME HIGH PRICE
Am. Broadcasting	63	68	7.8	102
Am. Can	51	54	5.9	64
Am. Cyanimid	26	33	26.9	48
Am. Elec. Pow.	36	40	11.1	47
Am. Enka	41	53	29.3	currently
Am. Home Prod.	56	57	1.7	67 ('68)
Am. Mach. & Fdry.	20	26	30.0	63
Am. Met. Climax	48	43	(10.5)	65
Am. Nat. Gas	35	43	22.8	55
Am. Smelt. & Ref.	72	69	(4.2)	78 ('68)
Am. Standard	32	46	33.3	currently
Am. Tel. & Tel.	51	56	9.8	75
Am. Tobacco	32	34	6.2	55

SELECTED GROWTH STOCKS

ISSUE	PRICE ON 1/2/68	PRICE ON 11/15/68	% '68 GAIN (LOSS) TO 11/15	ALL-TIME HIGH PRICE
Can. Javelin	11	14	27.2	30
Daryl	4	6	50.0	10
Franklin Mint	18	127	605.5	currently
Ogden Corp.	43	38	(11.6)	52 ('68)
Raymond Int.	18	27	50.0	39 ('68)
Warner-7 Arts	35	47	34.3	50

Twist it and turn it any way you want. I know you wouldn't buy *all* those blue chips, so pick any six—or three —or one. They had great gains, some of them; there have been years when we'd all love to have had a few like them. But they don't stack up.

Notice, too, that half the growth stocks listed hit their all-time highs in 1968. Including Ogden, which rang up the only loss for the period (ask yourself whether I rode it down).

What's the moral of the story? Simple. Good market or bad, many other stocks will outperform the blue chips. Not all other stocks, naturally, but selected growth stocks.

And that's what we've been talking about, isn't it? Selection?

Select a blue chip on occasion, if its fundamentals interest you. Like American Standard, which was merging like mad and so actually qualified as a special situation. But, ordinarily, look on the blues with a jaundiced eye, which should make a delightful color scheme—and should also help make you more money.

Chapter 25

Rule Number 15: DON'T GET FANCY

There are so many get-rich-quick temptations in the market. And the funny part is, you really don't need them to get rich quick. If they didn't have such get-poor-quicker qualities, all these slick operations would be great. But one characteristic of the market is the higher the chance for gain, the greater the risk.

That's why I link my policy of buying possibly risky growth stocks and situations with an inflexible policy of selling when they drop. It's the only way to cut the risk down to manageable size. And that's why you must not fool around with all the fancy-pants aberrations. Like selling short. Like day-trading. Like buying puts and calls. Like buying commodity futures.

Here's why they don't make sense:

Short-selling. When you buy a stock (there's no such things as "going long" or "buying long"; the opposite of "sell short" is "buy"), your risk is limited. It may be very great, indeed, but it is limited. If you pay $50 a share for a stock and it goes to absolute zero, you will lose $50 a share. No more, ever. But if you short a stock at $50 and it goes to $100 before you cover, you will lose $50 a share. If it goes to $150 you will lose $100 a share. Would you like to try for the next plateau? Don't think it hasn't happened.

Naturally, as a confirmed specuvestor, you will sell the $50 stock you bought before it gets to zero—long before. So isn't it just as natural to cover your short position long before the stock doubles? Not necessarily. And again it is the psychology of the market that rules your mind. When the stock you own declines, you have the feeling that your information was wrong, or the advice you got was wrong, or maybe you just got in too late (which was probably the case, at that). While the dreadful tendency of many people is to sit with that stock, for any one of a number of self-deluding reasons, the feeling of being wrong grows stronger as the stock goes lower.

That may not be the case with the holder of a short position. There's a certain kind of nut who gets into real trouble. When the stock rises after he goes short, he's disappointed, but its rise somehow confirms his strong feeling that it is too high. He doesn't regret having gotten into that situation, he just recognizes that he was a little early. The higher it gets, the surer he is that a tumble is imminent. He hates that stock because it can't do that to him. It's going up on nothing. Boy, is it going to come down. No amateur can be phlegmatic about a short sale—it involves you emotionally. And that's murder.

Your reaction may be exactly the opposite—in fact, brokers say the majority of small short-sellers are so scared that, in the classic pun of the market, they "run to cover" at the slightest rise in price. This is just as irrational as the actions of their more stubborn fellows. And it all works against your chances of making out on a short sale.

Don't get the idea you won't get caught up in this. You will. Furthermore, the cards are stacked against you in many ways. Like the general trend of the market. Up, up. And, sometimes, away.

Take the business of the "up tick." There's an innocent and thoroughly logical stock exchange rule that says you can't go short on a stock except at a price higher than was paid on the previous trade—an "up tick." Or it can be a trade at the same price as the last one, as long as the previous different price was lower—an "even tick," or a "zero-plus tick." Any selling pressure is a depressant, and, if there were no such rule, short sales would accelerate the decline. But the rule puts the short-seller at an immediate disadvantage because the stock is going up when you short it.

A tax ruling recently front-paged an example of a calamitous short venture tried by one couple back in 1963. They had the misfortune of selling 11,700 shares of Syntex short at that time. By the end of the year, when they finally covered, they were out $1,000,000. That's $85 a share. Why did these people let Syntex go up 85 points before they covered? Same reason you would—it's the hardest loss in the world to swallow.

So don't bite.

Day-trading. All covered in Chapter 1. It's not investing! It's not specuvesting. It's just plain crap-shooting. No sense to it and no need for it. In fact, you'll hear from your broker if your account shows a day-trading pattern. Today they don't like it, either.

Puts and calls. Again, I've covered the mechanics previously (p. 94). These devices are not for you because they cost too much in terms of a stock's movement. Here's a put offered in a recent advertisement. "Braniff Airways . . . 19⅝ 6 mos. 187.50." The stock had closed on the previous trading day at 21⅝. The offer means that, for a payment of $187.50, you could sell 100 shares of Braniff any time within the next six months at 19⅝. For you to break even (not counting commissions, etc.) Braniff would have to go down to 17¾. That's an 18 percent drop before you make dime one.

Here's a call, from the same ad: "Randolph Computer . . . 41 5 mos. 587.50." With the stock having closed at 41¾, a rise to 46⅞ would just bring you even—a gain of 13 percent.

It hurts to be that right and have nothing to show for it, and it should. Naturally, if Braniff dropped below 17¾ you'd start to make $100 a point, and that's the appeal. If Randolph went above 48⅜, $100 a point, too. But it's too big an if. The holder of a put or call is usually lucky to get part of his money back. He can exercise his option any time within the option period, but people are both optimistic and greedy, and the deal is rarely closed out before the end. Even if the stock moves in the right direction he exercises the put or call on the last day of the option for his profit or whatever he can recover. If Randolph went to 43⅞ he could get back about half his money by buying the 100 shares at 41 and selling them for a "profit" of $287.50. But he'd have a very real net loss on the deal. If it ended up above 48⅜ he'd make a buck.

When the stock goes the wrong way you lose the entire option price and just let it expire—presumably feeling very smart for not having bought or shorted the stock itself. But you weren't smart at all. Tell you who was. The dealer was—as was some big investor or fund or insurance company or some other agency that guaranteed to deliver the stock to the dealer if you exercised your option. These people have a standing arrangement to make stock available on these deals. They then get the lion's share of your option money, with only a commission going to the dealer. Why do they enter into this kind of a transaction? Because they know there's very little chance the stock will go far enough in the right direction for you to bother to exercise your option. Good reason? Discouraging reason.

The grim part is that the Little Guy is very likely to see options as a way of applying leverage with his money. Instead of using it to buy stocks, he places it all in options, figuring he can raise the money to exercise them if he makes out. And he just dribbles it away, with all the odds against him.

Remember what I said about not being forced into selling by a specific time, because the market or your stock is bound to be down at that time. That's one of the big problems with options. The market is not going to roll over for you on schedule. Not consistently, if ever.

"Once-a-week instructions to your broker take care of all trading details. Our weekly letter tells you where to buy, sell, take profits, or place stops. Learn to increase capital and income in these fast-moving markets that enable your funds to work ten times as hard as they can in common stocks."

That ad is talking about commodity futures. Sound too good to be true? Not a bit. Certainly, once-a-week instructions are enough for any broker. Then, too, it only says they'll tell you *"where* to buy, sell, take profits, or place stops," not *when*. Certainly you can "learn to increase capital and income," but that doesn't say you can apply what you learn. The markets are indeed "fast moving," all rightee, and they do "enable your funds to work ten times as hard as they can in common stocks."

They can work *up* ten times as fast, and they can work *down* ten times as fast. Fortunes are made ten times as fast and lost at the same mad pace. The market is the commodities market, where millionaires are in burlap and pork bellies are more precious than gold. Yea, than Mitch Feingold, as the Bible says.

I don't know anything about commodity futures. I don't want any more intimate acquaintance than the conversations I've had with assorted people who do know something about them. There is an occasional slight tendency to relate them to investing and the stock market. Don't you believe it.

Chapter 26

Rule Number 16: DUCK DIVIDENDS

Dividends are comforting. They're a light in the window and smoke rising from the chimney. They're a mother's smile and the good smell of fresh-baked bread. They are also a drag, a handicap, a security blanket, and an elaborate shrug of the shoulders.

Dividends drain off money that could better be used for expansion, debt retirement, research, and development. A company only pays dividends to make its stock more popular. Try to think of one other reason. Companies that are booming along, with new products and new markets opening up, don't need or want to pay dividends. Their stock is popular without dividends. They may make small payments that are a throwback to a less popular time or a concession to those who feel naked in a stock that has no dividend. But the yield of such stocks is seldom attractive because the price will have risen while the dividend payout didn't.

Conversely, companies whose stocks offer a high yield obviously feel they don't need the money. Or they may be under such tight government control that they can't use it (like utilities). Or it may, as I say, be their only bid for popularity.

Let's look at some yields (the annual dividend divided

by the current market price): IBM—.8%; Polaroid—.3%; Ling-Temco-Vought—1.4%; General Atlantic & Pacific Tea—5.2%; Great Western United—1.6%; Consolidated Edison—5.4%; Bethlehem Steel—5.1%.

Do you see any pattern? Take your monthly Stock Guide and leaf through it. Stagnant stocks (or stable, if you prefer positive thinking) have high yields. Dynamic stocks don't. In many cases it's a simple matter of arithmetic. As a price goes up, the yield goes down. But, conversely, some of the fattest yields are the result of a stock that ordinarily yields 3 percent, dropping a flock of points and ending up with a 5 percent yield on the same dividend. This, rather definitely, does not make it a good buy.

You will get some dividends when you invest—they simply come with some stocks, like giblets in a chicken. So you should understand yield. It is utterly fallacious to figure your yield on your purchase price. Some advisers tell you to, but that's not realistic. You have to figure yield on today's prices, because your equity is figured on today's price. The money you had in the stock a year ago has no bearing on the situation, whether it's more or less than you have today. You buy a stock at 20 and get a $1 dividend, and that's a 5 percent yield. If the stock goes to 40 with the same dividend, how can you think you're still getting 5 percent? Might as well say that the man who now buys it at 40 will get 5 percent. That's one you *should* argue with your friends.

Mind you, a dividend rise is a nice thing to happen to a stock you own, because flocks of people will always cotton to dividends—and some of them should, if they're retired or need the income. For you, it's just an extra puff of wind that moves your little boat faster.

Part of that income is outgo

Don't ever lose sight of the annoying fact that dividends are fully taxable as regular income. This can make them an expensive luxury if your bracket is comfortably high. And, naturally, following the precepts of this book will put you there in no time. Well, eventually, anyway.

I should mention, in this connection, the "tax-exempts." These are state, county, and municipal bonds whose interest is, by federal law, exempt from income taxes. The 3 to 4 percent yield offered by these bonds is, therefore, the equivalent of much higher yields available in some common stocks or in ordinary bonds. Naturally, their true value to you depends on your tax bracket. Expect no growth from them; they will simply stand there and deliver money like a cow in a milking machine. However, the specuvestor will find it far more profitable to raise the calves. Ignore bonds—including tax-exempts. Ignore dividends.

Chapter 27

Rule Number 17: KICK THE MUTUAL CRUTCH

You can't expect to get something for nothing. When you buy a mutual fund you buy more than the stocks that that fund holds. You also buy its management. You pay for your tiny percentage of the value of all those stocks; you pay your tiny percentage of the management fees.

In return you expect growth—and sometimes you get it. The twenty-one closed-end investment trusts on the New York Stock Exchange gained an average 28 percent in 1967. The seventeen mutuals averaged a 37 percent gain. It should be stated that 1967 was an exceptional year. In 1968 the fifteen biggest closed-end trusts gained only 6.6 percent, while the seventeen mutuals rose only 1.8 percent. The D-J Industrial Index, during that period, was up 4.3 perment. Non (I suppose) sequitur: my own equity rose well over 50 percent in 1968, but I charge myself very little in management fees.

You can't count on any growth at all, however. Hark to the saga of Gerald Tsai, apostle of the go-go fund (formerly called the "adrenalin fund" before the world turned sexy). Mr. Tsai, then well on the down side of forty, was the wonder of Wall Street in 1965, as long-time manager of the fabulously successful Fidelity group of funds. Quite naturally he left to start his own chain of funds, starting with the Manhattan Fund in early 1966. He planned to issue a not-too-modest 2,500,000 shares, but had become so famous that he quickly sold 27,000,000 at $10 each, of which 85 cents was sales commission.

In 1967 the asset value of the Manhattan Fund had risen a fine, fat 39.42 percent. But, strangely enough, between February and October of 1967 sentiment turned around to a point where the Manhattan Fund has been continually redeeming more of its shares than it was selling—for a net redemption of an embarrassing $124,000,000 in 1968.

I don't know why people changed their minds while the fund was still doing well, but later defections could easily be traced to the go-go funds' stop-stop performance. In 1968 Manhattan Fund was down a discouraging 6.91 percent. By the way, another of Tsai's babies, Fundex, had gained 6.2 percent, but a third, Hemisphere Fund, had dropped 7.8 percent.

He who lives by the sword shall die by the sword. And it is fitting that the man who practically invented high performance should take a beating when he falls off the wire —and fitting that such swings have led to a distressing (to the funds) trend toward trading in mutual shares.

Trading tit for tat

Old-timers will recall a blackface comedy team—horrors— called "The Two Black Crows" ("I'll meet you down at the Post Office. You take this chalk. If you get there before I do, you draw a white line. If I get there before you do, I'll rub it out.") Well, they had a saying, "Now we got reciprocity." So, with the SEC and Congress investigating like mad to see what adverse effects their in-and-out trading have on the market, the funds were feverishly working to prevent just such trading in their own shares. Investors, particularly very big ones, would buy the fund that was rising fastest, then sell and buy into another that had picked up the baton. Most distressing and hardly cricket. Now we got reciprocity.

Funds always had a provision by which you could buy their shares during most of the next trading day at the previous day's closing price. The biggest blowoff came on April 1, 1968, the day after President Johnson simultaneously announced that he would bring the North Vietnam bombing and his own Presidency to a halt.

The funds got clobbered. All day Monday, while the D-J Industrial Index had its sharpest rise in nearly five years, big plungers bought mutuals at Friday's prices—grossing as much as 4.5 percent gain on that one move. Since the charge on a $1,000,000 purchase drops to as low as 1 percent, they netted a fine haul on a sure thing.

The funds used to depend on devices such as denying dealers commissions on such trading and, reportedly, on keeping a private blacklist of such traders. But you can bet they'll have closed that door more tightly by the time you read this—and besides, where would you get a million bucks?

The fund investor's millstones

Obviously, funds have no claim whatsoever to the omniscience and prescience ascribed to them by their busy salesmen. But, like the fellow said to the frustrated programmer, "Don't get mad at the computer. After all, it's only human!" The funds are only human, so they make mistakes, too. Only they needn't make their mistakes on *your* money.

Above all, they have no real claim to the fees they charge. Most of the attacks on funds are directed at the "front-end load." But behind that obvious target lies an evidently universal overcharging for management fees, custodial fees, and maintenance fees.

212

Let's dispose of the "load" aspect first. More and more "no-load" funds are springing up, mainly because of the growing discontent with the practice of charging 8 percent to 9 percent sales commission, which you pay on any purchase of a load fund. If you buy such a fund on a contract, you really take a shellacking. Specifically, if you sign a ten-year contract with a load fund you will pay within the first two years a large part of the total commission applicable to the entire ten-year span. This is called a "front-end load." It works out so that up to 50 percent of your first year's payments go—not for shares in the fund—but for commissions to the salesman or dealer. If you change your mind and cash in during that time, you'll get a nasty surprise.

The Securities Exchange Commission's 1966 study showed that one-third of all buyers of front-end loads quit before the fourth year of their ten-year contracts, despite having, by then, paid full commission for the first five years of that contract. Since you can't foresee your future money needs, you can't be sure of being able to pay a certain sum monthly for ten years. But the funds and their salesmen can be sure you'll take care of them, because commissions come out first.

The answer, of course, was the no-load fund. More and more of them are becoming more and more popular today. But they still soak you. Their purchasers remain, for the most part, utterly ignorant of the true size of the management fee charged. This fee is covered by an innocent-sounding fraction of a percent per year. The charge runs up to 1 percent in some funds, which still sounds innocent. But a clearer look shows something surprising. The percentage is, quite naturally, paid on total assets, not on profit or appreciation. And that's a horse of another hue.

Say a fund has $100,000,000 in assets. It makes an actual 10 percent gain in the year. Very nice. The management fee is .75 percent—three-fourths of a percent. Fair enough. Except that means they actually get .75 percent of the full $110,000,000—or $825,000. That's 8¼ percent of the gain.

Surprise! That teentsy little three-quarters of a percent is one heck of a bite—and it's getting bigger. Especially in the years when there ain't no gain. In addition, there are usually custodial fees and bookkeeping fees that drain off more of the income.

A 1962 study by the Wharton School of Finance concluded that management fees bear no relationship either to the performance of the fund or to the cost of running the fund. It is also felt that, in these days of electronic data-processing, such fees are, in the word of one widely syndicated columnist, "outrageous."

There's another little aspect you never considered. If you buy into a fund that has a large amount of unrealized gains, you will eventually be paying a share of the tax on all those gains—despite having already paid for the gains themselves, which were figured into asset value when you bought your shares. This may or may not balance out when you sell your shares. If at that time the fund has liquidated a large portion of its holdings, you may be doubly hit.

Perhaps the best answer to the question as to whether your money is better invested by you than by a flock of distant experts is contained in this testimony given before the 1967 congressional hearings on the situation:

"In most instances, the benefits of portfolio diversification and professional management afforded by a mutual fund investment, but not by an investment in an individual stock, were completely offset by the much higher costs of the fund investment." The speaker was Mr. Manuel Cohen, Chairman of the Securities and Exchange Commission.

In the face of testimony such as this it is stomach-churning to read the recent let-'em-eat-cake statement of one broker. In justifying his firm's efforts to discourage small investors as unprofitable, he said the man with $500 to invest had no business buying common stock—"He should buy a mutual fund." As a friend used to say, "That fellow has a mind like a rapier—and it fits right inside his pointy little head."

214

The hedge fund

Of interest to you only because it is a new part of the Wall Street scene is the "hedge fund." This is a private operation of a group of rich investors, each of whom puts in upwards of $100,000 to participate. They pool their millions under a wild-eyed fund manager, untie his hands, and stand back.

This bird leverages the money to the hilt. He buys on margin and gets bank loans on the over-the-counter securities he buys. Part of this hoard he puts into stock and part he uses to go short (which is where the name "hedge" comes from). All in all he wheels and deals like nobody in recent market history, because he's answerable to no one except the big millionaires he's helping to make bigger.

The estimated $2,000,000,000 now operating in these funds exerts a power far beyond its size because it turns over so frequently. The commissions the hedge funds generate are reported to be more than one-third as great as those on all mutual fund trading combined. So they're big boys in the marketplace. Eat your heart out.

What funds do to the nonbuyer

There is considerably more concern about the effect of funds on the ordinary investor than on the holder of mutual shares. For one thing, there is no question they can and do swing the market. Today they account for close to one-half the annual volume on the Big Board—up from 22.8 percent in 1959. Having heard from Mr. Cohen on their value, let's hear from Mr. William McChesney Martin, Jr., chairman of the Federal Reserve Board, discussing the funds' power in a speech reported by *The Wall Street Journal*. He stated that they "may virtually corner the market in individual stocks (and may) create undesirably volatile price fluctuations."

Testimony before that same congressional committee

stated that funds make "apparently deliberate use in some cases of . . . buying power to run up stocks." One method is to purchase, say, 50,000 shares of a stock quietly—and than make a show of buying 10,000 more. The attendant interest and activity can handsomely increase the value of the original purchase.

Similarly, a fund can make considerable market activity in a stock by buying it and selling it a number of times in a short period without being detected. Funds report their positions only once every three months. If they hold the same number of shares in one report that they did in the last, it is generally assumed that there has been no change in their position. But a great deal may have transpired in the meantime. It is exactly like hitting teacher with a spitball and then being elaborately busy again when she turns around.

Brokerage houses have always worked closely with the funds in their drive for growth. This is natural, because the vast business that funds generate pays somewhat better than handling your account and mine, and a grateful fund can be a valuable customer. Furthermore, until late in 1968 it was the practice to reward cooperating firms even when no actual orders were placed with them. This was done with "give-ups," through which the house handling an order was instructed to give up part of its commission to some other firm that had done the fund a favor. After years of effort, the SEC got this cozy arrangement abolished. But new ways to get around the ban have been devised.

A *Wall Street Journal* analysis of the situation reported that a common practice is to recommend purchases to several funds at the same time, "sometimes before the brokerage house has even prepared formal research reports on the stock it recommends, and sometimes months before the same recommendations appear in the market letters sent to the public."

In one specific instance, referred to in our Preface, proceedings were brought against a large brokerage firm for leaking information of a serious earnings drop to fifteen investment companies before it was made available to the public.

All this makes the Little Guy's job a lot tougher—but it makes specuvesting itself all the more logical as an approach to investing. Your flexibility, your willingness to pyramid your holdings, your speed in reacting when your stock tumbles—whether or not caused by fund behavior— these are your sword and buckler in the fight to make a buck.

Don't buy mutuals. But if you can't join 'em, beat 'em. And share with me an ironic chuckle at Mr. Tsai's complaint that fund shareholders were "comparing results of Manhattan Fund with smaller speculative funds or even individual securities"—and were failing to realize that it's the long pull that counts.

On what meat doth this, our Caesar, feed? It looketh suspiciously like crow!

Chapter 28

Rule Number 18: DON'T FOLLOW ADVICE

Here I must admit to playing with words, because I'm really saying, "Don't just follow advice, use it."

The market consumes the robots, the copycats, the rigid conformists. It handsomely rewards the thinkers, the adaptors, the adjustables. Unfortunately, the less you know about the market, the more inclined you are to take advice and blindly act upon it. Actually, this is precisely the period in which you should have the most questions and the deepest doubts. Later, when your instincts are developed and your sensitivities honed, you may be able more easily to separate the actionable from the questionable. But for the first few years be a real skeptic and a doubter about advice.

There's such a snowstorm of advice around you that you couldn't follow it all if you wished. And it's often conflicting or downright confusing—like the Delphic Oracle, which meant different things to different interpreters. Double-talk is not a Wall Street invention, but it has reached refinement there. It's like an old boss of mine, who used metaphors so thoroughly mixed that you'd swear he got them out of a Waring Blendor. I remember the time he bawled out a man for an error in judgment. Shaking his finger under the fellow's nose, he shouted, "Just because you get in bed with the wrong woman is no reason for changing the sheets." Had a point there. Somewhere.

He's obviously been busy on Wall Street, I read, these days, about "blossoming lags in business indicators." The list is reported as "sharply mixed." We are told that . . . "not poverty, nor war, nor ignorance, nor education are the direct problems but there is also the prospective wealth and leisure and looselessness of life." I wonder if we couldn't strive for a little less looselessness of language, while we're at it.

No tipping

You must learn to differentiate between real advice and mere tips. Let me make a separation that may or may not help. Advice comes from your broker, from professional services, and from friends who have very thoroughly proved their reliability and good investing sense. Tips come from the rest of the world. They are suspect.

Develop armor against even the most persuasive tip. The only action it should inspire is checking it out with someone who really knows. This is especially true if someone whose judgment you don't really respect says something with which you happen to agree. Boy, is that a warning signal.

And resist the temptation to pass along advice or tips of your own—particularly in a loud voice while standing at the back of your broker's board room. Do you really want to be responsible for your friend losing his money? Tell him how to straighten out his wife or raise his kids; he can't ever measure the effects of that bad advice. But keep out of his investment life. He may not know Rule Number 18, and you'll lose a pal when he loses his shirt.

Investigate before you invest

That's another of Wall Street's favorite lines, but pertinent to our point of not following advice blindly. One of the curses of the market, as well as one of its chief advantages, is that you can act so easily. When you buy a power mower, you plan and shop and compare before you buy. But you can and will spend—don't dignify it with the word "invest" or it will prove you miss the point—thousands of dollars with no more attention than a two-minute phone call. And the strange part is that you're spending time on the wrong purchase. You could get a fair shake from virtually *any* of the dozens of power mowers on the market, because the manufacturer and the store buyer do your spade work for you—and even guarantee the product. Yet nobody but you has anything to lose when you buy a stock; and in fact, everyone but you may have quite a bit to gain.

Don't move too fast. Look into it; think it over; check it out. If you're told you have to hurry, be even more insistent on examining the proposition. The ultimate in hurry is the "boiler room" operation that still bilks thousands of suckers of millions of dollars. In that operation, the stranger on the phone stresses that you must act quickly. But even more money is probably lost by following friendly, well-intentioned, but misinformed advice without questioning it.

What about this book?

Okay, apply that same course of action to all the advice and rules I've been feeding you. At least to the extent that you think it all through until you understand and are comfortable with it. But recognize, going in, that a lot of it is very controversial, and that you'll get plenty of argument. Just so you give it a fair shake and don't let someone's self-interest talk you out of anything I've been out-lining. A fund salesman can make mincemeat of any point you or I might bring up, because he'll be trained to do it.

But then, there's no sense arguing Communism with a Marxist, either.

Advice on buying advice

You may well want to buy an advisory service. I never have, but it may be a very good idea for you. You will have an opportunity to spend anything from $1 to $1,200 to get such guidance. There is even a service that helps you pick the right service.

A characteristic of the services, quite naturally, is that they are periodical—every week or at least every month. The market is entirely too volatile to permit anything less frequent to be much help. Trouble is, this makes them expensive—starting at $1.50 a week. As they will tell you, this is little enough for advice that may make you thousands, the sting being further eased by being tax-deductible.

Let me simply state that you don't need these services in order to prosper. You will be exposed to more options through them, among which you will have to pick and choose. They often contradict each other, and no one of them is right all the time—few, in fact, being right most of the time. Plus which there are degrees of rightness. You are not wrong in recommending a stock that goes up 10 percent, but you are a lot more right in recommending one that goes up 50 percent. So, with various degrees of recti-tude, they trumpet their successes and ignore their failures; with no real accountability or Reckoning Day by which you can judge their effectiveness.

The SEC has finally cracked down on the advertising and promotion these services put out. The latest ruling is that they are not to overstate the case by featuring their past winners, unless they make clear the percentage of instances in which they were right. This resulted in a gratifying decrease in this type of claim.

Perhaps the greatest point against these services, from the standpoint of the Little Guy, is that he doesn't use them even when he buys them. Trading seldom and busy elsewhere, he is just not set up to assimilate the flood of material a regular service provides. In too many cases it stacks up with the *National Geographic*s, to be read some day. But Pago Pago will still be there when he finally gets to the *Geographic*s, while the investment situation will long since have vanished.

So his subscription lapses, testimony to his failure to extract value from the advice he bought. To cover the range of possibilities, I should say that he fails to renew because (*a*) he didn't read the advice, (*b*) he didn't follow the advice, or (*c*) he followed it and was disappointed. I believe the most convincing argument for a service would be an advertisement featuring its renewal rate. I don't ever expect to see one.

Your broker gets many of these services, and maintains a reading room in which you can devour them. Talk to him about them; familiarize yourself with them. Then buy them if you find they offer any hope of help. They all make introductory offers for anything from $4 to $25. If you don't mind being forever on their mailing list, try a trial and judge for yourself; they must be helping someone beside the staff.

Before leaving the subject of advisory services, I must acknowledge that those that use computer techniques are introducing new rules to the old ball game. There is no question that electronic data-processing, with its tremendous capacity for analysis and computation, will be able to assist in investment decisions to an extent we've never known. Two questions will remain—which computer service to buy (conscious of the "garbage in, garbage out" problem of programming), and whether the small investor can ever get enough out to justify the cost of subscribing.

222

It will probably always be better to use your broker's subscriptions as your own source.

A wry note

The New York Stock Exchange publishes tons of advisory and explanatory material, some of which is sold to brokers for distribution and some of which is offered direct. They also provide brokerage houses with outlines for two lengthy investment courses to be put on for the public. I wrote to them, explaining about this book and stating that I wanted to list the material available and also would like to see the course outlines; since I had not had good experience with brokerage house lectures.

Back came a letter suggesting that I come down and talk it over. Two subways and a taxi later, on the agreed-upon day, I was ushered in and asked to talk about my book—which I was not really down there to do. However, I explained it briefly, and the gentleman nodded. "Tell me," he said, tenting his fingers, "are you writing this in order to get more of the low- and middle-income group to invest?"

"No," I told him, "I'm writing it in order to make money."

The interview went downhill from there.

The New York Stock Exchange lives in a dream world typified by their slogan, "Own your share of American Business." People buy stocks to make money, not to be patriotic or to feel important. New York State made the same mistake in launching its lottery. Instead of featuring the big winnings that were possible, all posters and ads were headlined, "Your one best chance to help education."

At least horse players are consciously being humorous when they refer to their pastime as "improving the breed." But to get pompous about stocks and lotteries is to lose touch with the people—and to lose touch is to lose the ability to help and to advise.

Since I've had lots of advice from the financial fraternity —much of it very good—I will return the favor with this admonition. Put a sign on your desks where you can see it every morning. The sign should say. "The public is only in this to make a buck; it is my job to help them do it while I make mine."

Incidentally, the NYSE course outlines are excellent— it's the individual broker who louses them up.

Chapter 29

Rule Number 19: NEVER TOUCH YOUR STOCKS

That says it all. With your account in street name, you don't even need a handshake to make a transaction. No muss, no fuss. No lost certificates, no trips to the Post Office. It's the only way to go.

You never need handle money except when you deposit it in the account. If you ever do need to withdraw any, a couple of days' notice will get it to you. When you're fully invested you'll have to sell something first, but if you have a credit balance in your cash account (in which you make over-the-counter transactions) or in your margin account, you can draw it all out. If you have buying power in your margin account, you can draw out part.

But don't take money out unless you really have to—it never gets back in. And even if it does, you've broken stride. If you have to pay income tax on realized gains, try to find the money elsewhere. Have your employer increase the withholding, in anticipation of gains; you get back any that's not needed, and it makes a nice windfall.

That goes for dividends that happen to come your way. Leave them in the account as grist for the mill. Pay the tax some other way. Make that account grow. It's your secret, numbered bank account in Switzerland, your horde of illegal gold coins, rubies stolen from an idol's eyes—anything but MONEY.

Unless you can lose the feeling that you're working with money, you'll never make it big. I dealt for many years with the minor manager of a major client's advertising, a man whose greatest curse was his keen ability to translate a budget into familiar things. A spread in *Life* was "a fine home"; a new brochure was a Chris-Craft cruiser; a week's push on radio was "more than our President's salary." If we'd had TV in those days he'd have been reduced to a quivering hulk, trying to find a homely parallel for a million-dollar half hour.

His only other accomplishment was picked up in a college art course. On every piece of artwork he would lay two long steel rules, to make sure the perspective was true —that everything had a vanishing point. Fortunately, one long-overdue day, his management found his.

Don't touch your stocks or they'll start to vanish, too.

Don't think like you

You will have to rise above your normal approach to life and living in order to specuvest properly. Not to become a spendthrift or a high-roller or a wastrel, but to become a money manager on a new scale, able to view commitments in the tens of thousands of dollars as mere chess moves. The only way this can be achieved is to leave your stocks and your money out of reach. This is an absolute essential. You must always maintain the cheerful fiction that the money's there to be spent any time you need it. But don't need it. Feed it.

Chapter 30

Rule Number 20: DON'T BE AFRAID TO PANIC

Knowing that I had sold a plunging stock and then rather quickly bought it back on recovery, a friend once said to me, "Did you ever figure out how much more you'd be ahead if you had just let it alone?" Because he is very bright and genuinely interested, I broke my own rule against trying to straighten out my fellow man. I explained, as I have to you, that it is simply "buying insurance." You cannot ride a stock down because it is your own money you are losing. In many cases, the stock you sell will continue to slide and your wisdom becomes obvious. In others, if the stock goes back up to the moon, you are losing nothing except opportunity. If you didn't get on it again, your insurance payment was that lost opportunity. If you did buy it again, higher than your selling price, your payment was the difference between what you got and what you paid, plus commissions. But just as frequently you will have a net gain on the transaction because you'll buy back in at a lower level than your sale.

Anyone would credit you with a coup if you did that. But you're not in this for plaudits, so you're every bit as

227

right when you sell just before a good recovery as you are just before a further drop. When in doubt, get out—only when the stock is actually falling, of course, but then without a qualm and without subsequent regrets. Every purchase is a new purchase, and has no relationship to anything you ever did in that stock before. Every decision must be made without regard to whether you may look foolish, but simply whether you protect your money and preserve the chance to make more.

Item (Sell, buy back higher): Franklin Mint—buy at 18½, January 11, 1968; buy more at 23⅛, February 6; after dropping from 36 sell both at 31, February 27; after recovery from 28 buy same amount back at 31 on March 28; add more at 60⅜, May 13; sell that purchase at 72 on July 29 after dropping from 90; buy smaller quantity back at 110¼ on October 22.

Does that seem like indecision or churning? Then you haven't been paying attention. A retreat from 36 to 31 in February certainly provided a sell signal (to put it the way the big boys do). It was a speculative stock that had already risen from 6; even though sound, it was in short supply and could easily have dropped another 10 points. But the company had tremendous earnings potential and a very promotion-minded management. So a recovery to 31 said "buy" again. At 60 it was still going strong, so I purchased again—only to sell that lot in a retreat that darn near had me dumping the entire holding. But a recovery from 68 kept me in, and I bought again after it broke the magic number of 100. (It split two for one at 120 and kept going).

Item (Sell, buy back lower): Ogilvy & Mather—buy at 22 when first issued, April 26, 1966; sell at 19, May 23; buy at 10⅜ on the way back from 8, September 14, 1966; sell at 12½ in another retreat, March 9, 1967. Since I worked for the firm, loyalty might have kept me aboard all the way to 8 and back again. Instead, I had the use of the money for most of that time and just about broke even on the transactions. This, of course, was sheer coincidence, since breaking even is a stupid goal. Only another drop chased me out the second time—not the fact that I'd gotten my bait back. A year later it was back in the twenties, without me.

The strange case of the reluctant advisers

A very peculiar factor creeps in when a professional gives or sells you advice as to buying a stock. This applies to your broker and, in the case of more affluent investors, to their financial advisers or paid portfolio managers. These worthies are almost always reluctant to close out a bad position into which they have put you. When one of their recommendations plummets, pure judgment can go down the drain with it. Their reaction can be very defensive and potentially dangerous.

Then the familiar and somewhat contemptuous, "Don't panic," gets the volume turned up. If, which certainly shouldn't ever be the case, you have given them discretionary powers, they will hold on tenaciously. If you do your own deciding, they will argue strongly against any order to sell. Selling is a reflection on their skills and knowledge and, if the man is paid, on his value to you.

With your broker, this "don't panic" advice seems virtuous indeed, since he is thereby talking himself out of a commission. But his reluctance to act may very well be inspired by an unconscious inability to admit to having been wrong. So guard against it or you may go for a sleigh ride.

The one who has the most to lose—the investor himself —is best fitted to make the decision, if only because it's his money. Provided you have developed the proper attitude, you will feel no necessity to prove anything at all and will be able to make these decisions with amazing detachment.

The decision will *always* be to sell, rather than to ride it down. This will apply whether you have a gain or a loss on the stock, and whether you have to wrestle your broker to do it. Just be calm, but firm.

The one time when it is most difficult to sell a dropping stock is just after you've bought it. This is also the time when an adviser most passionately opposes such a sale. But just remember what I said about the stock not caring when you bought it or at what level. A point is a dollar, regardless of the timing—and the principle of protecting your principal applies the instant you own the stock. It's a futile feeling to go in and out of a stock at a loss in a couple of days, but it's excellent discipline. And can be very good sense.

Chickens can outfly eagles

Fear is healthy. In the army it can keep you alive—and that goes for the stock market, too. It pays to be chicken because it's too easy to get shot down when you start to fly high. Beware the feeling of wheeling and dealing. Overconfidence is a lot more dangerous than timidity, because overconfidence can lose your money while timidity will usually just prevent you from making as much as you should.

The market is always dangerous and difficult. No one has an easy time of it. My relish at the plight of the fund managers in 1968 is given a bitter taste by the aptness of the familiar John Donne quote: "Do not ask for whom the bell tolls—it tolls for thee." If these mighty men with their millions and machines can't call them right, then how can I? And how can you?

We can't. We'll always be wrong more often than we're right. And so our only hope must lie in what we do when we find we're wrong, and what we do when we find we're right. Our skill at handling the pitiful little list of stocks we own stands between us and failure. On it we must build that towering structure which will make us rich and independent. And the foundation stone is fear.

Two kinds of fear—one must go

I touched on the role of fear in survival in wartime. Now let me draw a further parallel. A soldier knows two kinds of fear—of being killed, and of visibly letting his fellows down. These balance to permit a properly cautious performance of his duty. They form a natural team that, unfortunately, is part of every other endeavor in life. Fear of failure and fear of looking bad.

In the market, this cozy team is made up of fear of losing money and fear of looking foolish. *You must eliminate any fear of looking foolish.* The one thing that never matters is how you look. That's why you're told to talk about your failures. That's why you're told not to argue with your friends' nonsensities. That's why you're told to sell when the signs say sell. You're not in this to make good impressions but to make money. You make enough money and you won't have to care who thinks you're a nut. Believe me, however, the best they'll ever grant you is that you're a lucky nut.

In our tightly knit society, we're all conformists—even those who rigidly nonconform. We all look over our shoulders; we all bend our necks to someone for a reassuring pat on the head. But, on just this one occasion, say to hell with your fellow man and his opinion. If you want to sell, sell! Think I'm overdramatizing this very simple act? Wait till your broker tells you, "Don't panic," and let's see where your manhood goes.

Chapter 31

HOW THE MEDICINE TASTES

And there it is—all wrapped up in a neat package and tied with a pretty bow. A friend says, slyly, "Why would you spend your time writing a book if you can make so much money in the market?" It's the age-old smuggery. "Those who can't write advertising *teach* advertising." Or engineering, or any of a dozen lucrative trades.

I can make money in the market. Year in and year out. I take my own medicine and it tastes great. Because you need the reassurance and are entitled to it, I'll tell you just how well I've done and, roughly, how I did it. You can believe what I say, and you can be damn sure I'm not inflating my earnings, because the Internal Revenue Department has fellows who can read, too—and I don't need a bill for back taxes, thank you.

After five years of "investing," my equity was down 20 percent. From that point, without any fresh money, my equity has gone up 600 percent in a little over six years. Some years have been better than others, and 1968 was a doozy, thanks in large part to one well-handled stock. But I've never had a bad year.

Mind you, I've had my ups and downs within any calendar year—and so will you because you're dealing with a most unruly beast. Sometimes November and December save the record and sometimes they knock the hell out of it, but rigid record-keeping such as the next chapter prescribes, has shown me to be steadily ahead. And, except for the mistakes that helped me develop them, I did it by adhering to the rules I've just spelled out.

Why write the book? For royalties, of course. For *spendable income*—because I never touch my investments (except to put my kids through college, and I'll replace that money). It takes a long time, even at 30 percent or more a year, to build a small account into the comfortable fortune you and I are planning on.

Let's look at the record

You don't remember it, but that was Al Smith's once-famous electioneering line. The taunts and taglines of yesteryear's elections are about as difficult to make sense out of as the records of past stock dealings. "Check everything with Sydney" ranks somewhat below "Tippecanoe and Tyler, too" in comprehensibility.

The whys of past stock purchases are just as dim, and might very well be dull as well. Who knows what I saw in CBS in 1962 that sent me into it for 20 shares at 44⅞? Who cares? But the record is clear that six weeks later it was the rise to 48 that inspired purchase of another 20 and, in another two months, 10 more at 53. With splits and distributions I had 104 shares by 1964, and my $2,500 investment had turned an $1,800 profit when I sold them.

A stock named Astrodata, a small company in the new telemetry field and suchlike, was getting a bit of a play in 1963. A hundred shares at 16⅝, followed by another at 20¾, turned into a thousand-dollar profit within the month, from a sale at 24. I mention it because the stock saw 7½ by 1967, then showed a spark again in 1968 that had me in at 18 for another try. It quickly went to 29 before the tumble started again. The point is simple:

Tasting stocks pays off over long periods of time, because you never stop watching a stock once you've owned it.

Were you investing in 1965? Did you buy the airlines? The jets were proving so maintenance-free that profits looked CAVU, as we used to say in the big war. And before they went SNAFU, in 1968, the stocks did handsomely for their owners.

My record was spotty. I saw them moving, liked the reasons. Into Pam Am at 29⅛ in January, 1965—then out at 29¼ in April, after it went up a bit and slid back. A hundred-dollar loss in KLM from selling at 38⅝, only a few months before it took off to 155 (the sin was not buying it back when it started to zoom).

Eastern and I pulled beautifully together for a long-term rise of 40 points in 1965. I couldn't resist taking my profits on December 29, in order to throw them over into the 1966 tax, for whatever good that did me. It would have been better to hold the 100 shares for the 1967 two-for-one split and a high of 60 on the new shares. But hindsight won't make money, and in this case foresight certainly did. But it's a two-way street, and I lost part of it back a year later when some momentary problem dropped Eastern from the 86 I then paid on a Monday to the 68⅞ I got when I sold on Friday. Remember that doggone roller coaster. (P.S. The shares as I write this are 26—the equivalent of only 52 on the old shares. It doesn't pay just to sit.)

Blow-by-blow of the way to go

But why just dabble in the past? I'll lay out the whole story of the last two years or so, and if you can get any nourishment out of it go ahead. You'll find I did some bright things and I did some dumb things, but I'd learned how to handle both, so the result was good gains.

There's rarely a time in the market when you know exactly what to do, and when you're most confident you're most likely to be wrong. It's somewhat like a job I held not too long ago. We had two bosses—one of whom liked to feel that God's in his Heaven and all's right with the world; the other operated under the basic assumption that everything would go to pieces if he didn't handle every detail. We used to say that the one didn't want you to bring him any problems and the other didn't want you to bring him any solutions.

The market presents that kind of a tightrope. And don't hate me for stumbling badly on occasion (as indeed I also did at times on the aforementioned job). To err is human —to profit in spite of it is divine.

Collins Radio was getting good recommendations in late 1966. Avionics and communications systems, you know. Earnings in 1964—$1.08; 1965—$2.04; 1966—$3.36. Glamour in spades, with earnings to back it up. So I bought 70 shares in November, 1966, at 57; then rounded it out the following March at 77. It soared by midsummer, so I passed the magic six-month mark with the first purchase and sold at 98 in August as it backslid. But discipline forced me out a month short of long term with the rest when it rallied the following week, then dropped to the 100 at which I finally sold. (Collins reached 117 that fall, but sank into the 60's in early 1968. I bought again when I thought it was recovering at 66 in September, but it dropped 4 points in a week and chased me out once more. It then strayed into the 40's. I'll be in it another time.)

General Instrument rode the semiconductor wave for quite a while before it got seasick and whoopsed in late '67, dropping from 86 to 40 in just six months. I got in fairly early, in December, 1966—but my 48 had only turned to 53 when I sold it prematurely. That's the kind of error you'd think anybody'd love to make, but not if you firmly believe in my average-up approach—in which case you realize that you can't survive on 5-point gains.

Studebaker (now Studebaker-Worthington) had a stormy career that culminated in a one-for-five reverse split in 1965. Its price chart looks like a cardiogram. With luck and a conviction that management was going to make it work, I got on at 38 in January of 1967 and off at 64 eight months later. Why sell? Because it was dropping. And to prove my point I bought twice as much three months later at 51, and got another 8 points out of the dear stock before I sold in February, 1968. Missed the next rise to 65, but tune in tomorrow.

Despite my work on the Shell Oil account I became intrigued by a very tough "small" East Coast operator named Hess Oil & Chemical. They were expanding rapidly from a small chain of discount gas stations to a fully integrated operation—which means from crude, through refining, to marketing. And they were great marketers. My disloyalty earned me 8 points, from 27 to 34, in December, 1967. The stock fooled around in a 7- or 8-point range till March of '68, when it took off to an eventual 67 without me—since I was busy with even better possibilities.

Don't get the idea I dug up all these marvelous deals myself, because I don't work that way, and you mustn't, either. Remember—buy a stock that's moving up and being talked about. All these I've named qualified under those vital rules.

Sometimes, of course, those qualifications weren't enough —and don't be surprised when they're not. Zayre, an acquisition-minded apparel chain, looked good at 35¾ in February, 1967—but not so good back at 36, ten months later. Holding it would have gotten me to 60 before it started to retreat again. But it was dropping, so I had to sell it at that bargain 36.

Brokers tell me, "Yes, but they never get back in again." Don't let that be true of you. Get out, watch it, then get back if actions and prospects say you should. Zayre's subsequent rise found me invested elsewhere, but I would have gotten back in if I could have.

Like with Seven Arts, man. This California producer of TV shows and animated films had early bought the TV rights to thousands of movies, including all Warner Brothers' vast production. TV was starting to clamor for these oldies. Seven Arts' earnings and stock prices started to rise. A hundred shares at 29 in March, 1967, were joined by 100 more at 32, two weeks later. They went to 42 within the year, then started dropping back. I sold the second purchase at 37 in February, 1968, and watched the stock's narrow trading range for three months, still holding the first purchase. Seven Arts bought Warner Brothers, like a guppy swallowing a trout, and I took 200 more at 36 when a rise began. In earliest '69 lovely merger stabs by Kinney and National General moved the stock suddenly to 64. Backsliding persuaded me to lighten the load a bit, so I sold 100 (against my highest price) at 61, in a move that paid for an awful lot of stupidities. The rest went later at 56.

Did almost all the right things with Ogden Corp., too. It's a conglomerate that's eternally determined to be more so, with an eye only for going concerns that can be made to go faster. March, 1967, saw a 200-share purchase at 24. June 5 brought another 100 at 27, and two days later 100 more at 30. Now that's a sizable hunk of my capital, but would you believe another 100 at 42 in January, 1968?

The bubble broke at 52 late that month, with the government wielding the pin by threatening to investigate the whole conglomerate idea. I sold my later purchases at 46, 45, and 44 as Ogden hit the skids. But with a foolish reluctance to take the fat profits, I held my original buy all the way down to 37 before selling in August. The gain I thereby let slip away would have paid the tax on all the profits made on my handling of that issue. So we never stop learning.

Anybody heard of Control Data? Bet your life you have. It's not a bad trade when you take three thousand idle dollars and turn a $500 profit in ten days. But when it's Control Data and you sell it at 68 in April, 1967, your ego gets a jolt to see it hit 160 by year's end. Of course, with that stock's crazy action you can always catch the brass ring next time around. It's been to 100 and back to 160 since then—but a couple of stabs in 1969 lost me small amounts when I got out of phase.

237

I handled LTV Aerospace stupidly in 1967, too—without the balm of a quick, fat gain. LTV is part of the Ling empire, and it's gooey with glamour—airplanes and missiles and space hardware galore. A purchase at 38 in June, 1967, made sense, and another at 46 in December followed my sainted precepts. But the bottom fell out so swiftly and so inexplicably in the next six weeks that I finally sold it all at 37 for an unpleasant loss. Good riddance, as a matter of fact, at least as of this writing—but I didn't move fast enough either in buying more on the way up or in selling on the way down. While you can't win 'em all, it doesn't feel good to be right and just handle things badly.

Dribs and drabs—mostly drab

There was a mixed bag of little stocks that won't mean much to you. But remember, a point is a dollar whether it's Control Data or Piece-a-Pizza, so don't snub the ones that don't get in the columns. I mentioned Daryl, bought in July '67 at 2¾ and hovering nicely at about triple that now. Dalto Electronics was an out-and-out O/C tip with a rising price to back it up. And if I tell you not to act on tips, it won't keep you from doing so once in a while if the source is really knowledgeable. So maybe a $900 buy will build you a $600 gain in three months, as it did for me with Dalto, whatever that is.

And maybe a $3,000 splurge will bring you a $600 loss in five months, as it did for me in Kenrich, whatever ditto.

Or Tronchemics—in at 3⅞, out at 2¼ with roughly half the money surviving, considering commissions.

Try Safe Flight, with a much-needed aircraft landing system nobody seemed to need. Two months without getting off the ground convinced me my money was needed elsewhere. But it cost only a $155 loss to taste it.

Spooner Minerals and Oils had promise that it fulfilled after my 50 shares were bought and then sold with a towering $81 loss. The 6 it reached would have made my buy at

$2\frac{7}{8}$ a happy one, but three months seemed long enough to wait. And I wanted the money for Abex, which I told about in an earlier chapter and which earned a dozen points on several hundred shares in three short months of 1968.

Minting money

The year 1968 had started with a purchase of General Numismatics at $18\frac{1}{2}$. I covered that operation earlier, too, in Chapter 12. I scared out of it a couple of times (by then it was called "Franklin Mint") but always went back in, so I benefited from a fabulous series of moves that took it up to 120 *after* splitting two for one. The record goes like this: Bought 1/11/68 at $18\frac{1}{2}$; more on 2/6/68 at $23\frac{1}{8}$; sold it all on 2/28/68 when it slid from 36 to 30; bought half back 3/28/68 at 31, then the rest April Fool's Day at the same price; half as much again on 5/13/68 at $60\frac{3}{8}$, to be sold 7/29/68 at 72 in a drop from 82; bought a few more shares at $110\frac{1}{4}$ on 10/22/68, just in time for the split announcement.

Year's end saw it hit 90 on the new shares (180 on the old), then slide to 73, where in a series of December moves I shorted it all against the box. That protected my profit yet moved it over into 1969, which I figured might not be as successful as '68. Oh, ye of little faith—it zoomed again. I delivered half in January, 1969, to cover part of the short. But I decided to keep the rest because it had already gone back to 88, so I bought shares to cover the rest of the December short sale. (This gave me a 15-point loss on the short transaction but retained my original long-term position.) Got it?

Within the month I could and did sell it at 107 to put the cherry on the sundae for that time around.

Fairchild Camera has been another yo-yo, and I caught the sweep very handily in 1968. This space and instruments company has been in and out of my portfolio through the years, but it's a dangerous one to play with. Adjusted for a 50 percent split in 1967, it's been as high as 150 and as low as 52, within a two-year span. But even that doesn't tell the off-again-on-again story, because it zipped from the 100's to the 50's, to the 90's, to the 60's— all in little more than a year.

I got it on the way back up, with 100 shares at 57 in March of 1968, plus another 100 two weeks later at 69. Got out at 75 on the way down from 90, in May. With wide swingers like FCI you have to permit a greater drop than with more conservative-acting stocks. Otherwise you'd be in and out twice a day.

There's a fantastically big construction outfit named Raymond International that builds things like harbors and airports. The father of a friend of mine was big in the company, so I hear Raymond all the time. They've got a constant backlog that looks like a baseball scoreboard in the final inning, but they never seem to make a proper buck. However RII moved up from the midteens to 21 in March, 1968, on the smell of an earnings rise, so I bought 100 shares. Foolishly I waited five months to buy more at 39¼—half a point below the absolute top. Two months later I was out at 31, with a net loss of about $100. Yecch!

Might as well also confess to my boo-boo on Conjecture Mining—a delightful name if ever I heard one. With a long-flooded mine made suddenly valuable by the rising price of silver, they figured it would pay to spend big money to pump it out. Every self-respecting gambler should own a mining stock, so I bought 1,000 shares at $1.03. In four months it had soared to $3.00, so it made sense to buy a thousand more. I suspect that, when the mine was drained, all they found was a ring around the sides—but whatever the reason, it was down to $1.25 when I sold the whole kaboodle to get a little more than half my money back.

You may notice—you sly one, you—that I've missed all the marvelous rise in computer "software," like with Leasco Data Processing and all the jazzy group that start with "computer" or "data." Well, for some reason I did—largely because I was busy elsewhere. But there will always be a hundred good stocks you miss for every one you own, so that's a simple shrug of the shoulders.

At least I did get interested in a computer terminal device that turns an ordinary dial phone into an extension of a central computer. Carried around by a salesman, for instance, it puts purchase orders directly into the whole computerized delivery system and suchlike. A company named Mite and one named Stelma cooked this one up, and Mite was rising, over the counter. So I bought 200 shares at 14½, then 100 more at 18. It promptly fell back to 14, whereupon I sold the later purchase. Since then it's gone on the AMEX, touched 22 and then dropped. I got out at 18 in a February, 1969, sell-off.

Stelma acted much more the lady. I got it in October, 1968, at 34, with more the next month at 40. A nice takeover bid strengthened it to 58, but I optimistically let it drop back to 46 before I sold in January, 1969, for what was still a fine profit.

To buy or not to buy

I'm glad to say that by early February, 1969, my "tilt" signals had me almost solidly in cash. Moore-McCormack, bought for a take-over move, was still in the fold when the market hit the skids in mid-month (35 D-J points in one week). A stock named Scientific Resources had come and gone for a 5-point loss. Two hundred Warner Bros.–Seven Arts had seemed worth holding for the merger that was imminent. Daryl still had not dropped, but the rest of my money was sitting on the sidelines, waiting.

How did I know a tumble was due? How does a fish detect a coming storm? By being part of the elements—by feeling—by instinct. But most importantly in my case, and in the case of anyone who follows the rules this book expounds, the simple compulsion to sell a falling stock had made me unload. And the absence of clearly strong and well-sponsored issues had kept me from reinvesting that money. Because of this I can be and always will be hurt by a falling market. But I won't be crippled. And when the inevitable recovery began, I got in again—and was fully invested for the fabulous late-April run-up that developed.

Will you do as well? Mind your "Twenty Rules" and the answer has to be a "yes" as smug as the paragraph you've just been reading.

Chapter 32

KEEPING RECORDS AND CUTTING TAXES

Records are a nuisance in one way, and kind of fun in another. But they're essential, no matter how you look at them. Furthermore, the back of an old envelope will very definitely not do. Decide now to treat your investing like the business it is—and that means keeping orderly records.

You need a loose-leaf notebook with both printed columnar sheets and plain lined sheets. Ask to see the book in which your broker keeps his handwritten record of your account. You'll want something like it. The sheets may be any convenient size, but the pocket size is rather small for entering the information you need, so don't plan to carry your records around. Keep them at home and carry a list of your current holdings (issue, number of shares, price, and purchase date) on a card in your wallet.

You can buy specially printed stock-record sheets at a large stationer's. But just ask your broker to give you a dozen of the kind he uses—he'll be glad to, because proper records at home cut client questions and he's all for that. Then buy a notebook of the same size with lined paper, and you're all set. Use the heavy first sheet of the notebook as a divider between the two sections.

In Section 1, a typical printed sheet will have the following headings:

DESCRIPTION	BOUGHT			SOLD			APPROXIMATE		
	DATE	NO. OF SHARES	PRICE	DATE	NO. OF SHARES	PRICE	PROFIT	LOSS	
CCE	3/27/69	100	58½ / 5894.88	6/9/69	100	72⅞ / 7236.08	1342.21		S
	4/10/69	100	73¼ / 7321.28	6/9/69	100	73⅛ / 7261.04		60.24	S

To familiarize yourself with the symbol, use it instead of the name; you'll find the symbol in your *Stock Guide,* or you can ask your broker. Most over-the-counter stocks don't have symbols.

Many printed forms don't have a column for the buying price and selling price in dollars and cents because they're made up for brokers, who don't need that record. You do, so divide the "price" box as shown, and list both. Be sure to note in some unused column whether the gain or loss is long term (LT)—at least six months and one day—or short term (ST). It will be handy for tax calculations.

If you don't want to bother with printed sheets and are hot for drawing lines, do-it-yourself.

Leave several spaces under each issue, because you may be adding to your holding of that issue. Or it may split or earn a stock dividend, which must be duly noted.

Your broker's a bookkeeper

Every time you buy or sell, your broker will send you a "confirmation." These are precious, so keep them in an envelope—preferably one of those red accordion affairs, "business letter" size. Keep one for "Current Holdings," the issues you have bought and have not yet sold. When you sell, fish out the matching purchase confirmation from

244

"Current Holdings," do your arithmetic on it, and enter the profit or loss in your notebook. Then staple them together (paper clips pick up other papers and are dangerous) and stow them in another envelope marked "Round Trip."

When you sell, draw a pencil line through the correct shares in the "Bought" column. If you sell only part of a purchase, figure the cost per share, including commissions, etc. The cost of the shares sold is the number of shares sold multiplied by that overall cost per share. Make a new entry for the remaining shares. Beginners like to apply the entire cost of a purchase against the sale of a portion of it, when they have a profit, and then pretend the remainder was free. Not only is that a dangerous viewpoint, it is illegal and will foul up your tax return.

Your broker also sends you monthly statements. These contain a record of all transactions, as well as of dividends paid and stock splits or stock dividends (both called "distributions"). You will receive two statements; one for your margin account and one for your "cash" account. The margin account statement will also show the current interest charge. This will be added to your debit balance, or subtracted from your credit balance if you're in a cash position. Both statements conclude with a list of your holdings as of the end of that month.

Check these statements against your records. Do the arithmetic. *Mistakes happen.* Politely question anything you don't understand or agree with.

In Section 2, the lined pages of your notebook, designate a page for cash dividends for the current year. For each stock leave four lines for the quarterly payments. Enter them as they appear on your monthly statements.

Check your equity monthly

Specuvesting calls for knowing where you are at all times. And here's where the fun comes in. Near the first of every month work out your exact position, where you are and how far you've come.

On one of the lined pages, list all your holdings, number of shares, latest closing price, and name of issue. Multiply and enter the value of each holding. Add them all up and get the total *value* of your portfolio.

Enter that as "value"; write under it the amount you owe on your margin account (call your broker that afternoon so you get the latest figure; you may have traded or received dividends since your statement was made up). Subtract the two, then add on any credit balance in your cash account. (Do not add the "buying power" in your margin account.) That gives you your total *equity*—how much you'd get if you sold everything. It's okay to ignore commissions, because you don't have to be that exact.

To see how you're doing, you will want to make two further, simple calculations. To get your percentage of gain over investment, subtract your total investment— every dollar you've put in to date—from your equity. The remainder is your gain. Divide it by the total investment and you'll get your percentage of gain. What do you mean, *loss?*

To determine how you're doing for the year, subtract your January total equity from the latest month's. (Okay, if you do have a temporary loss, subtract the latest month's figure from January's.) Divide the remainder by the January figure. Dividing gives you your percent of gain (loss) for the year. Compare it to the D-J gain (loss) and feel smug.

Keep a continuous record of gains and losses

It's useful as well as interesting to record your gains and losses. You don't have to be elaborate. Just the date, the issue, and four ruled columns. Two of the columns are "Short-term Gains" and "Short-term Losses," the other two are "Long-term Gains" and "Long-term Losses."

When you get your confirmation and post the information on your other record sheet, enter the name and date, plus the gain or loss in the proper column. Then, as often as you feel like, do the arithmetic and write in the net short-term and net long-term situations, year to date.

At tax time, as covered later on, you'll have to do a detailed report on the transactions for Uncle Sam. But this running record is just to give you a continual feel for how your realized gains or losses are shaping up.

One key item to look for. A well-run specuvesting account will show a preponderance of long-term gains and short-term losses—a reflection of the old Wall Street saw, "Cut your losses and let your profits run."

Tax matters (but not much)

Some people let the tax bite cripple their entire thinking. The sensible specuvestor takes it in stride and considers it just one more commission to pay. It's an inconvenience, it's a drag, but it is rarely a factor in the actions taken by the successful investor. Let's dispose of that chimera first, then we'll quickly review how the taxes apply, and finally cover some slim possibilities for taking the edge off them.

An unreasoning distaste for paying taxes loses investors a lot of money in the market. As pointed out in the very beginning, timing is of the utmost importance. That timing should almost exclusively be subject to market considerations. The market and the particular stock don't know or care about your tax problems, so those problems can't enter into your timing except in rare cases (Chapter 8).

If you ever get the notion you don't want to realize a gain because you don't want to pay the tax, ask yourself one question: Would I feel good if my boss suddenly gave me that for a raise? That ought to put it into focus. You pay tax on a raise, too—but everybody wants one. Unions sit down and strike, individuals sit up and beg; but everybody loves a raise. Grab that gain, too—and let the taxes fall where they may.

What the taxes consist of

Everything said here applies to federal income taxes only. The tax reforms that are now under discussion may even change a lot of it sooner or later. It does not pretend to be a complete study, but just a once-over-lightly in the hope that you'll feel more at home with the subject. I strongly advise you have your return filled out by an expert (the cost of which service is deductible). If I could think of any more disclaimers I'd put them in.

Anyway, let's start with the items on which you pay taxes:

Capital gains. Long-term or short-term, they're both properly called "capital gains." They are, literally, a growth of your capital, rather than a payment of some kind. Today, they become long term after six months and one day. The number of days in the month doesn't matter, *so sell after six calendar months and one day.* The period begins the day *after* you buy and ends the day you sell. Buy on June 11, the six-month period begins June 12 and ends December 11. You can sell on December 12 and count it as long term. A quirk: If you buy on the last day of the month, you must hold it until the first day of the seventh succeeding month (buy April 30, sell November 1).

Short-term gains are taxed as regular income. You pay your regular tax on one-half the long-term gains, with a maximum of 25 percent (not including surtax, if there is one). This is one provision they're trying to change.

Dividends. Unless they are "capital gains dividends," you pay on them as regular income.

Capital gains dividends. In most cases they are taxed as long-term gains, no matter how long you've held the shares on which they're paid. The cost basis of your shares is not affected, however.

Nontaxable dividends. These are a return of your capital and would do you more good if the company held them and put them to work. You pay no tax, but you should subtract the total from the original cost of your shares, "reducing your cost basis." They are a tribute to the gullibility of the investor, since they pretend to be a big deal but really consist of giving you back your own money—with the share value dropping an equal amount. But since you won't be buying the mutual funds that usually spawn them, what do you care?

Stock dividends. If the dividend is in extra shares of the company whose shares you hold, it isn't taxable. You add it to your previous holdings and adjust the per-share cost basis. They become long-term when the original shares do, regardless of how long you've held the new shares.

Spin-off. When you receive, as dividend, shares of a company other than the one you hold, it gets kind of complicated and works differently for different situations. Check your broker, and, if he doesn't know, see a tax expert.

Rights. Subscription rights are normally not taxable as income. If you sell them they represent a capital gain, figured from the date you bought the shares on which they were granted. If you exercise them (turn them in for shares of the stock), your cost for that new stock is the subscription price you pay, and the term is figured from the date on which you purchase the new shares. If you let them lapse, you're careless. But it's another way to avoid paying any tax, at that.

Warrants. If you buy and sell them, your gains are figured just as for stocks—the holding period starting with the date of purchase. If you buy them and exercise them, add their cost to the cost of exercising them as your cost basis for the shares of stock you receive. Then the holding period on the new shares starts the day after you exercise the warrants.

Conversions. If a convertible bond or convertible preferred is turned in for the stipulated shares of the issuing company, there is no tax on the transaction itself. The cost basis for the common is the purchase cost of the convertible securities, and the holding period begins with the date of the earlier purchase.

Transfers. Your state may charge a transfer tax on the sale of securities (except bonds). This is deductible from ordinary income. In a busy account this can really add up. Check your sell confirmations (no tax on purchases). You can add these taxes up and deduct them from ordinary income, the way you do other state taxes; but then be sure to *add* the tax on to the amount you report as realized from each sale. You can't take the deduction twice. Maybe you'll prefer just to leave it in the "net amount" realized. But if you sold many shares, for long-term gains, half the tax on a nickel a share (tops) may buy a good dinner. Federal transfer taxes are not separately deductible but are just part of your costs.

Short sales, puts, and calls. Darned if I'm going to help you on these. You shouldn't be indulging.

Dulling the tax ax

There are certain steps you'll want to know about that may help you keep your federal income taxes at a big, fat minimum. But first recognize that there is very little you can or should do about them. A lot of the tax-oriented, year-end activity you hear about is inspired by brokers in an honest attempt to whoop up some extra business. Just remember that they can't lose and you can. In fact, except in rare cases I'll try to make clear, you probably *will*.

There are only two basic situations in which positive, tax-saving action is flatly recommended for the specuvestor:

1. If you have heavy realized gains and stiff, unrealized losses, you may wish to take the losses to offset some of the gains.

2. If, near the year's end, the action of a stock on which you have large gains indicates that you should sell it, you may wish to postpone the gain till the next year. This is covered on page 252, selling short against the box.

In addition there are two iffy situations that have to do with next year's income expectations:

3. If the current year's total income is higher than you expect next year's to be, you may want to take losses and postpone gains.

4. If the reverse is true, you may want to take gains and postpone realizing losses.

Otherwise you should rule out all the much-touted "tax switching," "doubling up," or other devices aimed solely at shaving your taxes and building someone else's profits. Commissions and other considerations make these moves, in the main, nonsense. Categorical statement number 9,642: *It usually does not pay to take any action for tax purposes only, if you're a Little Guy.*

Here are details of these four situations and how to handle them:

1. Taking a loss to gain. You have realized handsome gains throughout the year and, I should hope, have not realized sufficient losses to offset them. But you do have some holdings that show losses and that you are considering selling. Since you are a specuvestor, this means the stocks have dropped sharply in price and you are afraid of another or a continuing drop. By selling them and taking your loss now you will help offset your realized gains and will save on this year's tax. Or, if you have paper losses in shaky stocks *beyond* your gains, you can apply up to $1,000 in losses against regular income, with the rest applicable in following years.

Whether the loss is long term or short term makes no

difference. Sell the stock and take the loss, but only if normal specuvesting rules indicate the wisdom of such a sale. You can establish a loss for the current year by selling the stock any day right up to and including the last trading day of the year.

"Sensible men often get advantage and profit from the most awkward circumstances. We should learn how to do that and practice it, like the man who flung a stone at his dog but missed and hit his stepmother, whereupon he exclaimed, 'Well, not so bad after all!' " (Plutarch).

2. Your only permissible short. The only other time when a tax move unquestionably makes sense is when you want to realize a gain that is slipping away, but you don't want to add to the current year's income. This will happen when you have already realized unusually high net gains, or made an unusual amount of money in some other way— or when you figure next year's income will be lower for any reason. You can actually freeze your profit immediately and have it apply on next year's taxes.

The device is a simple one called going short "against the box." It means you sell short the same number of shares you already hold. The name comes from the supposition that you now have those shares in your safe deposit box.

When going short against the box, you don't have to put up any extra money if you make it clear to your broker that this is your intention. It will be so noted on your confirmation. Surprisingly, you can use the proceeds of the sale immediately to reinvest, but are not credited with the gain until after the first of the year when you close out the transaction. The holding term ends when you go short, not when you cover, so that period cannot be used to turn a short-term gain into long term. You cover your short position by telling your broker to deliver your stock against it.

3 & 4. Adjusting to next year's income. Aside from shorting against the box to save a deteriorating situation, the entire question of taking or postponing gains and losses may be sharpened by an expected income differential. A loss is more valuable when your total income is higher; a gain when your income is lower. Either situation may prompt you to stretch things a bit.

For example, if you have an unusually high income in the current year, you may want to take losses, even in a stock in which you still have specuvesting faith. That move is described under "the hesitation waltz" on page 257. Or, in the opposite circumstance, a stock on which you have good gains may be sitting, relatively stagnant, at year's end. Ordinarily, stagnancy after a sharp rise is not a reason for selling because it may well be a period of consolidation preparatory to another climb. But if this year's income is relatively low, the scales might be tipped in favor of selling immediately and taking the gain. Again, hold the money to reinvest if it starts to move up once more. A stock sold with a gain may be repurchased immediately.

Neither of these moves makes much sense unless income changes are expected—and may not even then. Plot it out thoroughly *before* you move. To establish a *gain* for any reason you must be sure to place the sell order at least five trading days before the end of the year, or the gain won't count in the current year. This is the period between sale and the "settlement date," when money and stocks have to change hands. It used to be four days, before the brokerage firms' back rooms fell so far behind. They're currently showing so little progress straightening this mess out that you may need ten days lead by the time you read this, so better check. If you slip up, ask your broker about making the transaction "for cash," which you can do even on the last trading day.

Today's loss, tomorrow's deduction

I don't expect you to have big losses. If you do, you haven't been selling soon enough on the downturn. However, you should understand the provision that allows you to deduct up to $1,000 in capital losses from ordinary income this year—and to carry over any additional loss indefinitely, until you use it up at the rate of $1,000 a year. Thus a loss, while noticeably inferior to a gain, has its compensations since it comes right off the top, where the tax rate is highest, and it can be used forever till used up. This permanency of a loss is one of the reasons why people in high tax brackets can take a different view of highly speculative situations than we can. If you're in an 80 percent bracket, the 25 percent long-term capital gains tax looks mighty attractive. Particularly since, even if you guess wrong and get a big net loss, it actually costs only 20 cents on the dollar, and can be carried over till used up.

Short-term vs. long-term

Short-term is six months or less, long-term is six months plus one day or more. You have to merge all short-term gains with all short-term losses—and all long-term gains with all long-term losses—before you can start using the two kinds against each other. You will probably end up with a net gain or loss in each category. At that point any short-term losses can be used to reduce long-term gains. You could also use net long-term losses to reduce net short-term gains, if that's the way it works out.

Any short-term gains left over will be taxed as ordinary income; any remaining long-term gains will be divided in half, then taxed at the same rate. Got it? You put down *one-half* the long-term gain and pay your regular rate (plus the surtax, if any).

If losses are left over, you can apply up to $1,000 of them against income for the year the losses are incurred—and then apply $1,000 worth every year till it's all used up. To do that, you have to designate the amount of short-term gains and of long-term gains you're carrying over, because they have to be applied against their own category in following years, too.

There's a point at which the question of long-term/short-term might become important at the end of the year. If you find you have more short-term losses than short-term gains, you know you can take some additional short-term gains without paying taxes on them. This can be better than applying those leftover short-term losses against long-term gains because the latter incur less tax anyway. But remember the warning not to get carried away by tax-based decisions.

What's all this about a "wash sale"?

The Feds have a rule that says if you sell a stock at a loss and then buy the same stock back within thirty days, it is a "wash." That means you are still considered as owning the same stock, so you can't, as yet, take the loss on the first trade. However, your cost basis for the new shares will be the cost of the new shares *plus the loss that was voided by the premature repurchase.* You merely postpone the loss. You can, in effect, still take it at a future date (or, I hope, deduct it from the gain resulting from your repurchase). This should be your course of action if the stock you sold, but still like, comes alive before the thirty days are up. The heck with taxes—you're in this to make money, not to avoid paying taxes.

A sale is still a wash if you purchase "substantially identical" securities within the thirty-day period. Stock of a different company in the same industry is not "substantially identical" see ("the mixer," page 257). But warrants, convertible bonds, or convertible preferreds of the same company usually are.

Tax tangos and phony fandangos

If you're so inclined, you can do a lot of scurrying around at year's end, all in the name of cutting taxes. You will be abetted in this by the brokerage houses, which are full of dandy suggestions for fancy footwork. However, it is rarely profitable to take action other than that outlined above, for the sole purpose of cutting taxes. Therefore, you will usually be wise to pass up year-end invitations to such popular dances as these:

The two-step. A very simply step-close-step, set to a fast beat. You want to take a gain, to offset some severe losses. In this way you will not have to pay any tax on the gain. But you still like the stock. So you simply sell the risen stock and buy it back the next day. This is permissible when you have a gain, though not when you have a loss (wash sale). But since you can carry over a loss indefinitely, applying $1,000 a year to gains or income, this move is rarely advantageous. Perhaps if you know that next year's income will be a lot higher, and both the loss and the gain involve several thousand dollars, it would pay to match them up this year rather than apply only the $1,000 carry-over against the same gain next year. Better ask a tax expert about your particular case. Chances are his fee will be a lot less than the commissions he'll save you with a flat "no."

The double shuffle. This rather wearing polka is danced with two partners. You have a loss, which you'd like to take, but you don't want to close out your position in the stock. So you double up, you buy an equal number of shares of the same stock. Hold both lots for thirty days and sell the original on the following day. This has to be timed so that the thirty days end before the final trading day, or you won't get the loss credited to the current year. But don't fool with it at all! Why tie up a double amount of your money for thirty days in a stock you want to sell? As a specuvestor, if it's dropped enough to merit selling, sell. If it hasn't, hold it. But don't compound your dilemma by buying more, even for a limited time. You must have better things to do with your buying power—like letting it sit

256

safely in your account till you spot an issue that really looks good.

The hesitation waltz. A more stately version of the previous number. You want to take a loss to offset some gains you've realized but you still basically like the stock. So you sell, any time up to the last trading day of the year, then buy the same stock back after thirty-one days. Repurchasing sooner would constitute a wash sale, as we've already covered. It might make sense to do this deliberately in rare cases, but you shouldn't have enough of a loss to make it worthwhile. You might, of course, do it inadvertently by selling a stock you are convinced is dangerous, and then having it recover. But to say, "I-am-selling-this-stock-and-will-buy-it-back-in-thirty-one-days," brings a nonmarket consideration into your specuvesting and that's not good. The commissions aren't good, either.

The mixer. This is a great little ice-breaker, which involves changing partners without missing a beat. You have a loss you want to establish, so you sell that holding and simultaneously match it up with the same amount invested in some other issue. What other issue? Well, brokerage firms supply long lists of "tax-switching" suggestions, all based on the neat supposition that (*a*) one stock in an industry is about as good as another or (*b*) since you don't know which is better anyway, what's the difference? Oh, they'll match them up very carefully and scientifically so that you can feel quite comfortable, but the whole idea is based either on fatalism or cynicism. Remember, there is only one reason for selling a stock—namely, that it is dropping dangerously. It is entirely too pat to suppose that, of all the stocks on the market, another in the same industry will give you the one best chance for using that same equity more advantageously.

In any dance, the orchestra gets paid. Always consider that bite when you are invited to trip the light fantastic, with taxes calling the tune. It takes a mighty big loss to

257

make enough on tax savings to pay the piper—uh, the broker.

Odds and loose ends

Little pieces of information you might be able to use:

—Paper gains and losses don't get taxed. Too elementary? Sorry about that.

—Capital gains dividends and distributions are sometimes included in the same check with dividends. Don't lose the notice that tells you how much is "gains."

—The first $100 in dividends is excluded from your taxable income. If you and your wife file a joint return, you're each entitled to a $100 deduction. But she has to have securities in her name that pay at least that amount. If her securities pay only $50 in dividends you can deduct only $150, jointly. You can't give her any of yours.

—Capital gains dividends are *not* to be included in that $100 deduction.

—If you're unlucky (or stupid) enough to get caught with stock in a company on which trading has been suspended, you cannot take a gain or a loss. You actually have to sell the securities or they don't figure.

—A married couple filing jointly can deduct only $1,000 of surplus losses; filing separately they can deduct $1,000 apiece if each has incurred the loss in his or her own securities.

—An investment club, unless incorporated, should have its treasurer prepare a statement listing all sales as long or short term; the net gain or loss; all dividends, itemized. This, divided by the number of members, is each member's share in the year's business. Each pays his own tax, reporting all those details. Don't let it slip by.

258

—Add up all the interest charges on your margin account's monthly statements. These are to be deducted from income, just as any other interest charges are. Naturally, this may substantially reduce the cost of doing business on margin.

—Try to pay the taxes on your account out of regular income, or out of the bank. Try, desperately, to leave your investments alone.

—Because many people do sell securities to pay taxes, there is often a sell-off in the entire market early in April.

—There is also likely to be "tax-selling" in December, which can depress the market, and which may make it a bad time to sell—another reason for avoiding the fancy dances described earlier.

How to record gains and losses

You'll want to tally up gains and losses before the end of each year to see if there really is anything you should do to help your tax picture. Also, you'll have to submit a detailed schedule of them with your income tax form later. Fortunately, printed forms exist that make it very simple.

Your broker can probably give or mail you a handy brochure that details all the foregoing (in somewhat different terms), and contains suitable forms. If you use a tax accountant or service, they can supply you with equally useful ones. Or you can buy a pad of them at a large stationer's. Just ask for a "capital gain or loss" form.

Be sure to add into your losses any carry-overs from the previous year. This must be divided according to short-term or long-term characteristics.

Of course, after a couple of years as a specuvestor, you won't have any such carry-over problems. If you do, you'll just be drummed out of the corps.

In that, let me wish you good luck—and the good sense to make the most of it when you have it.

Chapter 33

HOW TO MAKE MONEY IN A BEAR MARKET

This seems like a fitting note on which to end. You can beat these debacles, too. Batten the hatches. Sell your stocks when they drop appreciably. Sit on your money till you find a stock with good fundamentals that is going up. Buy it. But stay largely uncommitted. Your specuvesting technique will have gotten you out early—the trick is not to get sucked back in too soon.

The best way to make money in a bear market is to sell out and then sit it out. You will eventually buy in at bargain prices, and benefit from the sharp rise that follows such markets. But it doesn't happen soon. Oh, the discipline required to wait out all the "technical corrections" and the "rebounds from an oversold condition." To resist your broker's "I think XYZ could be bought now." You won't be able to keep from nibbling—at least I'm not —but keep from making major commitments or you'll be worse off than those placid paupers who simply ride it down. Be patient and you will, indeed, be sitting pretty.

In case you've never been in a bear market, here's what one looks like:

Highs and Lows

MONDAY, JULY 28, 1969
NEW HIGHS—0
NEW LOWS—732

Abacus	Chris Craft	Fed Sign Sig	Jorgensen	Northrop	Spart Ind A
A C F Ind	Chris C cv pf	Fed Mfg Inv	Jostens	Northrop pf	Sparton Cp
Adams Exp	Chromally	Fieldcrst M	Joy Mfg	Nwt Bancp	Sperry Rnd
Adam Millis	Chrysler	Filtrol	Kaiser Alum	Nwst Ind	Sprague El
Addressog	Cin Sub Tel	Fst N City	Kaiser 57 pf	Nwst In pf A	Std Kollsmn
Aetna Lif C	C I T Financl	Fisher Sci	Kaiser 66 pf	Nwst Ind pf	Std Oil Cal
Air Prod	Cities Serv	Fluor Corp	Kaiser pf	Norton Co	Std Oil N J
Air Reductn	City Invest	Fly Tiger	Kals C 1.37 pf	Nort Sim2 pf	Siand Pkg
A J Indust	City Inv pf B	FMC Cp pf	KC Sou Ind	Oak Electro	Std Prudnt
Alcan Alum	Clev Cliff	Foote CB	Katy Ind	Occident Pet	Std Prud pf
Allegh Cp	Clev Elec Ill	Foote Miner	Kwack Berl	Occld P 4 pf	Slanray
Alleg Lud	Clevite	Foote Min pf	Kays Roth	Occld 3.60 pf	Starrett
Alleg Lud pf	Clevite pf	Ford Mot	Keller Indus	Ogden Corp	Stauff Chem
Allied Chem	Clorox	For McKess	Kennamet	Ogden Cp pf	Stevens J P
Allied Super	Cluett Peo	Fore McK pf	Kyl Chk Del	Okla GE	Stoke Van C
Alpha P C	Cluett P 1 pf	Fost Wheel.	Ky Util	Okla N Gas	Stone Web
Alcoa	CNA Finl	Fruehf Corp	Kerr McGee	Olin Math	Slone Cont
A M B A C Ind	CNA F pf A	Fuqua Ind	Keyst Con In	Omark Ind	Stude Worth
Amerce Esn	Colg Palm	GAF Corp	Kidde & Co	Oneida Ltd	Stude W pf A
Amrce Es pf	Collins Rad	GAF Cp pf	Kidde pf B	Opelika Mfg	Suburb Gas
Amer Hess	Colo Int Cp	Gamb Skog	Kings D Str	Otis Elev	Suburb Prop
Ame Hess pf	Colo So 1 pf	Gannett Co	Kiny pf D wi	Outlet Co	Su Crest
Am Airlin	Colt Indust	Garlock Inc	Koehring	Over Trans	Sun Oil
Am Brdcast	Colt In 4.25 pf	Gatewy Ind	Koppers Co	Owens Crng	Sun Oil pf
Am Can pf	Colum Gas	Gen Am Inv	Kroehler	Owens Ill	Sundstrnd
Am Cement	Colum Pict	Gen Cable	Lab Elect	Oxfd Ind A	Super Oil
Am Cry Sug	Col So Ohio	Gen Dynam	Laclede Gas	Pac Int Ex	Swift Co
Am Distill	Comb Engin	Gen Elec	Lanvin Ritz	Pacific Ltg	Swingline
A Dual Vest	Coml Solv	Gen Fds	Latrobe Stl	Pac Sw Airl	Syborn Corp
Am Exp Ind	Comw Ed pf	Gen Host	Lear Siegler	Pan Am	Taft Brdcst
Am Hoist	Comput Sci	Gen Mills	Leasc Dat pf	Panh EPL	Talcott Nat
Am Invest	Coarac Corp	Gen Motors	Leasewy Td	Parker Pen	Talley Ind
Am Mch Fd	Con Edis	Gen P Cem	Leh Port C	Penn Cent	Tandy Corp
Am Motors	Con Ed 6 pf	Gen Stl Ind	Leh Val Ind	Pennz Unit	Tech Mater
Am Photo	Con Ed 5 pf	Gen Tel El	Leonard Ref	Pen U 1.33 pf	Tenneco
Am Rsch wi	Con Fds pf A	Gen Time	Lever F Cap	Peoples Drg	Tenneco pf
Am Seating	Con Nat Gas	Gen Tire	Lib O Frd pf	Pepsi Botl	Texaco
Am So Afr	Cont Air L	Genesco Inc	Libb Mc Nl	Perfect Flm	Texaco wi
Am Sugar	Cont Cp pf A	Getty Oil	Liberty Cp	Pet Inc pf	Tex Gas Tra
Am W Wks	Cont Oil	Giant P Cem	Librty Loan	Peter Paul	Tex Gas T pf
Ametek	Cont Steel	Glen Ald	Ling Tem V	Petroleum	Tex Glf Sul
Amsted	Cont Teleph	Glen A 3.15 pf	Ling TV AA	Phelps Dod	Tex P Ld T
Anch Hock	Cook Unit	Glen Ald 3 pf	Ling TV S pf	Philips Ind	Textron
Arch Dan	Cooper Ind	Globe Un	Lockhd Airc	Phill Pet	Txln 2.08 pf
Arlans D Str	Copwd Steel	Goodrich	Lendntwn	Pit Forging	Txln 1.40 pf
Armco Stl	Corinth Brd	Goodyear	Lone S Cem	Plough Inc	Thrift Drug
Armst Rub	Cox Brdcst	Gord Jwly A	Long Isl Lt	Portec Inc	Time Inc
Ashland Oil	C P C Intl	Gould Batt	Lo..ral Corp	Port Gen El	Timk R Bear
Assd Brew	Crow Coll	Gran City Stl	Lowensin	Preemier Ind	Tobin Pack
Assd D Gds	Crown Zellr	Gray Drug	Ludlow Cp	Prem Ind pf	Tootsie Roll
Assd Spring	C T S Corp	Gt Atl Pac	Lukens Stl	Prod Rsrch	Trn W Air 2 pf
Assd Transp	Cudahy Co	Gt Nor Pap	Lyke Yng pf	Pub SvcCol	Transam
Atlas Cp	Cudahy pf	Gt Wn Un pf	MacDonal	Publick Ind	Transcon wi
Aurora Plas	Curtiss Wrt	Gt Wash Inv	Madison Fd	Pueblo Sup	Transitron
Auto Sprlkir	Curt Wr A	Greyhnd	Mad S Gar	Purex Corp	Triangl Ind
Avco Corp	Dana Corp	Grummn Cp	Manh Ind	Quaker Oat	T S C Ind
Aztec Oil G	Dayco Corp	Gulf Oil	Man Han	Rapid Am pf	T S C Ind pf
Baker O T	Dayco Cp wi	Gulf Resrcs	MAPCO Inc	RCA	U G I Corp
Bachy Oil	Dayco				U M C Ind

Think you can buck a market like that? You can't—but you can still make money by rolling with the punches and riding with the winners that crop up in any market. But mainly by waiting out the storm. Man—that's specuvesting!

GLOSSARY

ACCOUNT EXECUTIVE: The brokerage house employee with whom you do business. Also called a Registered Representative, Customer's Man, "my broker," or sometimes less complimentary names. (*See* Broker)

ACQUISITION: The lesser of the merged in a merger. The company, in such an operation, which is not the "survivor."

ACTIVITY: The number of shares traded in the period designated. The term can apply to a single stock or the whole market. The amount of activity can be as important as the actual movement of a stock or of the market.

ADJUSTED: Changed to take certain developments into account. Earnings are adjusted to the new number of shares when a split or stock dividend takes place. Usually indicated by the letter "a."

AMERICAN EXCHANGE: Until 1921 called the Curb Exchange because it was located outside, on the street. Located in New York.

AMEX: Nickname for the American Exchange. (*See* American Exchange)

ANALYST: Someone whose business it is to explore and report on the potentialities of a company and its stock. A trained and dedicated expert who pores over a company's records, prowls its plants, haunts its headquarters, and badgers its officers so as to get enough information to give you a professional non-opinion.

ANNUALIZE: To project a quarter's or a half's earnings into an annual expectation.

ANNUAL RATE: The total dividends paid by a company during one business year, exclusive of extras.

ANNUAL REPORT: The financial statement issued to stockholders every year by a corporation. It shows, in too much detail for your purposes, the assets, liabilities, earnings, etc. It is a selling tool to convince current shareholders that all is well and to persuade others that they're missing something. Nevertheless see one at your broker's whenever

263

you're considering a stock. Annual reports usually tell a lot about operations in the various divisions. And you'll see some of the purtiest industrial photography anywhere.

APPRECIATE: Increase, grow, gain. A stock appreciates when its price goes up. And that's certainly appreciated.

ARBITRAGE: This is so complicated that you can forget it. It's a method of buying one form of a stock and selling another form of the same stock simultaneously at a higher price—the difference usually measured in pennies. If you tried it, you'd be eaten up by commissions, but a member of the Exchange doesn't pay them, so he can make out. For instance, he'll buy a convertible bond and immediately sell the number of shares of stock which it is convertible into. He only does this if he's figured in advance that he can't lose. I said it was complicated.

ASSETS: The net worth of a corporation. A combination of fixed assets (buildings, land, machinery), current assets (cash, accounts receivable, inventories), and intangible assets (good will, patents).

ASSET VALUE: The total assets of a corporation divided by the number of common shares. It's a comfort to some people if the asset value equals or exceeds the stock's price, since even liquidation would get them their bait back. But that's a silly reason to buy a stock. (See Assets)

AT THE CLOSE: An order to buy or sell a specific stock at the closing price. Most often used in day-trading, and not a good idea since you're flying blind.

AT THE MARKET: An order to buy or sell a stock at the best price obtainable when the order reaches the floor. Usually the sensible way to conduct your business.

AT THE OPENING: An order put in before the opening of trading. All such orders are lumped together by the Specialist and matched up so that they all "get off" at a single price. Sometimes a flood of buy or sell orders will delay the opening of a stock until such matching can be accomplished—which can take minutes, hours, or even days. (See Specialist)

AVERAGE: A measurement of the current state of the market. It is meaningful only when compared with past performance of the same average. The Dow Jones Industrial Average is the most famous and the most frequently attacked. All others are designed to be improvements and maybe they are; but since most of us watch the D-J, it not only reports and reflects the market, it actually influences it. It uses only 30 stocks, applying a divisor to their total price. The divisor changes every time a stock split or a stock dividend is declared. Just follow them—don't try to understand them.

AVERAGE DOWN: A popular sucker play which consists of buying additional shares of a stock which has dropped in price. This is done to lower the price which must be reached before the purchaser can break even. It's a good way to compound your troubles.

BALANCE SHEET: A statement showing, in dollars, a company's assets, capital, and liabilities.

BEAR: A person who believes the market is going to experience a severe, long-term decline. (*See* Bull)

BID-ASKED: "Bid" is what someone is willing to pay for a share of a certain stock; "asked" is what someone is willing to sell that share for. In many cases, particularly over-the-counter, these prices are purely theoretical, but they give you an approximation of what you'll pay or get for the stock.

BIG BOARD: The New York Stock Exchange, often written as the NYSE —which, in our day of pronouncing all organization initials, is nice.

BLUE CHIP: Common stock in a huge, well-known company, known for its stability in price, earnings, and dividends and for the quality of its products or services.

BOARD ROOM: The very important-sounding name given the room where a brokerage firm displays the changing stock prices to the public. It is usually full when the market is rising and empty when it's falling—just when stocks should be watched most closely.

BOILER ROOM: Generic name for any operation which pushes questionable stock onto a gullible public. Derived from the noise level caused by a battery of phones being used by the high-pressure salesmen at work. Never buy if (a) you are being rushed, (b) you are promised a sure profit, (c) you cannot check the firm soliciting you.

BOND: A note promising to pay a specific sum (usually $1,000) at maturity. A bond carries a specific interest, as contrasted to the dividend paid on stock. There are several types of bond, but they are income vehicles and fight a losing battle against inflation. Unlike common stock, they do not represent a share in the company, but only a loan to it.

BOOK VALUE: The amount arrived at by adding the assets of a company and deducting the liabilities (including the liquidation price of any preferred issues), and then dividing by the number of common shares outstanding. Subject to lots of variables, including shenanigans.

BREAK OUT: A chartist's term used when a stock rises or falls beyond a point previously reached one or more times, or beyond a trend line established over a period of time. This, supposedly, signifies a continuation in the same direction. The more times the stock has bumped into that point without passing it (or the more points that have coincided with the trend line), the farther the breaking-out stock is supposed to rise or fall. So many people believe it that they can actually make it happen.

BROKER: The man who handles your account or the firm which employs him. The word originally meant a dispenser of wines; someone who broaches a cask. This may explain why it's sometimes better to talk to your broker before lunch.

BULL: The opposite of a bear; someone who believes the market is going to rise. No one knows where the terms originated.

BUYING POWER: In a margin account, the amount of money which you may invest in addition to your current holdings. This rises as your stocks do, but once "in your account," it is never taken away, even if your stocks decline. This loaves-and-fishes miracle is caused by your broker's desire to lend you as much as he possibly can with the sure knowledge that he'll make money on both commissions and interest charges.

BUYING RANGE: A mythical area in a stock's decline selected by your broker as a probable turnaround point. This area changes from broker to broker and doesn't exist at all if you have no buying power with which to inspire his prognostic powers.

CALL: To force conversion of a convertible bond or preferred issue. A company may do this (under conditions beneficial to the holders) in order to switch from paying interest or a fixed dividend to paying a dividend which is proportionate to the earnings. "Call" also refers to an option to buy shares of a stock at a certain price at a specified date. This is in expectation of a price rise. (*See* Put, Margin Call)

CALLABLE: Redeemable; referring to a bond or preferred issue which can be redeemed under specified conditions before reaching maturity.

CAPITAL APPRECIATION: A fancy name for gains. As in most businesses (notably data processing) Wall Street never says in one syllable what it can say in eight.

CAPITALIZATION: Total value of all the securities issued by a company. The value given the common stock is usually that at which it was originally issued.

CASH FLOW: A way of reporting a company's net income by adding to it all the depreciation, amortization, and other bookkeeping deductions. This gives a better picture of the vitality of a company and its ability to conduct business on the cash which it generates, without additional financing.

CASH SALE: A special transaction which calls for delivery of the stock and payment the same day the trade is made instead of within five trading days as in a "regular way" trade. It is used at year's end to cram in a gain or loss which would otherwise be counted in the following year.

CHART: To keep track of stock price movement; or the graph which results from such record keeping. There are several kinds of charting systems, all of which aspire to predict future moves from past actions. They keep thousands out of mischief.

CHURN: To buy and sell stocks at a needlessly rapid pace. Supposedly, some brokers do this to generate commissions. If they do, it's the investor's fault for being too permissive or too greedy.

CLOSE: The end of the trading day.

CLOSED-END FUND: An investment trust which does not continue to sell new shares. Its shares are traded on an exchange like any other stock. (*See* Open-End Fund)

CLOSED-END INVESTMENT TRUST: (*See* Closed-End Fund, Mutual Fund)

COMMODITIES: Foods and materials "traded" on commodities exchanges throughout the country. Contracts for future delivery (futures) of specific quantities of these items are bought and sold like stocks. The items range from goodies, like bleachable tallow, through exotics like copra, to what-is-its like palladium. Stay away.

COMMON STOCKS: Shares in a company as contrasted to promissory notes from a company (bonds) or stock which has a priority on dividends (preferred).

COMPOSITE: An average or index comprised of a number of stocks in various areas, notably Standard & Poor or Dow Jones Composites, which include industrials, railroads, and utilities.

CONE: One of a number of terms used by chartists to describe the formations appearing on their charts. It's all very pseudoscientific and comforting and probably results in a better chance of success than flipping a coin.

CONFIRMATION: The record of a sale, purchase, or distribution sent you by your broker.

CONGLOMERATE: An acquisition-minded corporation which consists of many divisions active in a variety of fields. This kind of organization used to be called a holding company, which implied mere ownership and financial participation. Today's conglomerates provide managerial assistance and actively run their various divisions, usually separate companies which have been acquired intact.

CONVERSION PRICE: The cost of the common shares for which a convertible bond or preferred share may be exchanged. In practice, such a bond or preferred is usually convertible into a specific number of shares. Dividing that number into the $1,000 face value of the bond or preferred gives you the conversion price. When the market price of the common rises beyond the conversion price it becomes profitable to convert.

CONVERTIBLE: A bond or preferred share which may be turned in for a specific number of common shares. This conversion may also be forced by the issuing company ("called"). (*See* Call)

CORNER: A classic maneuver which consists of buying enough stock to give the buyer or group of buyers control of the stock and, therefore, of its price. The principal effect is to squeeze anyone who has gone short and must, therefore, buy the stock to cover. In the bad old days cornering was done purposely and wrecked many a wheeler-dealer. Today, it's rare—and then largely inadvertent.

CORRECTION: A term used by the Street to explain away any awkward change in the expected price trend of a stock or group of stocks. It implies that the drop is temporary and nothing to worry about, or that the rise is to be of brief duration. It's a vague attempt at the precision which is quite naturally beyond the skills of even the most knowing observers and analysts.

COUPON: The portion of a "bearer bond" which must be cut off and mailed in to the issuing company when interest is due. Bearer bonds do not have the owner's name registered with the company, so the company will pay only on submission of the coupon.

COVER: To close out a short position by buying a number of shares equal to those previously sold short and delivering them against the sale.

CROSS: A privately arranged sale of a large amount of stock between two individuals, groups, firms, or funds. The transaction does not reach the Exchange floor but must be done with Exchange permission. (*See* Exchange Distribution)

CUMULATIVE PREFERRED: A type of preferred stock which provides for accumulating any dividends which are passed (not payed) and paying them off in subsequent years when the company's earnings permit.

CURB EXCHANGE: (*See* Amex)

CUSTOMER'S MAN: (*See* Account Executive)

CYCLICAL: A stock which (or a company whose stock) rises and falls with the business cycle rather than independently. For example: steels, construction, clothing.

CYLINDER: (*See* Cone)

DAY ORDER: A buy or sell order good only during the trading day on which it is issued.

DAY-TRADE: The practice of buying and selling stock (or selling short and covering) within a single trading day. Day-Trading multiplies your buying power immensely (and your likelihood of loss even more) .

DEALER: A person (or firm) buying for and selling from his own account rather than acting as an agent or broker. A dealer profits by selling his stock at a higher price than he buys it, just like an investor or trader, but actually he operates a store, with an inventory of stock. You will most often make use of dealers in purchasing odd lots (less than 100 shares) or over-the-counter stocks. Your order will be placed with your broker, as usual. He will arrange the transaction through a dealer.

DEBENTURE: A type of bond not secured by a specific mortgage or property lien. (*See* Bond)

DEBIT BALANCE: The amount owing on a margin account.

DEFENSIVE ISSUE: A mythical security blanket which is supposed to protect investors from sharp losses in bad times. Unfortunately, it usually protects them from worthwhile gains in a good market, too. Utilities and foods are typically considered defensive issues.

DEPLETION: An accounting term referring to the law which recognizes that natural resources are exhaustible and that profits from their consumption are, therefore, in theory, one-time only. Companies (oil, metal and coal mining, etc.) as a result can deduct a "depletion allowance" from earnings. Depletion is what makes millionaires a leading Texas export.

DILUTION: The effect of bringing out an additional stock issue, selling Treasury Stock, or otherwise increasing the number of shares of stock outstanding. Dilution cuts the earnings pie into smaller pieces, decreasing the amount available for dividends (although not always decreasing the dividends) and the value of each share of stock previously outstanding. Shareholders are given a right (literally) to buy a percentage of new shares equivalent to the increase in shares outstanding. (*See* Rights)

DISCOUNT: The difference between a stock's price and its actual value when the value is higher; in the case of an investment trust, between its price and its asset value (the amount you would get if you redeemed a share). Also, the action of the market which balances out a future value; it "discounts" an earnings increase, a dividend hike, or an unfavorable development by bidding the stock up or down before the events actually take place. (*See* Premium)

DISCOUNT RATE: The interest rate charged by Federal Reserve Banks on loans made to its member banks. The discount rate directly affects the interest charged businesses or individuals by all lending institutions. The Federal Reserve Board therefore has the power to make money "tighter" by raising the discount rate in order to cool down the economy and, theoretically, slow inflation. The term "Credit Crunch" has become a popular way of describing this action. It has the effect of distressing and, therefore, depressing the stock market, because it indirectly affects earnings by making expansion more costly.

DISCRETIONARY ACCOUNT: An arrangement giving the broker (or a financial manager) the right to buy or sell without specific instruction. This indiscretion is often practiced by people who were bright enough to get the money in the first place but are too stupid to handle it.

DISTRIBUTION: The assignment of additional shares to a shareholder following a split, stock dividend, or spin-off. Also an arranged selling of a large block of stock without using the trading floor.

DIVIDENDS: Payments made by a company to holders of common or preferred shares. On common stock, the dividend is voted, usually quarterly, by the board of directors, and rises or falls with the company's earnings. On preferred shares the dividend is usually a fixed amount.

DOLLAR COST AVERAGING: Buying an issue by investing a specific amount in it at regular intervals, regardless of the number of shares it buys at the time. The inexorable, long-term rise in the stock market makes this a good way to insure gains, but they probably won't be spectacular and you must stick with it. (*See* M.I.P.)

DOUBLE TOP (BOTTOM): Chartists' term referring to the chart pattern formed when a stock twice rises to the same high and then drops back, or (bottom) drops twice and recovers. The double top looks like an "M"; the double bottom like a "W." Both signify a stock resistance zone which, if penetrated on a subsequent move, indicates continued advance (top) or decline (bottom). You can bet on it. You can also bet on which sparrow will fly off the fence first.

DOUBLE UP: Most frequently the practice of buying more of a stock on which you already have a loss so that, thirtyone days later, you can sell the original shares to establish the loss for tax purposes. Don't let them snow you into it.

DOWNSIDE RISK: Something there is always very little of in a stock being recommended. Patter for "likelihood of dropping."

DOW-JONES: Publisher of *The Wall Street Journal* but usually a reference to the Dow-Jones Industrial Index, earliest and best known of the "averages." Composed of 30 leading industrial stocks, the DJI is a number which indicates with much questioned precision the state of the market. (*See* Average, Index)

EARNINGS: Usually the net annual earnings after taxes, and most usually the net annual earnings divided by the number of shares of common stock outstanding. Earnings are generally reported every quarter, however, so you'll see "three-month," "six-month," and "nine-month" together with those of the same periods of the previous year.

EFFICIENT MARKET THEORY: This is the theory that, since the stock market is an auction in which people bid only what they think the stock is worth, each day's bidding is based on all knowledge obtainable to date. The market, therefore, discounts everything in the past and starts fresh each morning. Yup! (*See* Random Walk)

EQUITY: For your purposes, the amount by which the value of all the stocks you own exceeds the debit balance in your margin account.

EVEN TICK: (*See* Up Tick)

EXCHANGE DISTRIBUTION: When a customer wants to sell a large holding, the broker sometimes handles it himself. He gets orders from his other customers, offers the block on the trading floor, then buys it himself. It's the same as a "cross," but carried out on the trading floor for some obscure reason that needn't bother us. (*See* Cross, Secondary)

EX-DIVIDEND: "Without the current dividend." Stocks which are ex-dividend are listed in the tables with a small "x" before the number of shares traded. If you buy such a stock it means you're too late to get the recently declared dividend. The price of the stock is reduced by the amount of the dividend at the opening of the day that it goes "ex."

EXERCISE: To exchange your "rights" for their equivalent in stock, or to buy or sell stock which you have optioned with a put or call. Oh heck, it only means "to use." (*See* Rights, Put, and Call)

EXPIRE: To lapse. Rights and options expire on specific dates. If a company in which you own stock offers rights, you must either sell them or exercise them by the expiration date or they become worthless.

EX-RIGHTS: "Without the just-distributed rights." (*See* Ex-Dividend)

FILL OR KILL ORDER: An order to buy or sell (usually at a specific price) which must be executed as soon as it reaches the floor. If it is not, the order is cancelled. (*See* Stopped Stock)

FISCAL YEAR: If a company balances its books on December 31, they go by the calendar year; if on any other date, they use a fiscal year. The Government's fiscal year ends June 30. From the size of the deficit they rack up each time, you'd swear it was February 29.

FLAG: (*see* Cone)

FLOAT: Slang term for the number of a company's shares which are available for purchase. A small float makes a volatile stock. It also means to market a new issue or obtain a loan, but that has a disreputable tone.

FLOOR: The part of an Exchange in which actual trading takes place. Also, in charting, a support level from which a stock has previously rebounded.

FRONT-END LOAD: The hunk of money that goes to the salesman in certain mutual funds. It can eat up practically all of your first year's payments, if you are on a contract basis of so much per month. But it serves you right for not trusting yourself to make your own investment decisions.

FOREIGN ISSUE: Means just what it says. But things get complicated with ADR (American Depositary Receipts), Interest Equalization Taxes, and such. So ask your broker about them when you buy a foreign stock, including most Canadian issues.

FUNDAMENTALS: The rock-solid facts and figures about sales growth, earnings growth, debt, market prospects, etc. The things that say "yes" after other factors have said "How about that!"

FUTURES: (*See* Commodities)

GLAMOUR STOCK: Somewhat like a glamour girl—its beauty is in the eye of the beholder—only likely to fade more quickly. Any issue that's getting a big play because of solid fact rather than wild hopes, except that the only solid fact may be that the purchasers have wild hopes.

GNP: "Gross National Product." A measure of our economic health constructed by adding up the value of all the shoes and ships and sealing wax produced in a calendar year.

GO PUBLIC: To sell shares of a company to the public on an Exchange or over-the-counter. It involves registration with the SEC and some other rigmarole. But don't get the idea that it means there's any value in a stock or worth in a company. All they have to do is to tell the whole truth, and it can be pretty grim.

GROWTH: Usually "earnings growth," which will be accompanied by price gains, as a rule. "Growth" and "glamour" are often bedfellows. (*See* Glamour Stock)

GTC: "Good till cancel"; an order to buy or sell at a specific price. It remains an order until you tell the broker to cancel it. You can also put in an order as "today only," "good this week," or "good this month."

GO-GO FUND: A fund dedicated to amassing capital gains in a hurry. It tends, therefore, to be in and out of stocks faster than used to be the practice with funds—and to invest in issues which conservative funds might ignore or even deplore. (*See* Mutual Fund)

GIVE-UP: A practice whereby one brokerage firm gives part of its commission on a transaction to another brokerage firm. Also, between individual brokers on referred business. The SEC has cracked down on this because the funds were using the practice to reward firms which, supposedly, had been helpful—almost like a finder's fee. The SEC thought it was bad and I'd agree, if I understood it all.

GAINS: Ain't no dog food, baby!

HEDGE FUND: A high-risk fund, usually conducted for a small group of large investors. Became a factor in 1968. "Hedge" refers to practice of shorting stocks on occasion; not usually done by standard funds.

HEAD AND SHOULDERS: The chartists' dream formation. Briefly, it occurs after a good rise. The stock falls off, recovers to a higher point, falls off to the same lower point reached before, and recovers to the point reached by the initial good rise. The first rise was the "left shoulder," the higher rise the "head," the next rise the "right shoulder." If the price (and the chart line) drops below the recovery point ("the neck line"), it will continue down (maybe).

HIGH (NEW): The highest price reached by a stock or an index. Naturally there are daily highs, all-time highs, year's highs.

INDEX: Actually, a yardstick by which any statistic is measured against the same statistic in a selected base year (e.g., the Federal Reserve Board Production Index). Most commonly, though, a stock "average" such as the Dow-Jones Industrial Average or its brothers, the D-J Railroads Average, Utilities Average, or Composite Average. While the D-J is the oldest and best known, you'll run into Standard & Poor's similar group, and others, including those put out by the NYSE and Amex—perversely called "Index." (*See* Average)

INDICATOR: (*See* Index)

INDUSTRIAL AVERAGE: (*See* Index)

INSIDER: Don't expect me to define this, because even the SEC can't —or doesn't choose to. The term used to apply only to an officer of a company. Recent cases have stretched it to cover anybody who knows something the public doesn't. Today you can get in trouble for profiting on, or even passing along, information overheard in an elevator. One more reason for not acting on tips.

ISSUE: Securities of a company. Also the act of putting those securities on the market for the first time. One company may have many issues.

INVESTMENT CLUB: A group of investors who pool their resources for one of several reasons: they don't feel up to making investment decisions individually; they can invest small sums regularly without having commissions kill them; or they like to join clubs.

LEVERAGE: It's hard to be brief on this but not worth being lengthy about. When a company that has both common and preferred issues does poorly, the interest which *must* be paid on the preferred adversely affects the per-share earnings of the common. That effect is "leverage." It works the other way too; when earnings rise, interest payments remain the same, so per-share earnings go up disproportionately fast compared to the total rise in earnings.

LIMIT: An order to buy or sell at a specified price or better. (*See* Stop)

LISTED: Stock traded on an Exchange, as compared with an issue sold only privately or over-the-counter.

LITTLE GUY: Us.

LOAD: That part of your payments to an open-end investment company (mutual) which goes for commissions and other distribution costs. A "front-end load" lumps most such costs into the first year or two of a contract. Don't contract for such shares unless you fully understand this bite. Then don't contract for such shares. (*See* No-Load Fund)

LOCKED IN: A stupid phrase meaning unable to sell because the person has (a) too large a loss, or (b) too large a gain, or (c) too small a brain. It belongs in no one's vocabulary.

LONG: The opposite of "short." I don't think the word is officially sanctioned, but being "long" means owning shares of a company.

LONG-TERM CAPITAL GAIN: What you have if you hold a stock longer than six months and one day and sell at a profit. The income tax is roughly half that levied on profits on stock held a lesser length of time with a maximum of 50 percent whatever your bracket. This is subject to change under pending tax reforms. (*See* Short-Term Capital Gain)

LOW (NEW): (*See* High)

MAINTENANCE REQUIREMENT: The percentage of equity which must be kept in a margin account to conform to rules established by the brokerage house, influenced by the Federal Reserve Board's margin requirements. Confused? Might as well stay that way. What it means is that if your stocks have gone down a lot (but not enough to necessitate a margin call) you'll lose some of the money realized on the next sale. It will go to reduce the amount you owe the broker. There's a cute ruling that lets you use the entire amount, though, if you reinvest before the end of the same trading day. (*See* Margin, Margin Call)

MANIPULATION: Shh! Dirty word.

MARGIN: The percentage the customer must put up when he borrows from the broker to buy stocks. It is set by the Federal Reserve Board and has ranged from 10 percent to 100 percent (in fact, a cash purchase). Also the act of buying a stock on margin.

MARGIN CALL: The demand made by the broker for additional money or securities when a margin customer's equity falls below a minimum percentage. If not met, the broker must sell enough of the margined securities to bring the customer's equity up to the required percentage of his holdings. It never happens to a good specuvestor.

MARKET ORDER: An order to buy a specified number of shares of a security at the best price obtainable when presented to the trading floor. "At the market."

MATURITY: The date on which a bond or other loan comes due.

MERGER: The marriage of two firms into one, sanctified by Uncle.

MIP: The New York Stock Exchange's "Monthly Investment Plan," which lets you invest a regular amount in an issue every month, regardless of the price of that issue. You own shares and fractions of shares, and get dividends or fractions of dividends.

MUTUAL FUND: A company formed to invest other people's money in the market. It sells shares in itself, and the purchasers own a corresponding percentage of all its holdings (after management fees, maintenance, and sundries are charged off). Technically only open-end investment trusts (funds) are mutuals. (*See* Open-End Fund)

274

NET CHANGE: The change in a stock's price from the closing price on the previous trading day.

NEW ISSUE: A stock offering made to the public for the first time.

NO-LOAD FUND: A mutual fund which does not take the salesman's commission and other costs out of the payments which the investor makes. (*See* Load)

NYSE: (*See* Big Board)

NONTAXABLE DIVIDENDS: Usually dividends which are "returns of capital," a favorite trick for cajoling shareholders of companies which don't have much earnings. It seems so great to receive a "nontaxable distribution," but they may only be giving you back part of your own money and, for tax purposes, you have to reduce your cost basis by that much. It's like giving you a lick of your own ice cream cone.

OBJECTIVE: The price you expect a stock to reach. Unless you are a seer, astrologist, necromancer, or fool, just shrug when someone asks, "What is your objective for that stock?" Or tells you what his is.

ODD LOT: No, Clyde, not the investors. It means less than the specified "round lot," which is usually a hundred shares, but can be only ten shares in some inactive stocks. (*See* Odd-Lot Index)

ODD-LOT INDEX: The buy/sell ratio of all transactions of less than a round lot. Tradition and sad fact is that odd lotters are wrong so frequently that if the index says the Little Guys are selling, it means a market rise; if buying, head for the storm cellar.

OFFER OR QUOTE: An order to buy a certain number of shares at the offer price (asked) or, if that price has been raised, to give you the new quote. This ensures that you will get a chance to buy at the new price without the carte blanche given by a market order. Used for exceptionally volatile stocks.

ON BALANCE: Preponderately. If more factors look good than bad, for example, "on balance" the outlook is favorable.

OPEN-END FUND: The type of investment trust (mutual fund) which continually sells its shares to the public and redeems them itself. (*See* Closed-End Fund)

OPTION: Can mean an agreement given to an employee to permit him to buy, up to a specified future date, a specific number of shares at a possibly lower price (usually the price on the agreement date). Also a put or call. (*See* Put, Call)

OUTSTANDING STOCK: Not an editorial appraisal of a stock but merely the total supply which has been issued, not counting any Treasury Stock. (*See* Treasury Stock)

OVERHEAD SUPPLY: A big block of stock which someone is determined to sell. It will probably be offered in "small" lots so as not to depress the market. But it *will* darned well depress it till the stuff is all sold. The Street always knows about it.

OVERSOLD: The condition in which a stock or the market is thought to have reacted too violently downward to some development. (*See* Technical)

OVER-THE-COUNTER: Publicly held but not sold on an Exchange. Also called "unlisted" although these issues may be listed in your daily paper.

PAINT THE TAPE: Appear recurrently on the tape; said of a stock which is getting big volume in relatively small lots.

PAPER PROFITS: It's all paper profits, baby. And paper losses. They are every bit as real as realized profits, and you pay no taxes on 'em.

PAR: The dollar value of a common share as stated in the company's charter. Quite meaningless thereafter.

PARTICIPATING PREFERRED: A preferred stock on which the dividend is raised on a specified basis when the common dividend is raised.

PENNY STOCK: Any stock under a dollar. Most of these are on the Canadian Exchange. It's a term of contempt. No stock is a good buy because it's cheap or a bad buy because it's high in price. Other factors are what count.

PINK SHEETS: The daily reports of bid and asked prices of over-the-counter stocks. See them at your broker's.

PLUS TICK: A stock transaction made at a higher price than the preceding transaction in the same stock. Also called an "up tick." A short sale may be made only on a plus tick or a "zero-plus tick," which is a transaction at the same price as the one preceding it when the latest price movement was upward.

POINT: One dollar in the price of a stock. Also one digit in an index or stock average. But it's ten dollars in the price of a $1,000 bond.

POINT AND FIGURE: A type of chart which disregards fractions and plots only moves of a full point, regardless of the time it takes to make that move. In practice, the unit is usually half a point for stocks under $20 and three points for stocks over $80. Ask your broker—it pays to be curious.

POSITION: "Everything in life," say the cynics. In the market it simply means holding shares of a stock. You "take a position" when you buy.

PREMIUM: The amount by which the price exceeds the measurable value of any security. (*See* Discount)

PRICE/EARNINGS RATIO: The current price of a share of stock divided by the annual earnings per share. It is a measure used in deciding whether a stock is overpriced or underpriced, but you might as well measure your feet with a rubber band when buying shoes. Certainly, consider the P/E, but only in relation to other stocks in the same field.

PRIME RATE: The rate charged by the Federal Reserve Board for money loaned to its member banks. It affects all interest rates and is increasingly being used to attempt to control inflation by discouraging borrowing and, therefore, spending. Rots of ruck.

PROJECTION: A forecast of earnings or whatever.

PROXY (FIGHT): A "proxy" is a signed authorization given by a shareholder to the board of a company to vote his shares a certain way. A "proxy fight" is a struggle by two factions to influence the shareholders to vote a particular way.

PUT: An option to *sell* a specific number of shares of a certain security at a set price prior to a certain date. You buy a put in expectation of a stock going down. (*See* Call)

PYRAMID: A negative sounding word applied to the very sensible practice of reinvesting profits and using any increased buying power built up in a margin account. Also said of buying more of a rising stock.

QUOTE: The current bid and asked prices of any security.

RAIDER: An entrepreneur (to put it politely) who buys control of a company in order to milk it of assets rather than to run it successfully.

RANDOM WALK: A theory which holds that nothing which was known yesterday will affect a stock today; therefore your guess is as good as mine as to what will happen in the future. The opposite of charting, it is also called the "efficient market" theory. A great comfort and better than active stupidity when it comes to picking stocks. (*See* Efficient Market Theory)

REACTION: A gain or a loss in a stock or in the market itself following a sharp or prolonged move in the other direction. One of Wall Street's many meaningless terms, but it sounds wise.

REALIZE: To turn a paper profit or loss into an actual gain or loss by selling a holding or closing out a short position. (*See* Paper Profits)

RECORD DATE: The date on which you must be recorded on a company's books as a shareholder if you are to receive a dividend or be allowed a vote at a stockholders' meeting.

REDEEM: To pay off holders of a bond. (*See* Call)

REGIONAL EXCHANGE: Any U.S. Stock Exchange other than the NYSE, Amex, or National.

RESISTANCE (AREA, LEVEL): In charting (and the term is widely used by non-chartists for the same thing), the point at which a stock or the market has previously turned around in a descent or ascent. In theory, it will have trouble breaking through and will tend to rebound. It is considered very significant and scares watchers into action frequently enough to give the theory some validity.

REVERSE SPLIT: Well, what would *you* call it when a number of shares are turned into one? This is done when a stock's price has dropped very low, usually well under 10.

RIGHTS: Permission to buy newly authorized shares at a specific price, usually lower than the market price. Rights are given to its current stockholders by a company which plans to issue additional shares to the general public. This keeps a shareholder's equity in the company from being diluted. The rights have a value of their own, so should be exercised or sold before expiration, which isn't usually a very long time. (*See* Exercise)

ROUND LOT: A number of shares, usually one hundred, which qualifies for a smaller commission rate than a lesser number. In such a case, if you order a hundred and fifty shares, your broker will charge you on the basis of one round lot and an odd lot of fifty shares. (*See* Odd-Lot)

ROUND TRIP: The full cycle of purchase and sale of a specific number of shares; or, in going short, the selling short and subsequent covering of the sale.

SAUCER: In charting, a long, shallow depression which shows that a stock has been at a low point for a long time. The longer that base is (sometimes years) the stronger is the buy signal when it starts to climb again. If it breaks through the previous, long-ago lip level, zowie. All good, clean fun.

SEC: The Securities and Exchange Commission, watchdog and stalwart defender of your welfare.

SECONDARY (DISTRIBUTION): Sale of a large block of stock held by an individual or group, by offering it privately to investors. It is handled by a broker, or group of brokers, rather than on the trading floor so as to keep the sale from depressing the market price—which it usually does anyway by draining off buying power.

SELL OFF: Go down in price.

SENIOR CAPITAL: Securities or other claims which get first dibs on earnings, prior to the common. (*See* Senior Security)

SENIOR SECURITY: A bond or preferred issue on which interest or dividends must be paid before any dividends are paid on the common. It has nothing to do with age or years, but simply means it takes precedence.

SHARE: A definite fraction of a company, owned in common, as distinct from a bond, which is a loan to the company and carries no ownership privileges such as dividends or votes.

SHORT SALE: The sale of borrowed stock, in the belief that the price will drop so as to enable subsequent repurchases at a lower price. The difference between the sale price and later purchase price (minus commissions, etc.) constitutes the profit. Or the loss, man, or the loss.

SHORT AGAINST THE BOX: The device of going short the number of shares of a stock which you already own. This can later be covered by delivering the stock (or, if you change your mind, by purchasing the same number on the market and delivering them). It is a means of freezing a gain so that it can be applied at a later date, usually in the following year, for tax purposes.

SHORT INTEREST: The number of shares of an issue which have been sold short and not covered by a given date. A large short interest, paradoxically, is considered excellent potential support for a stock, since it must eventually be covered by buying shares on the market. Any demand constitutes support.

SHORT-TERM CAPITAL GAIN: A profit realized from sale of a security (or covering a short sale) held less than six months and one day. The income tax on this transaction is calculated as on regular income. (*See* Long-Term Capital Gain)

SIGNAL: A charting term meaning any of a number of occult formations which tell the the initiates that something specific is going to take place. "Buy signal" and "sell signal" are synomyms for "I guess."

SPECIAL SITUATION: Any stock which looks good to your broker for reasons which he can't really explain. Seriously, folks, a stock in a company which ordinarily wouldn't be a good buy, measured by the usual yardsticks, but which is made attractive by a particular development. Could be a take-over bid, a discovery, or some other circumstance outside its usual pattern.

SPECIALIST: A member of an Exchange who is responsible for "maintaining an orderly market" in certain stocks. There are more than 350 of them on the NYSE. They buy and sell for their own accounts and execute orders for brokers. No connection with Chic Sale.

SPECULATOR: One who buys a stock in the belief something will happen to make it go up—or sells it short in the belief something will happen to make it go down. He may know or think he knows what it will be; the chief difference between him and "investors" is that he doesn't wait for it to happen. This mild definition will suit only confirmed speculators.

SPECUVESTING: Mine own term for a golden middle road between speculating and long-term investing. A flexible, opportunistic approach characterized by boldness, patience, and iron discipline. Only practiced by excellent fellows and gifted ladies.

SPIN-OFF: To distribute, to its shareholders, shares in another firm held by a company. If a company wishes to, or is ordered to, divest itself of a subsidiary company or of shares held in some other firm, it may simply give all the shares to its own shareholders and you should be so lucky.

SPLIT: To divide a share of stock into a specific number of pieces which become the new shares. Usually done to reduce the market price, sometimes to produce additional shares for use in acquisitions or to qualify for registration on an Exchange. Don't ever forget your holding has no greater value after a split than before.

SPREADS, STRADDLES, STRIPS, AND STRAPS: Kinds of fancy option buying in which you should have no interest. (*See* Put, Call)

STOCK DIVIDEND: A popular but basically meaningless dividend paid in stock instead of cash. In reality a junior grade split; by NYSE rules less than 25 percent, but usually less than ten. A stock dividend does not usually increase your equity in a company; it merely gives you more pieces and makes the ones you already hold correspondingly smaller.

STOP: Also a "Stop Order": An order to sell specified shares if a transaction takes place at or below a specified price. Less frequently, an order to buy if a transaction takes place at or above a certain price. It becomes a market order when this happens, so don't kid yourself that *your* transaction will take place at that price. (*See* Stop Limit, Stop Loss, Market Order)

STOP LIMIT: This differs from a "stop" or "stop order" in that a transaction at or below the "stop price" (in a stop limit, a sell order) does not become a market order. Instead it becomes an order to sell at that price or better. A stop limit buy order, naturally, becomes an order to buy at that price or better. If the specialist can't get it off at "that price or better," the transaction will not go through. (*See* Stop, Stop Loss, Market Order)

STOP LOSS: Despite common use of the phrase, there ain't no such animal. It's too good to be true. (*See* Stop, Stop Limit)

STOPPED STOCK: A guarantee given by a specialist to your broker that he will execute your order at a specific price or better. If the specialist thinks the price may shortly change in your favor, he will "stop" the specified number of shares at the current price and try to buy it for less (or sell it for more, if yours is a sell order). If he can't, you can at least be sure of trading at that price. You can't lose by the endeavor.

STREET NAME: The term indicating that securities are held for the investor in the broker's name, rather than the investor's. All margin accounts are in "street name." You can also have them so designated if you buy for cash but don't want to hold the stocks. A very sensible, uncomplicating move.

STRONG HANDS: A loose designation for institutions and knowledgeable investors (presumably large), who won't panic out of a stock on a decline and thereby cause a further drop. At the bottom of a decline, the stock is assumed to be in strong hands, with all the timid

Little Guys scared out. It is better to be weak and whole than never to have sold at all.

SUBSCRIPTION RIGHTS: (*See* Rights)

SUSPEND: Usually "suspend trading." The act of stopping trading in a specific stock for any of several reasons: a drastic change in the company's fortune which is causing excessive volume and price change, suspicion of skulduggery, a suit or other action. Also to prohibit an individual or firm from doing business as punishment for transgression of some kind.

SYMBOL: The letters assigned an issue of stock and used to represent that stock in making and reporting transactions.

TAX SWITCHING: A year-end activity, very profitable to the brokers but of little value to most investors. It consists of selling securities in which you might want to realize a gain or loss for tax purposes and buying another issue, usually in the same industry, which has an equal or better chance of performing well. Taxes are usually the worst possible reason for acting—and the false assumption that one issue or company is much like any other can lead to expensive follies.

TECHNICAL: Said of a stock's or the market's price movement which it characterizes, meaning that it was not significant in the long run but merely a temporary change in direction. (*See* Oversold)

TENDER: An offer to a company's shareholders to buy their shares at a stipulated price or exchange them for a specific amount of another company's stock. Often done by outsiders to get control of a company. In many cases there is advance agreement that no shares will actually be accepted if the offerer fails to get a specified number of shares in response to his tender.

THIN: When applied to the market it means relatively little activity; of a stock it means few shares are outstanding. (*See* Float, Outstanding Stock)

TODAY ONLY: An order which is to be executed before the close of trading or not at all. Also used as "this week only," and "this month only." The former means by Friday's close (or that of the last trading day) ; the latter means "before the close of the last trading day of this calendar month."

TRADE; A transaction, either buy or sell. Naturally, you can't have one without the other, so it is truly a trade of cash for stock.

TRADER: One who buys and sells stock very rapidly for his own account. He tries to catch short swings and is not interested in the long pull. A tough way to make a buck—but an easy way to lose many.

TRADING CROWD: A very esoteric term for the people on the floor of an exchange who actually make the transactions. It always sounds a bit like calling a group of men "chaps."

TRANSFER TAX: A tax levied by some states (New York) on the sale or transfer of securities. It is paid by the seller (or former owner, if no money changes hands).

TREASURY STOCK: Stock which has been issued by a company and then reacquired. No dividends are paid on it and it carries no voting rights.

TREND LINE: In charting, a line drawn to connect any three lowest points in the jagged path made by a rising stock—or highest points touched by a descending stock. You extend that line into the future, and if the chart line breaks through, it supposedly signifies further movement in the direction of the breakthrough. (*See* Break Out)

UP TICK: (*See* Plus Tick)

UNDERWRITER (s) : The firm or syndicate of firms which contracts to sell to the public and to institutions a new issue or a large block of stocks or bonds already issued.

UNLISTED: (See Over-the-Counter)

UTILITY AVERAGE: An index or average of selected utility stocks. (*See* Average)

VOLUME: The number of shares traded during a specified period—either of a specific issue or of an entire Exchange.

WARRANT: The right to buy a certain security at a specified price, either up to a particular time or in perpetuity.

WEAK HANDS: (*See* Strong Hands)

WHEN ISSUED: The designation for the new shares of a stock which has recently split, or for shares which have been authorized but not yet issued. These will trade for later delivery when the certificates are actually available. Abbreviated as "wi."

WASH SALE: A situation caused by the repurchase within 31 days of securities which have been sold at a loss. For tax purposes, it is considered that no sale has taken place. The new cost basis becomes the cost of the original shares plus or minus the difference between the sale price of the original shares and the cost price of the new shares.

WRITE OFF: To charge an expense against a specified time period.

YIELD: The percentage determined by dividing a stock's previous year's dividends by the *current* price of the stock. There is a tendency, sanctioned by the NYSE, to divide the annual dividend by the price you originally paid for the stock. This makes you feel good, providing the stock has risen, but is somewhat like measuring your son's foot size by looking at his baby shoes. You don't have in a stock what you originally put into that stock, but exactly what that stock is worth right now. So don't kid yourself on what your money is yielding. If the price has risen and the dividend hasn't, your yield has dropped.

ZERO-PLUS TICK: (*See* Plus Tick)

INDEX

ABOUT THE AUTHOR

LEWIS OWEN, a veteran of thirty-three years on Madison Avenue, has just retired from advertising to devote himself to watching Wall Street and studying the American Revolutionary period. HOW WALL STREET DOUBLES MY MONEY EVERY THREE YEARS: *The No-Nonsense Guide to Steady Stock Market Profits* is the direct result of his investment experiences, which have enabled him to retire at the age of 53. He lives in Oradell, New Jersey, and summers at Sag Harbor, Long Island, with his wife, Esther, and (on occasion) their two grown children, Rick and Patty.